MDCCCXLVIII
HAHNEMANN
UNIVERSITY
CURA ANIMARUM · ERUDITIO ARTIS
PHILADELPHIA
MEDICINAE

HAHNEMANN UNIVERSITY
LIBRARY

THE HEALING WEB

SOCIAL NETWORKS
AND HUMAN SURVIVAL

THE
HEALING WEB

SOCIAL NETWORKS
AND HUMAN SURVIVAL

MARC PILISUK
SUSAN HILLIER PARKS

University Press of New England

HANOVER AND LONDON, 1986

University Press of New England

Brandeis University
Brown University
Clark University
University of Connecticut
Dartmouth College
University of New Hampshire
University of Rhode Island
Tufts University
University of Vermont

© 1986 by University Press of New England

Printed in the United States of America

Library of Congress Cataloging-in-Publication Data

Pilisuk, Marc.
  The healing web.

    1. Social medicine. 2. Healing—Social aspects.
3. Interpersonal relations. I. Parks, Susan Hillier.
II. Title.
RA418.P54   1986   306.4   85–26290
ISBN 0–87451–360–X

In memory of my father,
Louis Pilisuk, whose life was a
lesson in caring

MP

To the memory of
Marshall DuWayne Krumenacker,
who practiced what he preached

SHP

CONTENTS

PREFACE

This is a book about caring. To write on a topic so inherently subjective presented a substantial challenge to us as social scientists steeped in the traditions of academia. This challenge was not the only one.

Our intent when we began this book was to bring together, under one cover, the multitude of interdisciplinary approaches to the study of supportive connections. Given the plethora of studies all related to the area of social support, this goal proved to be no small feat. Caring and social support are in no way confined topics. We read and we wrote—about social support and health, about loneliness, and about friendships and families. We reviewed the political requirements for more cohesive communities and the place of human caring in broader social issues such as inequality and nuclear war.

As we progressed with the manuscript, however, it became apparent that a critical lack within the body of social and behavioral science studies was a political and psychological synthesis of their importance. Studies appropriate for journal publication are, of necessity, small, representing one part of the elephant. What emerged as we fit these pieces of scientific research together was a message that is humanistic in both a personal and a political sense. Much like streams and tributaries that merge to form a vigorous river, the evidence merged to form a message more compelling than we had imagined it would be.

The case we present is that actual human interdependence is far greater than our contemporary values recognize. Understanding this interdependence is critical to our health, our sense of belonging, and even the survival of the human community. Where interdependence is nourished, it provides a healing web with remarkable powers for regeneration of the human potential. To survive—both individually and socially—we must reconnect with the ecology of our humanity, which is inseparable from the ecology of our world.

The Healing Web: Social Networks and Human Survival is written for different audiences. It is for scientists interested in how caring relationships can be measured and in how such relationships can actually affect the body's resistance to disease. It is also written for professionals in health and human services, concerned with the creation and facilitation of supportive social networks and healthy social arrangements. To our surprise, however, the book that emerged is written primarily for any person concerned about society, for it deals with the nature of the human bond and its development and changes over a lifetime.

We would like to express deep appreciation to the network of people who provided us support in the form of encouragement, feedback, and tangible help. Particular thanks is given to George Albee, Carolyn Attneave, Barbara Brandes, Carman Carillo, Susan Chandler, Sydney Cobb, John Conger, Leonard Duhl, Judy Frank, Bill Goldman, Ed Gottlieb, Paula Heady, Nick Higgenbotham, Barbara Israel, Maddi Marcus, Martha Mednick, Meredith Minkler, Mary Beth Montgomery, Ellen Morris, Stan Oservitz, Robert Perrucci, Tracey Revenson, Seymour Sarason, Harry Specht, Leonard Syme, Elizabeth Young, Xiao Jian Zhao, and a group of wonderfully helpful reference librarians. We appreciate the essential support provided by the University of California, Davis, and the Agricultural Experiment Station.

A special note of appreciation goes to Tom McFarland of New England University Press for his faith in our manuscript over a long period of time, and to Mary Crittendon, the managing editor of the manuscript. We also want to give heartfelt thanks to some special members of our own support networks—Phyllis Pilisuk, Tammy Pilisuk, Jeffrey Pilisuk, Charlotte Pilisuk, Jim Parks, Jennifer Hillier Parks, Brian Gore, and Elaine Russell. Without their humor, help, and daily caring, the task of completing the manuscript would have been insurmountable.

Davis, California   M.P.
October 1985   S.H.P.

THE
HEALING WEB

SOCIAL NETWORKS
AND HUMAN SURVIVAL

INTRODUCTION

THE INTEREST IN SOCIAL SUPPORT

If self-expression was a theme of the 1970s, social support is surely a contender for the theme of the 1980s. Caring exchanges among people have been a matter of popular concern, with support groups for every special interest or problem and for the more pervasive problem of loneliness currently described and advertised in popular magazines and newsletters across the country.

Mental health professionals, nurses, social workers, and physicians, also noting the benefits of close social ties, have gotten into the act, studying and encouraging among people those bonds that are apparently so important to our health and to our adjustment. Social scientists from the fields of epidemiology, psychology, and sociology have been actively involved in studying three very important questions: What is happening to the family as a support giver? How does social support actually affect our health? Why does social connection matter to the human psyche? Writers and social critics have also been wondering why there is this sudden profound interest in relationships. What is happening to our society to cause this increasing fascination with social support even as our isolation increases?

In this book, we wish to make sense of this flurry of interest. We believe there is value in looking at the phenomenon as a whole, that some

1

insights into the changing human condition may be obtained by doing so. Here, under one cover, we ask, Does support or love really provide resistance to illness? Can we survive, as individuals or as a planet, without caring relationships? Can contemporary families meet the supportive needs of their members? Are the creative, nonfamilial forms of support a basis for enduring relationships? How can the helpers, the providers of concerned care, be helped?

Beyond the question of the relevance of social support to individual health or to local community cohesion, there are yet other concerns that reflect the broader importance of social support. The quality of social bonds reflects a changing, technologically oriented economy. Child care, for example, requires special social linkages. How does a community provide adequate funds for quality child care when its fiscal resources are needed to attract branches of multinational firms, which in turn employ the parents of that child?

The issue of equality is also related to social support. What, for example, does caring mean in a world with increasing starvation and homelessness? Additionally, war and peace relate to social relationships. Can people's concerns about war play a part in the formation of national decisions that jeopardize the fate of loved ones? Here we enter the arena of the politics of a caring community, for basic to each separate inquiry is one underlying concern: Can we survive, as individuals or as a planet, without a profound change in our attention to caring relationships?

In this book, these questions and others are addressed and an underlying thesis emerges: the unchecked movement toward autonomy in modern society threatens all of us if it is not balanced with a conscious movement toward interdependence. If interdependence is understood, then the advantages of individual development can be preserved while building a stronger and more supportive social fabric.

The questions we have raised are, in a sense, broader than most inquiries into social support. We therefore find ourselves dipping into many fields in the social and behavioral sciences, ranging from psychoneuroimmunology to social exchange, and into issues of philosophy. This breadth is necessary precisely because the causes of loneliness and the consequences of inadequate social support networks are so diverse—affecting factors ranging from the biochemistry of our resistence to illness to the political economy of inequality; from the psychological attributes of relationships to the cultural values placed upon caring and healing; from the probability of the continuation of the nuclear family to the probability of nuclear war.

Needless to say, we cannot do justice to the research in every area. To bring coherence to so broad an undertaking, certain themes recur. First, we assume a life-span perspective, examining social support over different stages of life as well as by gender and across the generations of recent history. Second, we take a systems perspective, examining specific relationships against a more general structure in which these relationships find meaning. This viewpoint may be seen in our review of caring roles in the family, where some of the disruptive changes that have occurred are viewed as products of evolving belief systems and of economic patterns rather than as the fault of men or women. Similarly, in examining what is to be done, the more microscopic innovations in individual caring are examined against the background of related conditions. Some broader circumstances increase the need for care, and others constrain the resources that make caring relationships possible.

Third, we have chosen to make a special point of relating social support to issues of inequality and of human survival. As human beings, our devotion to one another is surely related to the problems of hunger and to our capacities to prevent a nuclear winter. The relationship of social support to broad social issues is greater than is obvious.

Finally, we have written a book that expresses a point of view and a value premise. We believe that people need one another in more ways than the contemporary scene invites. We also believe that this need is a good thing for the individual and for society. The case we have built is based upon evidence that, in fact, supports this contention. It is based upon what is known and not upon nostalgia, but because the issue is so complex we have had to be selective. We want our bias to be known in advance.

THE CONSEQUENCES OF IMPERMANENCE

The meanings we affix to people and things and the values we live by reflect our place in the network of reciprocal relationships comprising the social order. For most of the history of humankind, the particular web in which an individual was enmeshed throughout the life cycle consisted of a group of perhaps 15 to 150 individuals. They were linked to one another typically by kinship but almost always economically, socially, and spiritually. This group provided individuals with social support without forethought or intent. Writing in 1936, anthropologist Ralph Linton referred to this fundamental social unit as "the band." He expressed the hope that growing industrialization would not push society further toward a collection of rootless individuals searching in vain for the bands they had lost.

What was feared then is a reality now. We are a society on the move. We moved out of the central cities to find a touch of green, clearer air, less turbulence, and less crime, and we returned to avoid the monetary and emotional costs of commuting or the dependence on our cars for every errand. Our society recreates itself by escaping through travel and maintains commitments to relatives by an occasional uprooting trip for the holidays. Our households are moved with greater frequency than the British, the French, or the Japanese, and those who remain in place are surrounded by a parade of changing neighbors. Though most of us reside in reasonably close proximity to at least one living relative, many of our most important family ties are maintained from a distance.

Many people have gained from moving about by the opening of new directions and opportunities. There have also been costs—serious costs of being and feeling rootless, a pervasive loneliness, and an intense curiosity about personal relationships and how to find them and how or whether to make them last. Currently, both popular and scientific literature abound with accounts of the causes and consequences of the contemporary search for enduring social contacts. The products of this search are called *social support groups*. Whether we refer to formally established groups or to informal associations, a large number of social entities now consider the provision of social support a part of their explicit purposes.

Sometimes the difficulty in finding a natural bond or a convoy of close people is defined as the loss of community. Today, "community" is a vague term. For some of us, community means the place where we live. This definition is meant when appeals are made to keep the community clean or to keep crime out. But there is also a *sense* of community—a feeling of safety and comfort among people who know us. This feeling is what we once held toward the family doctor who made house visits and to the butcher who remembered your family's preferences and asked how your son's broken arm was mending. Seymour Sarason's (1974) work provides some feeling for the importance of a psychological sense of community and for the informal network building that helps it develop. For much of human history, this community was where one lived. Now it only rarely includes our neighbors. Most of us live in one place and find community somewhere else or not at all.

Social scientists who once studied nuclear and extended families or neighborhoods now have shifted to the study of social support networks. From a broad perspective, the concept of social support networks has become part of the discussion on how the social order performs its basic functions: reproduction and socialization of the young, dissemination of cultural values, control over disruptive forms of deviance, and basic care of members' physical, psychological, and social needs. With modernization, we have experienced mobility and the expectation of changes in vocation, in residence, in life-styles, and in social ties. Smaller family size, shorter durations of marriage, and increased mobility have contributed to making a society in which the bonds between people are more likely to be a product of the circumstances of time and place rather than a mandatory or continuing product of kinship or of the longtime neighborhood workplace. Jerome Frank (1979) has described our culture as the "instantaneous society," devoid of temporal continuity.

Traditional sources of enduring supportive contact have decreased. Consequently, certain subpopulations have experienced isolation and the detrimental effects to physical and mental health that follow. Other kinds of supportive ties in the form of mutual help groups, neighborhood helpers, and intentional, extended families have arisen to fill the gap. Human service agencies have adapted to the increasing reliance upon informal patterns of helping by recognizing these informal systems and by seeking to assist them.

The proposition that social ties are weakening assumes enormous proportions when one considers the evidence that people bereft of such ties are more likely to have problems. Many indicators of weakened bonds—a socially marginal lifestyle, vocational resettlement, or recent loss of spouse—appear to be related to an equally diverse set of health breakdowns. These ruptured ties are associated with cardiac disorders and accidents; with tuberculosis and psychosis. Whether such findings really hold up, how closely these factors are related, and what this relationship means to our concept of health makes up one set of issues to be addressed in this volume.

The contemporary disintegration of traditional ties is not a fact but rather an hypothesis with which many students of society differ. Here again, it will be useful to look more closely at the studies, to ask who has lost what kind of connections with whom and to examine what supportive connections have survived or been strengthened. Friendships, voluntary associations, informal helping networks and mutual help groups all have complicated our image of the state of natural helping. But what of professional helping? What do our *formal* ties contribute to our health, to our ability to reaffirm meaning in our lives?

Major cutbacks in public services have had a curious effect upon the attention paid to natural helping. In the absence of adequate support for professional services, there has been more recognition of the role of "natural helpers" in the community. The added respect for natural helping systems must surely be positive. But how, then, does the professional community best react to a client who is not an individual but an imperfectly working system of natural helping relationships? In response to this question, a new set of experiments in the delivery of human services is being developed, both within and between several professions. We will describe several of the more interesting experiments.

Determining how to allocate responsibility for caring for people between professionals, on one hand, and indigenous family, friends, or community volunteers, on the other, is not merely a matter of discovering the most appropriate ways to divide up the task. Natural helpers are not a cheap substitute, ready to fill in whenever professional providers of human services are pulled out. The natural helpers themselves need opportunities for recognition, for compensation, and for employment. A working mother, particularly a single parent, is typically too stressed and too poor to assume the full care of an elderly, disabled parent, even if she wants to do so. Clearly, helping the helpers and/or creating a more caring society are matters seriously constrained by social values and by the economic and political conditions influencing both our capacity and our incentive to care. We will therefore also have to look at that larger society and ask what kind of social policies and priorities encourage and nurture the phenomenon of interpersonal caring, and what policies stunt a caring society.

The new trends in human services aimed at strengthening supportive networks have arisen in parallel with a new trend in the social sciences. The concept of network analysis, borrowed originally from mathematical graph theory, has proven to be a tool of remarkable usefulness in the study of linkages among people. Primarily descriptive in nature, the concepts from network analysis have encouraged a more refined view of social ties, enabling us to make comparisons between one group and another using a language sufficiently rich to describe what transpires in social, emotional, and material exchanges among people. Studies in this framework have helped reveal the networks of older women, of single parents, of school-aged children, of separate minority groups, and of former mental patients. Network analysis also provides an ideal framework for the study of informal ties and mutual help associations.

Coinciding with the extreme developments of individualism and social isolation, there has been a simultaneous awakening of concerns for the ties that bind people into supportive and sometimes continuing social networks. We examine the reasons behind the current surge of interest in support groups. We also attempt to define the phenomenon of social support and to review its demonstrated relevance to human health and well-being. The concepts of network analysis currently being used to study the social support phenomenon will be examined, and we will review applications of the network concept to the building or rebuilding of social support networks. Throughout, we seek to find where we are on the path from bonding to separateness, from social contact to narcissism, from love to self-sufficiency. We will look at where we have been torn from our roots, and also what means we are finding for taking root again.

Like the infant separated from its mother, people wither and die when isolated from supportive networks. Although people are dying amidst a sea of broken ties and marginal contacts, life survives. The family, we find, has been buried prematurely, and nonfamily ties abound in more novel forms than we thought possible. New forms of caring are arising from the embers of older forms, and we have arrived at an opportune moment to take stock of our commitments to each other. The purpose of this book is to ask, "Are we modern Americans, with computers and televisions, psychoanalysts and designer drugs, still carriers of a human need for connection and nurturing? If so, do we care for each other sufficiently to make this tumble through civilization worth continuing?"

1
THE SOCIAL CONNECTION

WHO NEEDS IT?

    We are social animals. So be it. Our species is decisively social. Yet the form of our sociability fails to tell us, with certainty, either the degree of our interdependence or the necessity of our deep attachments. Other species are decisively social. Like us, the ants and bees, the social wasps and termites are able to move through life only in liasion with each other. The ants, as Lewis Thomas has noted, are embarrassingly like us.

> "They farm fungi, raise aphids as livestock, launch armies into wars, use chemical sprays to alarm or confuse their enemies, and capture slaves. The families of weaver ants engage in child labor, holding their larvae like shuttles to spin out the thread that sews the leaves together for the fungus gardens. They exchange information ceaselessly. They do everything but watch television." (1974:12)

As Thomas points out, however, the solitary meandering ant cannot be seen as having much on its mind. It has too few neurons directing its busy legs and jaws to have a mind, or even a thought. Only in groups of ants encircling a dead insect or in thousands of them crowded around a hill can one observe a planning, calculating, purposeful creature, an intelligent, responsive computer collecting exactly the right size matter for a particular phase of hill construction. Without the option for thought, the ant must manage this intricate social life with no possibility of caring for kin or for neighbors.

The individual ant has no chance to make it alone, at least in the long run. Like all living entities it survives only as part of a larger ecology, but its link to others in its colony is close indeed. An ant's existence and survival separated from others of its species is confused, short, and pointless. But what of humans? We also, admit it or not, are part of a larger ecology that sustains us.

The interdependence of people is special in its reliance upon a complex and tenuously balanced environment that provides for us the means to care for ourselves and for each other. Although Euro-American culture has more often than not viewed natural resources as existing only for exploitation, we now find we must learn what to do with the air and water we have polluted, the fossil fuels we have burned, the radiation we have released. We are inevitably a part of the world and it is only a strangely arrogant, cultural propensity toward development that has clouded our heritage from those who used sparingly and replaced with care. Some Indians of the Great Plains have used particular parts of plants for dyes. Only what was needed was picked. The unused parts of the plant were then saved for weaving or added to meal. Like those tribal game hunters of Africa who never harmed an animal not needed for food, this isolated example of Indian respect for the environment is part of an understanding of how our relationship with the ecology frames our inherent relationships with one another. The integration of these beliefs is seen in the Medicine Wheel—a symbol of health through connectedness and part of the concept of the Earth as Mother and giver of life.

Among the people of the plains—the Cheyenne, the Crow, and the Sioux—the story of the Medicine Wheel is a description of a way of life, of an understanding of the universe. Its deeper messages are conveyed by peace chiefs and teachers to all members of the nation. The Medicine Wheel, like the Judeo-Christian Bible, draws its lessons from a host of tales about people, and also about animated skies and waters and personified animals of the prairie. Its themes are clearly those of our interdependence with our surroundings. As Hyemeyohsts Storm writes in *Seven Arrows,* "The Medicine Wheel begins with the Touching of our Brothers and Sisters. Next it speaks to us of the Touching of the World around us, the animals, trees, grasses and all other living things. Finally, it teaches us to sing the Song of the World, and in this Way become Whole People." (1972:1)

The Indian concept of touching is fundamental. It is at least partly metaphorical, for it expresses a level of engagement with the world outside oneself which alone enables us to become one with life. People vary, according to this belief, in an infinite number of ways, but they are alike in their loneliness. This aloneness is considered the source of growth, but it is also said to be the cause of wars. Our love, hatred, greed, and generosity are all thought to emerge from this loneliness, from our desire to be needed and loved. Only through touching is our loneliness overcome. The process proceeds in two directions: we are touched by our surrounding world, and we extend ourselves to touch its nourishment. The belief in interdependence, more poetically captured by our Indian brothers and sisters, is found in all the world's great religions, and in many of its scientific writings as well. So, whether we recognize it or not, we are of our environment, acting upon it, dependent upon it, part of it.

What of our ties to other members of our species? Are we, like the ants, alive in meaningful ways only through our interdependence? Or, if true at one time, are we now undergoing a social and a psychological revolution making us more willing, more able to live free of binding ties? Unlike the ants, we have been self-consciously tied to one another by our images, our passions, and seemingly by our decisions. Is the human species approaching a threshold where we will, with new success, go it alone?

In some concepts regarding the human condition, the human being of the modern, postindustrial society is considered a different beast than even the forbearers of fifty years ago. The image of an atomized society of anomic individuals may be accurate and one to which *Homo sapiens* will soon adjust, perhaps for better, once the nostalgia of togetherness wears off. Huxley's *Brave New World* (1946) seemed robotlike despite the programmed happiness of its members, but perhaps the emerging human forms will be more creative because of their loss of bonds. Before we can predict a level of satisfaction for a rootless human race, however, it will be useful to examine just how basic is our connection to the social environment about us, to others of our species.

There are, of course, some obvious interconnections given our biology. Through sexual activity we produce children: Such sexual activity is a basic reaffirmation of human connectedness in a physical and a spiritual way. At least traditionally this has been the case. Contemporary successes with test tube babies and current research in genetics suggest the possibility of a less personal, less sexual way of reproducing our own kind. Experiments with cloning processes involving recombinant DNA even suggest the possibility of more genetically predictable offspring without sexual contact. Some comfort, however, must be taken from the observation that human sexuality has remained a matter of amazingly durable interest over the centuries. Sexual activity has been, and continues to be, an expression both of psychological and of physical connectedness. The question of how durable are our bonds, however, is not resolved by a discussion of sex by itself. We need other people for certain ends instrumental to our own needs and desires but the human connection concerning us here is deeper, generated by concern for another human being, perhaps by concern for all human beings. Sex without affection or attachment is not relevant to the issue of interdependence.

BIRTH AND BONDING

A compelling argument about the inherent inclination to make bonds stems from our knowledge of the first bonding relationship between mother and infant. It can be argued that, starting with birth, our infancy creates a special propensity for continued human contact.

When an infant is born, its relationship with the mother changes dramatically. The moment of birth ends a pregnancy that with labor and delivery, revives for the woman some basic fears of childhood—fears of mutilation, abandonment, and loss of love. The fears are both for herself and for the baby, and they are not without foundation. Some mothers are cut, torn, or injured, and some babies are born damaged or dead.

Following delivery, the mother, while in a state of physical weakness and emotional exhaustion, has a most important adjustment to make. She must claim her baby and make it emotionally a part of herself again. In this process, she will identify with those qualities in her own life that are reassuring, safe, and rewarding. This identification gives her the power to address the infant's demanding needs. That power is enhanced by the support the mother has experienced in her past and by the support she is experiencing at the time (Nuckolls, Cassell, and Kaplan 1972). The bonding relationship is particularly difficult for a mother who is not part of a supportive network, and even more so if her infant presents an irritable temperament (Crockenberg 1981).

The mother who cannot claim her baby and the rejected infant become precursors to more serious problems—beaten or physically or mentally abandoned children. Women, and men also, who feel neglected and less than human will in turn neglect their babies and treat them as less than human. Studies show that parents who abuse their children are likely to have been abused children themselves (Steele 1970; Parke and Collmer 1975).

Births which once took place in familiar home environments, have now become technical and impersonal events arranged largely for the convenience of the physician and the hospital (a far smaller percentage of babies, for example, are delivered on weekends than on Fridays). The impersonal and high-tech hospital environment transforms the magic of childbirth. Birthing is a time for the mother to regain contact with the baby's body, to touch it, to examine it with delight while marveling over tiny toes and crevices. Soon after, in close proximity with the father and other family members, claiming is reestablished by naming the child. The depth of the family claim and the security and support of both parents is likely to insulate against abuse and neglect (Morris 1968). Hospital routines too frequently curtail this process and are too rigid to listen to the mother's doubts and fears or to respond to her concerns about her baby and her own body. Rejection is more likely in such an environment.

When claiming does follow childbirth, the mother touches and holds the newborn, now a separate individual, nurses it, and quickly comes to love it. Typically, the infant, within its means, reciprocates. Much of life is a process in which a new level of association emerges when a new measure of separation occurs.

THE FIRST ATTACHMENTS

Our understanding of just what transpires in these early relationships owes much to the writings of Freud and to several later psychoanalysts of the object relations school of psychoanalysis. In their view, the origins of psychic life and the development of our psychological identities are closely tied to our relationship with other people. The theory uses the term "object" to designate persons or things of the environment external to oneself and significant to one's psychic life. The infant's earliest psychic experience likely recognizes those aspects of its environment most immediate to its needs. The long period during which the infant is highly dependent on surrounding adults emphasizes the special place these early "objects" hold in the child's development.

At first the infant is unaware of objects as such and, only in gradual stages, comes to differentiate itself from its surroundings. Its first images focus on the sensitive membranes of its own body, then on the breast or bottle. The objects are unstable at first, present only while being perceived, then gone. When the full-sized adult figure is first cognized, the scolding parent is probably not the same as the nursing parent. Gradually a whole person is recognized and recalled even after immediate physical needs are met. Later in the first year of life, the infant develops a strong and continuing relationship with the mother object. The early parent figures are the targets of rage as well as love, but in all cases there is believed to be an identification of the self with the parent object. The process of identification is an important part of the bonding relationship that permits further development of the infant's ability to master its own impulses and to deal with an external reality in which the needs and desires of another person are prominent. The many pathological consequences of a disruption in the relationship at this particular time have been explored in several studies and immortalized in films showing infants degenerating physically and psychologically following a separation from mother.[1]

[1] See for example Renee Spitz, *Grief: A Peril in Infancy*, and J. Robertson, *A Twoyearold Goes to the Hospital*.

Mary Ainsworth (1969) has gathered extensive data of her own and from many other researchers on the effects of mother-child contact and separation. Her conclusions focus upon a theory about attachment, perhaps most clearly described in the writings of John Bowlby, another scholar of infant social development.

"Attachment behavior is any form of behavior that results in a person attaining or maintaining proximity to some other clearly identified individual who is conceived as better able to cope with the world. It is most obvious whenever the person is frightened, fatigued, or sick, and is assuaged by comforting and caregiving. At other times the behavior is less in evidence. Nevertheless, the knowledge that an attachment figure is available and responsive provides a strong and pervasive feeling of security, and so encourages the person to value and continue the relationship. Whilst attachment behavior is at its most obvious in early childhood, it can be observed throughout the life cycle, especially in emergencies. Since it is seen in virtually all human beings (though in varying patterns), it is regarded as an integral part of human nature and one we share (to a varying extent) with members of other species. The biological function attributed to it is that of protection. To remain within easy access of a familiar individual known to be ready and willing to come to our aid in an emergency is clearly a good insurance policy, whatever our age." (1982:668)

This theory helps us to understand the depth of our fears about separation and loss. Just as it is functional for a deer in the forest to fear a crashing sound, whether or not it has previously experienced a negative association with the sound, so it is functional for human beings to be afraid of the separation from their caretakers. Bowlby's theory is ethological and evolutionary in nature, relating our inclination for attachment in infancy to our fundamental organic propensities. It is in the grand plan, the neurological wiring diagram of the human species, for the infant to become attached to a mother figure, who may be either the natural mother or a substitute principal caregiver. Under certain unusual circumstances, the basic plan is not met, and the baby receives too little satisfying interaction with one caregiver for attachment to occur. Some scholars have argued the existence of a pervasive, continuing effect of the infant-mother bond upon the developing child (Klaus and Kennel 1977). Others have questioned whether the evidence actually supports so strong a conclusion. That controversy lies beyond our concern. The bond does typically occur, and when it does, it provides an important first experience of attachment to another person (Klaus and Kennel 1977).

Ainsworth (1969) distinguishes one-year olds who have made a secure attachment from those who, from deficiencies in their interactions, have developed an "anxious attachment." The securely attached one-year olds are later more cooperative with and affectively more positive and less aggressive or avoidant toward their mothers and other less familiar adults. They emerge as more competent and sympathetic when interacting with their peers. In free play situations, they display more intense exploratory interests; and in problem solving situations, they are more enthusiastic, more persistent, and better able to elicit and accept their mother's help.

Object relations in the family play another major part in psychological development for the child of approximately three years of age. Again, the identification process is important, for here, while establishing what gratifications are appropriate with family members and which ones are taboo, the young child develops an aspect of its psychic life that introduces mandates of the social order. The introduction of conscience, of right and wrong, and of guilt produces a new level of social being. Through identification with a parent, the child takes into itself a particularly human set of ideals and admonitions. In fact, these identifications are said to form the basis of all conscience, all morality, all sense of responsibility to persons other than ourselves.

The degree to which such early attachments are basic is evidenced by the severity of consequences when the process does not take place. Infantile autism, a condition whereby the baby fails to distinguish the inanimate from people, and even fails to distinguish itself from the world of inanimate objects, is considered to be one consequence of the failure to bond (Bettleheim 1967). Those infants who survive the experience in a physical sense are believed more likely to develop psychopathic personalities—unable to develop an internal sense of caring and responsibility toward others. Surely the infant's attachment to another human is basic, then; but again, this knowledge does not fully resolve our original question. Are such relations merely an exception, a basic energizing shot that enhances social development at one stage of life but thereafter sets us loose to develop relatively autonomous selves? Although that first bonding experience gives us a capacity for empathy, for trust, and for caring, it may still be only one of the necessary tools. The critical experience insures a capacity, but capacity is not destiny. Having once been attached, we may be able to find attachment again—but must we? Does our psychological development actually provide us with an identity as bonding organisms throughout the seasons of our lives?

The concept of attachment was developed from observations of the behavior of infants and mothers. Can the concept be usefully applied to people at other stages of life? Some social scientists say yes. Robert Kahn and Toni Antonucci (1985) describe the various forms of stressors and the supportive resources used to deal with these stressors during different stages of life. They describe a "convoy" of fellow travelers—supportive companions—whose presence makes possible an accommodation to stressful, age-related challenges. Other social scientists look at the attachments we form as major factors in our inner feelings of competence throughout the life cycle (Bowlby 1982). Just as with the infant, the individual at any age makes overtures of attachment to others. Most frequently, the feedback received from the other person contributes to a sense of mastery and security. The person then feels less vulnerable or helpless and is more likely to have the confidence to take risks, to move in new directions, and to be creative.

Surely, then, we are assembling a case showing that the capacities for love, for caring, and for persistent attachments to another person are building during the early years of life and continuing to operate throughout the life cycle. For many of us, attachments do persist; but again, capacity is not actuality. The demanding conscience has grown perhaps more relaxed in current times, and children less fully nurtured may develop less propensity to bind themselves to the destiny of others. Is caring written into the human script? Are we inevitably and deeply interdependent? We have still not made the case.

TIES OF BLOOD

Perhaps the answer to our question about interdependency lies in our continued propensity to find families. One or another form of family has been found in every known society. Families have always been a prime setting for the determination of who and what we are. The family of origin, which raises us, defines our most fundamental attributes, and the family of orientation—a group formed partly by an act of decision—becomes the background for much of our adult experience and for the adventures of our children. Moreover, if we think of our associates as a convoy of persons passing with us through a shared life experience, it is the family, nuclear and extended, that is the likely source of long-term fellow travelers.

These familial or family-like ties are proving to be more important to our health than we had previously imagined. We are too accustomed, with our particular medical view of the body, to see ourselves as autonomous and skin-bounded creatures, in need of careful protection against the intrusion of microorganisms, sharp objects, or excessive demands on our time. A closer look, however, suggests that we are already contaminated, and fortunately so. We are the symbiotic hosts for a multitude of species—protozoa, bacteria, fungi—that share our respiratory passages, our intestines, and most of our organs (Thomas 1974). We are the hosts as well for our human confederates or guests, whose existence, like that of the protozoa, is vital to our own. The family, in particular, is like an outer layer or buffering membrane, reducing the likelihood of health breakdowns and cushioning us against the sometimes overwhelming stress of modern life (Caplan 1974). The family and related forms of supportive ties are proving vital to health, not only as part of our protection against disease but as a component of our recuperative powers. Our sudden separations and social isolation are translated into physical changes in our white blood cells, striking at the core of our immunity against disease. An individual closely linked to other persons with wider and more meaningful bonds appears to be, from what we can tell, better able to avoid and to recover from the greatest variety of illnesses (Cassell 1976; Cobb 1976; Pilisuk 1982).

On the other hand, the family can be a source of illness as well as of health. The work of Salvadore Minuchen demonstrates this fact, which every family therapist has observed. Minuchen's method was to measure change in anxiety by assessing levels of free fatty acid, an anxiety indicator, from blood samples taken every few minutes from each family member during a family therapy session. The two-hundred families participating all had children with serious illnesses. The remarkable finding was that shifting anxiety levels related closely to the theme of the moment. When the conversation focused on the ill child, the parents' levels of fatty acid remained normal and the child's level rose. When the focus shifted to a conflict between the parents, however, the child's anxiety dropped and the parents' elevated. The associated theory suggests that illness is a way of coping with the problems of living. The symptoms of one family member may be needed (and provoked) to maintain an equilibrium between other family members (Minuchin and Montalvo 1967; Minuchin, Rosmon, and Baker 1978). Again we are reminded that illness is not just an individual affair and that the family, like the psychological capacity to form attachments, does not assure one of healthy and supportive relationships.

For many individuals, however, the family does provide just that assurance of continued and supportive caring, but the number of individuals entwined in such families must surely be dwindling. More people live alone than ever before; extended families are often separated by great physical distance, and nuclear families are smaller and less stable than in the past. Social scientists disagree about how real is the decline of the family, and, if real, whether the change should be mourned or considered a change for the better. But change is the operative word. Our propensity to create families has not been met in recent years by our abilities to retain them as continuous forms for personal support. If we humans are deeply interdependent in some essential way, proof cannot be found in the modern history of the family.

THE MEANING OF SOCIAL SUPPORT

There are many ways to look upon the value of social ties. Sociologist Lynn Lofland (1982) reverses the question by asking what is lost when we are bereaved of such ties. She answers with a list of seven "threads" that tie people to one another. The first connecting threat is that of role partner. One cannot be a father without a child, a worker without an employer, a helper without a person in need. Role partners, particularly in secondary or formal relationships, are replaceable. But if our roles are part of our identities, our role partners are part of ourselves. The other connecting threads are the functions of mundane assistance, linkages to others, the creation and maintenance of self, support for comforting myths, reality maintenance, and the maintenance of possible futures. These "threads," in Lofland's view, are basic since they provide us with a sense of who we are, how we are comforted, what meaning we find in life, and what potential life holds for us. The list of "threads" has an informal and subjective flavor, but they do ring true to our common experience.

Other social scientists have tried to describe more systematically what is vital to the exchanges and relationships among people (Caplan 1974; Cobb and Erbe 1979; Gottlieb 1982; Mitchell and Trickett 1980; Moos and Billings 1982; Weiss 1969). In our own research, we have tried a simpler set of three types of supportive relationships: social (involving doing things with another person), instrumental (doing things for another person), and emotional (sharing feelings) (Pilisuk and Parks 1981). In later chapters, we will show how to describe and measure the different types of relationships among people and how the increasingly popular concept of network analysis may help in this task (Pilisuk and Parks 1982). For now, let us point out that the great variety of ways to describe the functions of the human connection is itself a testimonial to the basic importance of the phenomenon.

Social bonds are described abstractly by sociologists as the basic building blocks of the larger social order. They are described more graphically by writers, who wish to capture the depths of intimate attachments, and by still others (like therapists and ethnographers) who wish to focus upon either the nuances of tone and meaning in particular relationships or the variability relationships display from culture to culture, from person to person. From this diversity of description, we have arrived at our own definition of social support. It has two components: the first describes the types of exchange that transpire, the second describes the subjective meaning of these exchanges. Social support is the sum of the social, emotional, and instrumental[2] exchanges with which an individual is involved having the subjective consequence that the individual sees him or herself as an object of continuing value in the eyes of significant others. With social support,

---

[2] Instrumental exchanges here include physical and material assistance as well as information and guidance.

we are more secure in our interdependence. Without it, we are pushed toward greater independence and loneliness.

This sense of being cared about is possible because of the psychological capacity for empathy. Kenneth Clark (1980) has defined empathy as "the capacity of an individual to feel the needs, the aspirations, the frustrations, the joys, the sorrows, the anxieties, the hurt, indeed, the hunger of others as if they were his or her own." Because of empathy, we are less alone.

LONELINESS—EMOTIONAL AND SOCIAL[3]

Americans travel quite a bit, meet many people, but are still quite lonely. The actual pattern has been for one of five persons to change residence each year, with almost half the population relocating within five years (Shumaker and Stokols 1982). In recent times, this mobility has occurred for at least two major reasons: young, educated people are moving, often long distances, in search of more favorable environments (Miller 1977), and poor people move, more locally, as the economic and ethnic characteristics of their neighborhoods force them to relocate (Fairchild and Tucker 1982).

The effects of such moves vary greatly. Studies show there are many conditions wherein mobility leads to a variety of positive ties for some people (Rubenstein and Shaver 1982; Rossi and Shlay 1982; Stokols and Shumaker 1982). Some of the studies show, however, that many individuals are physically cut off from those people who once made a difference in their lives and that high rates of mobility are having deleterious consequences (Syme, Hyman and Enterline 1965; Brett 1980; Weiss 1973). Whether valued or detested, however, movement speaks of impermanence.

Our pattern of movement seems to deny elements of our human interdependence. We teach and preach independence and accept as a given that it is good to raise our children to be independent. Hence, we keep moving to find our own ways. We left the old country for the New World, we moved West after settling the East Coast. Always we left communities of people we knew for what we imagined to be opportunity.[4] Now we have no frontier, but we are still leaving each other. Our freedom has become a quest for independence, unchained by geography, by finances, or by social ties, and we continue to insist upon this freedom to relocate to another area, to quit jobs, to quit families, and to move on. The changing face of America

---

[3] A theoretical review of loneliness and its relation to friendship appears in chapter 4.

[4] For Native Americans, here before the white settlers, and for Afro-Americans, who came involuntarily, mobility has been more often a form of dispersion in the wake of the mobility of white people than a chance to increase opportunity.

reflects the triumph of rugged individualism. The individual is in many ways replacing the family as the basic social unit of society. The average household size has gone from 4.1 members in 1930 to 2.8 in 1980, and 42 percent of all new households are comprised of only one person (U.S. Department of Commerce, Bureau of Census 1982). With fewer bonds, though, we are more lonesome.

One national survey found that 26 percent of all Americans, more than fifty-million people, said that they had recently felt lonely. The two forms of loneliness found were *emotional loneliness* and *social loneliness* (Weiss 1973). The first is based upon the absence of a personal, intimate relationship or attachment. It is the more painful form, an anguished sense of isolation, of not being loved. The second form, social loneliness, is based upon a lack of social connectedness or sense of community. This form is likely to be experienced with feelings of nonacceptance or rejection, as well as with a sense of boredom. The distinction between emotional and social loneliness is important. Strong, close, emotionally supportive ties help confirm a sense of self-worth, a function different from that provided by a more diverse, loose community network. Diverse ties can give an important sense of meaning—of predictability—to life (Granovetter 1973). They provide a feeling that the world beyond one's nest, with all its minor confusion, conflicts, and challenges, is still understandable and safe. When social isolation occurs, as often follows a period of immigration, one sometimes finds what Peter Maris calls a return to *tribalism*, a reaffirmation of an earlier tribal identity that rejects the values of the new culture and the social loneliness of the new setting (Maris 1974). In chapter 4 we shall return to examine theories of loneliness as they relate to the meaning of friendship. For now, we look at loneliness because it is, in some ways, the reciprocal of social support.

When we feel we are not cared for, we also feel quite alone. But the perception of social support depends upon more than the actual amount of supportive contact available to us. Old people, more frequently than we wish to admit, find themselves substantially cut off from actual contacts with other people (Butler 1975). Yet old people are not, as a whole, the most likely group to perceive their aloneness. Several studies show young adults (below age twenty-five) to be the most lonely. Apparently, there is a disparity between actual contact with a social network and the perception among some older persons of adequate social support. Adequacy of support is obviously, therefore, a subjective matter. Perhaps those older persons who have had a lifetime history of social isolation are less likely to see themselves as lonely than those people who have been accustomed to having more social ties in the past. Still, in every age group, we find a large portion of the population telling the surveyors that they are lonely. Whatever people may gain from their separation from others, they are left with a sense of loneliness. The feeling shows that although many have lost either their capacity or their opportunity for attachments, their interdependence comes through in a sustained need to belong.

FINDING ONESELF AND CARING FOR OTHERS

Committed ties depend upon trust. The commitment the silent generation of the fifties made was to a social order that promised security in return for conformity. For the first time since the Great Depression, large numbers of people saw the opportunity to pursue a career, get married, and raise a family, all with financial security. The time was of rising consumerism, fueled by the first massive dosage of television. The good life on the installment plan accompanied this period of low tolerance for nonconformists of any type. The organization man, without face or opinions, commuted from a split-level home to the firm, sighed or applauded at the excesses of the McCarthy era, but never objected (Whyte 1956). Those not a part of the organization, aspired to it. People were committed to their own betterment and to the benefits available to their family members. The well-being of women, of minorities, of foreigners, of homosexuals, or of poor people was not in the public consciousness, and deviance was suspect (Riessman, Glazer and Denney 1969).

Small wonder, then that a generation reared alongside their parents' willingness to acquiesce lost faith in the social order of adults, whose ideals could so easily be bought for the price of security. Rejection of the goals and moral values of the established order brought pain to the traditional commitments made to families. Young people suspected their elders simply did not care, and in ever-increasing numbers they found ways to express their concern over racial injustice and over the ethics of the American intervention in Viet Nam (Flacks 1971; Keniston 1977). The revolt was deep indeed, but the rebellion was not only over injustice. Edgar Friedenburg, writing in the 1960s about *The Anti-American Generation,* observed wisely that the youth of the time were less distinguished by their feelings about America than by their feelings about feeling (Friedenberg 1971).

The rejection of adult morality, seen as hypocritical, brought about great experimentation in ways of living and relating. Within a decade, a revolution in sexual mores occurred. Before 1960 the established view on sexuality was that it was an extension of the deep feelings engendered with attachment to a family. Intimate relationships that differed from the norm, whether homosexual, extramarital, or premarital, were necessarily secret. For the most part, the choice regarding who was bedded down with whom at night was guided by whom we were willing to be seen with in public the next day.

The family, as Richard Sennett (1970a) has noted, has not always been a satisfactory place for the wholesome development of adult members. Women and men both began to move away from the family for sources of satisfaction and of challenge and intimacy. Individuals living separately or temporarily together found that, with financial security, they were free to find amicable companions and sex with nothing other than companionship and sex required in exchange. There came, of course, a loss of familiar and dependable ties, but this loss was consistent with the idea that other people are not entirely to be trusted. We became, through this process, somewhat preoccupied with ourselves.[5]

The great leap inward has been termed the "me decade" and "the new narcissism." It was accompanied by new concerns with physical well-being, from jogging and nutrition to hot tubs and meditation, from new psychotherapies to courses in sexuality and to new religious sects. For those less blessed, or less plagued, by the inner search, self-indulgence took the forms of escape to the casinos or to the head sets and to hitting the road in a camper truck. These pressures of the 1970s left a legacy of terms: "being number one," "finding my own space," "getting my act together." Concern with the self, however, became all-consuming and permitted insensitivity to others (Conger 1981). As the Ancients wisely understood, each present state evolves gradually into its accompanying state. Self-centeredness has evolved into selfishness, epitomized by the question, What's in it for me? In the classic Yuppie pattern of the 1980s, personal computers, individual retirement plans, and tax shelters have added a practical side to the concern over what is best for me. But it has always been the public sector that has provided the expression of concern for the health, the safety, the literacy, the education, the well-being, indeed the parks and libraries available to all people. The indulgence of our private selves has left us more a part of the competitive market economy than ever before in this century. It is in part a function of our despair, our impotence in being unable to redirect the dangerous course of public policy.

The uneasiness of America's contemporary hedonistic philosophy is captured in a book by pollster Daniel Yankelovich (1981), *New Rules: Searching for Self-Fulfillment in a World Turned Upside Down,* with surveys showing that 80 percent of all Americans now view their own search for self-fulfillment as a primary concern. Yankelovich writes:

---

[5] This cursory historical view of the changes in interpersonal ties is supplemented in chapter 3 with a historical view from the perspective of the family. Chapter 4 views these changes from a gender perspective, while Chapter 8 examines the roots of these changes in personal orientation, roots that lie in the corporate economy.

"When the war ended in the early seventies, the campuses quieted and the challenge to traditional mores spread beyond college life to find expression in the larger society: in the women's movement; in a further expansion of the consumer, environmental and quality-of-life movements (small is beautiful); in the emphasis on self-help, localism, and participation; in the hospice movement (death with dignity in a family environment); in the flood of books on cultivating the self; in the questioning of the scientific/technological world view; in greater acceptance of sexuality; in a new preoccupation with the body and physical fitness; in a revival of interest in nature and the natural; and, above all, in a search for the full rich life, ripe with leisure, new experience and enjoyment, as a replacement for the orderly, work-centered attitude of earlier decades." (1981:19)

Yet the pursuit of personal pleasure or of self-realization—whatever its contribution to human well-being—is not adequate. Each self-indulgent individual removes one potentially committed person from the pool of caring people, leaves one less person upon whom others can invest a sense of trust. Without a body of trusted and loved others, our very freedom makes us a slave to whims that cannot be satisfied for want of a standard to know when we have really arrived. Philip Slater (1976) warned us of just such delusions of individualism in his thoughtful *Pursuit of Loneliness*. With only self-interests as our values, we fall victim to fads, to empty commercial substitutes in a sequence of weekend self-improvement programs.

The achievement of an independent sense of identity is no small accomplishment. The movement toward individualism has surely opened a world of opportunity for many. For large numbers of women, in particular, it has meant a path away from de facto servitude. But psychologist Erik Erikson (1974) has called our attention to another aspect of mature development called "generativity." This term refers to rewards that can be gained only from contributions to the development and well-being of other people. Another psychologist, John Conger, provides an intriguing summation of just what is meant by self-realization. When examining our old stereotypes about the family, sex, and social roles, "it is important to . . . be aware that self realization is not synonymous with self indulgence, that concern for others is a necessary ingredient of concern for self and that there can be no true freedom without responsibility and commitment." (Conger 1981:1484). This lesson is about human interdependence, most visible in matters of health.

INTERDEPENDENCE IN HEALTH
AND THE WAYS OF DESPAIR
The importance of human interdependence is extremely clear but frequently ignored in matters of health. Numerous epidemiological as well as

experimental studies show, in some detail, just how strong the link is between our supportive ties and our resistence to physical or mental breakdowns. But the social nature of health is apparent in even more obvious ways. In a real sense, our health is not truly our own.

Look, for example, at the history of the fluorocarbon scare in the late 1970s: a major environmental hazard was damaging the earth's protective layer of ozone. The threat was brought on by the widespread use of fluorocarbons found, among other sources, in aerosol sprays. The convenience of sprays for a great many uses made them products for which busy folk were willing to pay. Therefore, manufacturers of all manner of products from household cleaners to insect repellents, found a profitable market in the sale of aerosols. Damage to the earth's protective layer of ozone began to permit penetration of dangerous, cancer-causing, ultraviolet rays to the earth. The effects were likely to be felt first by farm workers—persons who worked full days in the sunlight—rather than by the urban consumer or by the manufacturer. The health of the farm worker depended on the social conscience of others, although in this case, as in so many others, the help we give returns ultimately to ourselves.

This illustration is not unusual. Major health problems related to air and water quality or to industrial and consumer safety are obviously of this type. So, also, is the current problem of torture, now, according to such groups as Amnesty International, occurring at epidemic proportions. The future of socially responsible interdependence will determine what happens with the recurrent problems of hunger and malnutrition and with the most serious health threat of all—nuclear war.

The single, greatest threat to human health must be that of nuclear war. When one considers fully the effects of blast, firestorm, and radiation, and the disruption of basic services upon which we have become dependent for food, waste disposal, medical assistance, or transportation, it becomes easy to imagine Jonathan Schell's depiction of a barren and lifeless planet. Given the magnitude of this threat, surprisingly little has been done to assure us that no such event will occur. Beyond the details about how much deterrent force is enough or what specific actions reduce or increase the levels of threat, there are deeper matters restricting our ability to stop preparing for war. These hindrances result, in part, from an inability to recognize the degree to which all people are interdependent. Throughout history, it has been possible for some people to gain in status, in prosperity, in well-being, and even in health at the expense of others. Now, however, it is abundantly clear that our health, indeed our survival, depends upon our recognition of the interdependence of the human community.

Joanna Macy (1982) has illustrated the link between our ability to avoid a nuclear war and our connection to other people. Her analysis begins by describing the despair we feel about our inability to avoid the impending threat, and then continues with an account of our ability to bury such despair, like sweeping anxiety under the rug. Most often, we touch upon the topic of mass death with only a psychic numbing devoid of strong feelings (Lifton 1982). The suppression of despair, like the repression of any strong feeling, takes a heavy toll. It permits our daily routine to continue as if the horror were no longer present. But the suppression impoverishes our emotional and sensory life—leaving our flowers less bright and fragrant and our loves less ecstatic. The banishment of despair limits as well creative energies for fashioning new visions and new solutions. There is, in fact, so much about which to despair that those for whom the feeling breaks through conceal it from public view. Americans, in particular, rush in with solutions for every problem—ignoring those conditions for which we can find little hope of resolution.

Beneath the surface, unexpressed despair, like unexpressed grief, takes its toll. Macy writes:

> "So long as we see ourselves as essentially separate, competitive and ego identified beings it is difficult to respect the validity of our social despair, deriving as it does from interconnectedness. Both our capacity to grieve for others and our power to cope with this grief spring from the great matrix of relationships in which we take our being. Just as our pain is more than private, so is our resilience. We are, as open systems, sustained by flows of energy and information that extend beyond the reach of the conscious ego." (1981:41)

There are several tasks to be accomplished in working through our despair to the point at which we may be able to do something other than bury it or collapse under its strain. The first is to acknowledge its validity, for like pain, psychic disarray can be a healthy reaction. The second is to allow our full feeling to emerge and to imagine our apprehensions and darkest fears. Despair requires patient working and active waiting to acknowledge that our fears and our hopes are possibilities that must both go on and on. The resources to work through despair are fortunately not restricted to those which each of us has at the start. Rather, small "affinity groups" of like-minded, supportive people or our deep sense of an even broader community can provide us with the necessary courage and patience to work through it.

People can be relieved and energized by despair work. It is akin to the powers some claim to have found in overcoming the diagnosis of fatal cancer through psychic imagining in a supportive group context. And it also fills a void. Some of us have been left wondering why, after being "freed up," stimulated, relaxed, self-realized, and self-actualized by every promising growth therapy, we still feel at a loss. We will continue to feel this uneasiness until we can recognize the social source of our anxiety about our world and our children's future within it.

> "Despair work experienced in this fashion is consciousness raising in the truest sense of the term. It increases our awareness not only of the perils that face us but also of the promise inherent in the human heart. Whether we "make it" or not, whether our efforts to heal our world succeed or fail, we live them in so vivid a consciousness of our community that the most obvious and accurate word for it is love. And that seems in and of itself, a fulfillment." (Macy 1981:47)

We have arrived at a difficult historical moment during which we, through the planned actions of civilized human beings, may by design or by accident begin the nuclear war that will destroy not only our own culture but all people of all cultures, all birds, all mice, all insects, all microbes, and every blade of grass. The life that sustains us is also hostage to the decision we make.

The danger of sudden termination of all life by a nuclear war has meaning for our discussion of a society centered upon prompt satisfaction of self. Surely, the possibility of extinction casts a cloud of doubt upon enduring love. The threat of extinction drives love away from stronger attachments and toward more fragile moments where it can perish.

Carl Sagan (1983), the planetary astronomer and science educator, reminds us that, as far as we know, no other world has been graced with life. It is through the planetary perspective that time once again unfolds upon our consciousness. "What a waste it would be," he writes, "if after four billion years of tortuous biological evolution, after the deaths of trillions of slightly maladapted organisms so a few, like us, could be superbly adapted, if after all this, the dominant organism in the planet contrived its own annihilation."

If we are able to see beyond the moment, we can witness the danger of war, not only as an end to ourselves and our supporting ecology, but to our children, and to our children's children, and to the precious gift of life for endless centuries ahead. But how are we to appreciate the long view, to move from our separate preoccupations with ourselves to that recognition of our membership in an ongoing human community and in the surrounding life that supports our own over generations and endless centuries? Perhaps there is an interdependence visible in the exchanges between people that can channel our attachments and move us through our loneliness and our despair to a renewed dedication to life.

INTERDEPENDENCE UNBOUNDED BY TIME OR SPACE

Social exchange theories first introduced by sociologist George Homans (1962) and by psychologist Harold Kelley (1979) explained our continuing relationships to one another by assuming that we reinforce the behaviors of each other, reaping benefits even as we give. A basic tenet of exchange theory is that relationships stay in balance by exchanging rewards that reiterate the importance of the relationship. When one gives money, others repay with deference or with recognition of status. The exchange moves toward balance when all terms are considered. The theory has led to many successful studies of behavior in small groups, predicting who wants in, who wants out, who feels obligated, who contributes willingly. For our purpose, however, if social interactions are directly or indirectly repaid, then the case for strong personal interdependence may be weakened. Much that we do to obtain rewards we can stop doing when the rewards are no longer forthcoming—or no longer needed. However, if our balance sheet is not exclusively with an individual but with any of a large group of people, and if the balance sheet can be sustained over very long periods of time, then we come closer to genuine interdependence.

Carolyn Attneave (1981), a clinical psychologist and a Delaware Indian, has spoken of "interdependence unbound by time and space." Her examples will be helpful. One illustration came from her observation of a graduation ceremony, a ritual celebrating the achievement of a group of individuals. Upon closer scrutiny, it is clear that the autonomous, individual accomplishments performed over a clearly designated time represent the workings of many people over a much longer time period. Surely graduation notes the culmination of activities begun by a student prior to entering college. Surely parents who partake in the ritual have been long-term parties to the event being celebrated, as have teaching faculty, administrative staff, and fellow students. Moreover, many of the students are marking not a termination of study, but a continuation. Many will return in new roles to visit the faculty or to be the parents, friends, or faculty represented at future commencements. In truth, commencement celebrates an ending, a beginning, and a continuation of an effort clearly the product of a large number of reciprocal contributions. The illustration suggests two important facts about independent achievements. First, they are rarely independent, and second, interdependence, the more common state, does not contradict individual achievement. Rather, the two are complementary.

Attneave's second illustration comes from her experience as a family therapist helping a man who, because he himself had been adopted, thought his own children might be passing on inferior genetic endowments to their children. Through some good detective work, the man was able to discover the circumstances of his own adoption. After his mother's death during childbirth, he was adopted by a great aunt, so the people who raised him were truly his own aunts, cousins, and uncles. Following the practice advised by experts of that time, no one told him the identity of his real parents. The family history was pursued back five generations and revealed that the client was only one of a number of children in the history of the family who had been placed for adoption or foster care following some economic hardship, illness, or death. In every such case, someone in the family had come through. There was a balance between needing and giving that extended over generations. Needless to say, the man concluded his grandchild would come from good stock indeed. His accountant-style message summarized the supposed genetic strengths: "He will always be able to count on folks and to do his part. We may not be able to do it alone, but as a family we balance our books!" This heritage is certainly a fine one—and a wonderful example of interdependence across the generations.

Attneave presented the two examples during her commencement address for a Pennsylvania college. She was being honored as an outstanding family psychologist who had drawn from her own Indian background in contributing to her field. Her final example also drew upon her own heritage as a Leni Lenape (Delaware) Indian. Two groups, her people and the followers of William Penn, had been parties to a three hundred-year-old treaty—never broken during the signers' lifetimes. Mutual respect and an honorable agreement between equals represented a balanced book in the account of the time. The interdependence based on respect ended abruptly after the death of the signers. The Delaware people were crowded out of the eastern part of their hereditary lands. They were chased westward amidst a series of deaths and injustices, leaving a grave sense of despair upon the remaining 10 percent of the tribe who still survived one-hundred years later. In 1777 the Delaware tribe was assigned, in a gathering by all eastern tribes, the role of protecting all Christians—Indians and whites—from the growing storm between the colonists and the British. This role of peacemaker was misunderstood and resulted in further injustice. In 1778 the first treaty signed with another nation by the United States obliged the Delaware to leave Pennsylvania for all time, an agreement still observed. That treaty, ratified by the United States Congress, provided for a separate Indian state as an equal part of the new nation. Half a century later the scant one-hundred ninety-eight remaining families from the once populous tribe were settled in Oklahoma (then known as part of the Indian Territory) after having been removed from nine other states. But the Indian Territory was also settled by whites. Indians were finally made citizens in Oklahoma in 1907, giving the area a population sufficient to request statehood. But the rights to health care, education, and other guarantees purchased in exchange for land have never been fully honored.

For sensitive persons like Dr. Attneave, the return to her ancestral homeland has often been a painful reminder of a history of exploitation.

Yet, she returned as an invited guest at a college commencement honored for the application of her own cultural heritage to her professional work, an invitation that at least symbolically connoted respect for Indian people and cultures missing since the days of the first agreements three-hundred years before. Hence, Dr. Attneave found joy in the commencement ceremony, which she likened to the ceremonial ritual of young men of the tribe moving into the status of adulthood.

Her summary captures her concept of the interdependence of all people over all time:

"The intrinsic value of the parchment paper of the diploma is about that of a feather or a string of wampum—and the symbolic value is equally priceless. The tokens of affection today may be fountain pens, neckties, and pocket calculators, instead of beaded bags, new moccasins, or tools for straightening or fletching arrows. But at the symbolic and human level, they are the same.

For many of you it may be a real surprise to find your own life connected in this way to a people whom you have never really known. This, I think, is another characteristic of interdependence unbounded by time or place. It is often unrecognized as each person does these things that need to be done according to one's best talents and understandings of the moment. Occasionally, dramatically or in quiet insight, the pattern emerges clear and palpable. We savor it, appreciate one another, and then go on with our lives again, and interdependence, echoes like the resolving chord in a symphony, or the shared Amen that concludes a prayer in the liturgy. For me to be here, and join with you, represents the recognition that mutual respect, love and acceptance between peoples is possible. It is only possible as we find those things that are here for us to do, and as we work together to solve new and difficult problems—interdependently. Tomorrow there will be new tasks and new activities, and even new roles for us. Perhaps just as we here realize our interdependence, flowing from the obligations and dreams of the past, we also can glimpse its continuation into the future. Having kept true to the faith—our own and that of our predecessors, we arrived at this point today. Our joy in it may also make possible solutions to new problems as we move ahead, into the future." (Attneave 1981:12)

Let us summarize the discussion so far. Are we capable of genuine, caring attachments? Yes. Are we inevitably interdependent? Yes. Can we go on alone with concerns primarily for ourselves? No. Is there cause for despair regarding the state of our attachments to each other and to life? Yes. Is there reason for hope? Definitely. Join with us, then, in an inquiry into the changing forms our interdependence is taking and the effects these changes are having upon our health, our values, and our images of the future.

2
HEALTH AND SOCIAL SUPPORT

**CARING RELATIONSHIPS AND
IMMUNOLOGICAL PROTECTION**

Like the air we breathe—and like the interdependence of all people—the support we receive from others is often taken for granted. Sometimes social support helps us to feel connected to others—a good feeling, perhaps most fully appreciated when it is absent and we are lonely. The obvious subjective benefits that follow feelings of connectedness to other humans are but the tip of the iceberg in evaluating the benefits of caring relationships. There is now a mass of evidence to indicate that such support may be one of the critical factors distinguishing those who remain healthy from those who fall ill. Such evidence could dramatically change our understanding of the causes and meanings of illness. It would also suggest a major role for family, friends, neighbors, and for the mental health practitioner in the field of disease prevention and health promotion. In this chapter, we will assemble the evidence relating social support to health. Then we would like to ask some difficult questions. How do our thoughts and emotions affect our resistance to health breakdown? What special effect does social support

This chapter has been adapted from a paper by M. Pilisuk, Delivery of social support: The social innoculation, *American Journal of Orthopsychiatry,* 1982, *52*(1), 20–31.

have upon these psychological processes that, in turn, help or hinder our immunity from disease?

Social support is a contributing factor—one among several others—affecting our ability to resist illness. Some well-loved people fall ill and die prematurely; some isolates live long and healthy lives. But these occurrences are infrequent. For the most part, people tied closely to others are better able to stay well. To examine the potential link between isolation and illness, it is necessary to take a public health perspective. The approach starts with an examination of the health of large numbers of people. By examining the rates at which different populations fall ill (disease morbidity), by examining ages of death (mortality), and by looking at the conditions under which these rates change, we are in a position to make inferences about what conditions are linked to a particular disease, to illness generally, or to good health.

Several major reviews of the literature on social factors affecting disease morbidity and mortality rates have pointed to the importance of social support to health maintenance. Sidney Cobb's presidential address to the Society of Psychosomatic Medicine stated:

"The conclusion that supportive interactions among people are important is hardly new. What is new is the assembling of hard evidence that adequate social support can protect people in crisis from a wide variety of pathological states: from low birth weight to death, from arthritis through tuberculosis to depression, alcoholism, and other psychiatric illness. Furthermore, social support can reduce the amount of medication required and accelerate recovery and facilitate compliance with prescribed medical regimens" (1976:30).

John Cassell on the occasion of his presentation of the Fourth Wade Hampton Frost lecture,[1] concluded:

"with advancing knowledge, it is perhaps not too far-reaching to imagine preventive health service in which professionals are involved largely in the diagnostic aspects—identifying families and groups at high risk by virtue of their lack of fit with their social milieu and determining the particular nature and form of the social supports that can and should be strengthened if such people are to be protected from disease outcomes" (1976:121).

Incrementally, a case is being built with the evidence from epidemiological inquiry that strongly argues that social support is necessary for one's health.

We would like to review the building blocks of this case. Following this

---

[1]An annual, honorary award in the field of epidemiology.

review, we will offer a theory about how it is possible that love, or supportive and caring relationships, can affect the body's immune system, which protects us from pathology. If love really can prevent illness, or cure it, we surely have a lot of explaining to do.

SOCIAL MARGINALITY, SEPARATION, AND HEALTH

A placebo is an innocuous substitute that pacifies us without genuinely affecting our problems. A phony pill that we believe is a powerful antibiotic is a classic case. Prior to the use of penicillin and the sulpha drugs in the 1940s, many of the medications doctors administered were placebos. They were surprisingly effective, so much so that when a new drug is tested now, it must be shown to be more effective than a placebo. The strength of this healing power of belief has long been noticed, and it was augmented by our belief in the power of the physician—by our trust in the physician's concern for us. The physician, in turn, earned this trust by an intense interest in each patient, and in the patient's family as well.

A substantial change has now occurred: doctors know far more about specific diseases and their treatments and feel far less familiar with the human host in which the ailment is found. This specialization has been a product of a very particular approach to the accumulation of knowledge about illness. Experimental research in medicine has had dramatic effects in the prevention or treatment of diphtheria, smallpox, syphillis, and polio. By clearly identifying each separate disease state, its cause, its course, and its specific treatment, we have perhaps lost sight of some more basic principles underlying good health generally—elements that explain the amazing power of the placebo, particularly when administered by a trusted doctor.

Still, it is possible, as Dr. William Osler once suggested, to change our task and to describe the patient first and the illness later (cited in Cassell 1976). We may forget for the moment the characteristics of the pathogenic intruder and ask instead what is the state of the host. After all, we are all frequent and unknowing hosts to a wide variety of intruders, some benign and many potentially dangerous; yet, not all of us succumb. Following Osler's suggestion, we could temporarily drop the question of what type of illness the patient has and ask instead, "What type of patient has the illness?" When this approach is taken we find a remarkable similarity underlying a highly diverse set of physical and behavioral symptoms.

Persons who develop schizophrenia or serious depression or who are admitted for any form of psychiatric hospitalization are likely to share the problem of social marginality (Brown, Davidson, and Harris 1977; Brown and Harris 1978; Hammer 1963; Mishler and Scotch 1963). Additionally, this factor frequently characterizes the victims of suicide, alcoholism, and multiple accidents (Durkheim 1951; Pittman and Snyder 1962; Tillman and Hobbes 1949). The illustrations just cited link social connectedness to a variety of psychiatric or behavioral disorders. But other studies show the link to be broader still. Tuberculosis is most likely to be found among people who have little social support (Chen and Cobb, 1960; Holmes 1956). Harburg, Erfurt and Chape (1973) were able to show a relationship between hypertension and living in a census tract with little community cohesiveness. Even the likelihood of arthritis is favored by the absence of supportive linkages (Cobb et al. 1969). Social marginality is a state of weak and impermanent ties with one's community. In one extensive review of the scientific literature concerning higher mortality rates from all causes among the poor, the underlying factor affecting mortality was believed to be social marginality (Syme and Berkman 1976).

Many individuals whose social status could not be considered as socially marginal nonetheless appear to enter the high-risk category for illness when they experience an interruption in their predictable sources of social support. The most obvious cause of interrupted social ties is a physical move from one location to another. Sometimes, however, the situation changes dramatically although the person stays in the same locale. Persons who have been uprooted or who otherwise experience great disruption in either geographic or situational stability have been shown to have higher rates of sickness absenteeism at work than do their peers. For example, people moving from the small valleys in Appalachia to the company towns created by reopened coal mines showed an increase in illness. By looking at the family names of the workers, it was possible to estimate how many had relatives living in the town to which they had come. The amount of sickness absenteeism was significantly diminished for those moving into a community containing kinfolk (Cassell and Tyroler 1961). Higher rates of illness are found where a great deal of social dislocation has occurred and the converse appears in more stable communities. Very low rates of myocardial infarction (heart attack)—only 50 percent of national rates or even of the rates in nearby towns—were found in Roseta, a community distinguished by closely knit family and community relations (Stout et al. 1964). Research findings are also available to support the association of participation in a closely knit religious group with lowered incidence of cancer and heart disease (Phillips 1975).

Disturbed interpersonal relations have been related to several particular disorders. In the family of an alcoholic, there are often disturbances in the pattern of communication that actually support and perpetuate the drinking problem. A similar pattern of disruption in supportive relationships is found in families where the problem is not alcoholism, but something else. Disturbances in the family support pattern are related to difficulties in pregnancy and to suicide (Bunch 1972; Nuckolls, Cassell, and

Kaplan 1972; Orford 1975). A disruption in supportive family ties apparently better predicts *some* breakdown in health rather than a specific condition or illness. Illness susceptibility is also seemingly related to marital status. Married people have less illness in almost every category and greater longevity than do their single counterparts (Kraus and Lilienfeld 1959). The findings cannot be attributed to a biased selection of those initially able to obtain marriage partners since the differences favoring the married are also present in studies including widowed or divorced people (Bloom, Asher, and White 1978).

The importance of supportive ties is highlighted upon the death of a spouse. Among the newly bereaved, particularly among men, the rate of coronary mortality is substantially higher than that found for others of their age groups (Parkes, Benjamin, and Fitzgerald 1969). Bereavement brings unusually high susceptibility, not only to coronary disturbance, but to all forms of health and mental health breakdown. The health of a group of women was studied thirteen months after the death of their husbands. The group was divided into those who perceived their social support to be adequate and those who did not. Twenty-two percent of those who considered their support adequate described their health as poor. This percentage was compared with a poor health rating of 86 percent for those with inadequate social support. When a sample of those women with inadequate social support was provided with a program of supportive counseling, the number who viewed their health as poor went down to 13 percent. It seems reasonable to conclude that adverse health effects associated with bereavement are absent or at least reduced when the individual maintains close supportive relationships (Raphael 1977).

Among older persons, disrupted ties are a common fact of daily living, being associated with retirement, bereavement, or change in residence. Frequently, such losses produce severe depression, but not when the individual maintains even one close supportive confidante (Lowenthal and Haven 1968). Engel's study of the life circumstances surrounding 275 sudden deaths reported in newspaper accounts found that most commonly these mortalities (135 deaths) followed "an exceptionally traumatic disruption of close human relationship or the anniversary of the loss of a loved one" (Engel 1977). Apparently, then, to understand illness in the human being it is best to address not only the causes of specific illness, but also the cause of breakdown in general.

Some of the more compelling epidemiological studies in this area have appeared first as doctoral dissertations at the University of California, Berkeley, School of Public Health. One study showed severity of mental and behavioral disturbance to be clearly related to the degree and type of integration into a network of supportive relationships (Froland and Brodsky

1979). In a major cross-cultural study, coronary disease was found to be more frequent among Japanese men living in Hawaii than in Japan, and higher still among Japanese men in California. Careful examination of the California cases not subject to elevated blood pressures or to coronary disturbance showed that these men maintained a closer affiliation to traditional Japanese styles of life, language, and familial traditions, including strong family loyalties. The effect attributed to this lifestyle was completely independent of risk factors such as smoking, obesity, serum cholesterol, or diet (Marmot and Syme 1976).

Equally convincing is a large-scale longitudinal study of residents of Alameda County, California, that examined participants' social and health status, then followed their records of illness and death over a subsequent nine-year period. The study showed that disease morbidity and mortality rates, from all causes, were related to the individual's interpersonal ties at the start of the study. Those with more supportive social ties at the start of the study were less likely to become ill or to die during the nine years that followed. The relationship held for both sexes, for all ethnic groups, and across socioeconomic classes (Berkman and Syme 1978). The latter two studies are particularly noteworthy in relation to the question of whether it is isolation that generates pathology or pathology that generates the isolation. Lack of supportive contacts could lead to more frequent sickness, or, on the other hand, the ill person may be less able to retain close ties to others. Clearly, both phenomena occur, but there now exists evidence that cannot be explained by the isolation of individuals following breakdowns in health. The findings appear even more striking when one considers the obvious fact that not all social ties are supportive. Some people are surely made less healthy by repressive or otherwise destructive family or friends. Even negative ties did not erase the stronger, underlying association between social connectedness and health. The presence of predictable, familiar, and supportive others is apparently beneficial for good health.

The human epidemiological evidence is supported in nonhuman laboratory studies. Mice subjected to competitive feeding developed hypertension, but only if the other mice were strangers. Among litter mates, the mice managed their situation without getting sick over it (Henry and Cassel 1976). Chickens injected with neoplasms developed cancerous growths if they were placed among unfamiliar chickens. Staying with the familiar pecking order, however, prevented the growth (Gross 1973). Young goats subjected to repeated noxious stimuli in isolation showed symptoms of experimental neurosis, while the same situation, with the mother present evoked no symptoms (Liddell 1950).

The classic studies by Harlow and Harlow (1962) demonstrating the pathology-generating qualities of an artificial lactating wire mother, when contrasted to the presence of either the real Rhesus monkey mother or the touchable cloth substitute, are relevant here. This finding relates to the repeated studies by Bowlby (1973) about the debilitating effects of maternal separation, discussed in chapter 1. Taken together, the studies provide further support for the significance of supportive, familiar ties for health and well-being.

Serious questions have been raised regarding the direct extrapolation of experimental findings, mostly with animals, to conclusions about socio-psychological factors in human health. It is the apparent convergence, however, of so diverse a set of experimental and epidemiological findings that makes so compelling a case for the effects upon health of predictable and/or familiar social support.

SOCIAL NETWORKS AND MENTAL ILLNESSS

People with major psychiatric illness have social networks that differ from the normal population, or even from those individuals with less severe neurotic problems. The psychotic individual typically has a small primary network of about four or five family members with friendship ties being virtually nonexistent. In the opinion of family system therapists, ties among family members are not necessarily positive or supportive, particularly for the mentally ill for whom relationships are characterized by ambivalent feelings and an unequal balance of power (Heller 1978). Psychotic individuals have few opportunities for reciprocal relationships wherein they can care for others as well as receive care (Henderson et al. 1978; Horowitz et al. 1977; Mueller 1980; Pattison et al. 1975; Tolsdorf 1976).

People with less serious mental disorders also have certain distinguishing social network characteristics. Here the network seems to be somewhat larger, say ten to twelve persons. Frequently, there is a significant tie to someone who has moved far away or perhaps to someone no longer living. The active ties tend to be negative and with people not connected with one another (Henderson et al. 1978).

This pattern is quite different from the one we find among a normal or average population. What is considered normal is, of course, influenced by many things. If one takes the time to examine networks found in a large variety of settings, some very interesting consistencies appear. This is surprising, since different observers looking at different populations and using highly varied techniques to gather their information all tend to find something similar. The size of the typical network has been estimated for rural, urban, and suburban settings in the United States and for middle- and working-class neighborhoods in Britain. It has been estimated in various countries for such specific groups as mothers of young children and people living in underdeveloped villages in Africa. A typical person's social network, we find, consists of fewer than ten people who are intimately known, and most of whom are also well known to each other. Beyond this, the individual is likely to see an additional thirty or so individuals on a regular basis. The typical size of one's active social network, then, appears to be in the vicinity of forty people. The range varies from between twenty-five and fifty, and the people named in one individual's network need not be known to each other. Frequently, the people are grouped into six or seven clusters who know each other, with not much contact between the separate clusters. There is usually some contact across clusters but the groups tend to represent different activities or parts of an individual's life, for example, friends from a club who all know each other, or work associates who know one another but who may not know the club members (Pattison 1977; Leinhardt 1977; Turk 1970; Westermeyer 1980; Westermeyer and Pattison 1981).

One study in Portland, Oregon, used questionnaires to learn about clients from the three mental health service units (outpatient, day treatment, and full-time residential treatment) of a large, state run facility. Across the continent, another study used field observation to look at the residents of a single-room occupancy hotel in New York City. Both studies, using different populations and different measures, found that an individual's degree of psychiatric disability was related to network size and to the specific characteristics of the exchanges in which the person took part. More disturbed individuals had fewer complex relationships with others and fewer network relationships that were reciprocal (Froland, Brodsky et al. 1979; Sokolovsky et al. 1978). We find a further corroboration, in a study of Chinese American adults: frequency of contact with friends, neighbors, and Chinese American organizations predicted an absence of reported psychiatric symptoms (Lin et al. 1979).

The theory that social contact reduces the likelihood of mental illness makes a good deal of sense. It was once hypothesized that the paranoid patient establishes for himself or herself a pseudo-community in which delusions and hallucinations are true and verifiable (Cameron 1963). All of us are dependent upon conversations with the important others in our community for affirmation of our views of reality. Berger and Kellner state this conclusion most clearly:

"... the predictability and stability of the world, as socially defined, is dependent upon the strength and continuity of significant relations in which conversation about this world can be continually carried on ... reality of the world is sustained through conversation with significant others" (Berger and Kellner 1964:5).

The studies we have cited do not tell us whether deficiencies in the networks came before or after the symptoms of mental illness. Perhaps the question is not really that important. It seems likely that serious mental symptoms, on the one hand, and limited and disturbed interpersonal relationships, on the other, are probably part of the same phenomenon. These studies do not prove that embeddedness in a supportive network precludes serious mental disorder, but they are certainly consistent with the findings on other forms of illness and with laboratory studies. The conclusion seems inescapable.

Social support, apparently is good for one's health—both physical and mental. But how can this be? We have not yet asked about the means by which social support, the care people give and receive, can contribute to so broad a spectrum of immunological protection.

SOME CONTROVERSY ABOUT
HEALTH AND SOCIAL SUPPORT

Social support appears beneficial not only to the prevention of illness but to an alleviation of the strain associated with the work environment (LaRocco and Jones 1978). Surely the workplace is often a source of great pressure, and the beneficial consequence of supportive ties is worth noting. For the moment, however, our interest in this relationship is aroused by one particular study. This study tried to determine how socially supportive networks could be responsible for the apparent relationship between social support and successful accommodation to a new teaching position (Depner, Wethington, and Korshavn 1982). The study, while not directly related to illness, is important because it tried to distinguish clearly between three different views regarding the effective ingredient in social support. The first of these views is that social support works as a *buffer*. Under highly stressful circumstances, supportive ties help reduce the impact of the pressure, perhaps by moderating the meaning of the stressful events. The surrounding group of intimate family and friends acts like a filter for harmful events.

The *buffering* hypothesis differs somewhat from the *compensation* hypothesis. The latter assumes that the effects of the stressful event will come through with all the expected pain, but that the individual with social support will have better ways of coping with the circumstance and will thus use his or her resources in a compensatory way.

There is yet a third possibility considered in the study: that social support contributes to the successful adjustment and well-being of the individual in a direct manner, independent of the assistance such support provides in reducing the impact of external stressors. This latter hypothesis was the

best in predicting the successful adjustment of new teachers (Depner, Wethington, and Korshavn 1982). In this direct effect view, social support protects us by doing something to the type of person we are, providing us with
some inner strength to withstand the slings and arrows, and the germs, of
life.

It is not all that easy to distinguish these three views in our minds, no
less to demonstrate the clear superiority of one over another in scientific
studies. Supposedly, the buffering theory suggests that support is helpful
in reducing the incidence of health breakdowns, or related disturbances,
only among those under high levels of external stress. For example, one
study showed that women who had a close and intimate confidant were
better able to resist the depression following inordinate levels of stress
(Brown, Bhrolchaim, and Harris 1975). In fact, it was the widespread observation that stressful events are everywhere, though only some of us
break down from the exposure, that has made the issue of social support
so important to the field of public health. The argument makes sense, since
modern life is full of stressful change and the traditional sources of social
support are no longer always there.

Yet those who argue for a direct effect have been able to show that
some good comes from social support, whether or not the people studied
are living under highly stressful circumstances. In a study of 720 adults in
New Haven, Meyers and his colleagues (1975) found that a measure of
social integration predicted low incidence of psychiatric symptoms, regardless of the scores received on a measure of stressful life changes. Another
sample in Australia showed that stressors and the absence of social support
were both related to illness; however, the effects of the two were independent, that is, one did not need to be under duress to show the benefits of
support in avoiding psychological difficulties (Andrews and Tennant
1978a). In yet another study of depression, this time in a New York community, the authors again suggested that "the problems in social support
appear to have greater direct consequences on depression than does the
extent of recent exposure to stressful life events" (Dean, Lin, and Ensel
1981:92).

The debate does not end here, however, and one writer has suggested
what seems to be an eminently reasonable compromise: that social support
may act primarily as a buffer, but can also offer protection in its own right
(Turner 1982). Cohen and Wills (1984), after a most thorough review of
the available evidence, have come to a similar conclusion. Sometimes, support particularly suited to the stressful circumstances does apparently appear to reduce the likelihood of illness. In addition, integration into a continuing social network also provides a measure of protection, independent
of the presence of stressful circumstances. Perhaps we are ready to refer to

a more specific definition of social support and move onto a hypothesis on just what it provides.

A DEFINITION OF SOCIAL
SUPPORT AND A HYPOTHESIS

Some of the supporters of the buffering hypothesis have proposed that, since social support refers to so many different actions, the effects one might anticipate in protection against stress are likely to be quite varied. The argument is that, for a particular variety of stressful experience to be buffered, it must be met by a particularly appropriate form of social support (Cohen and McKay 1984). A study of social support for cancer patients measured only the particular assisting behavior that had occurred during the past week. The measure showed opposite effects for individuals who received chemotherapy or radiation treatment at the time of study than for those not under active treatment. With supportive attention, the treated groups benefited significantly in their psychological adjustment, but those not under such treatment showed a negative psychological result from support. Though the result appears to fit the buffering hypothesis, the research teams' careful discussion of the findings suggests there may be more afoot. After all, supportive attention may undermine a person's sense of mastery. It could suggest to some that their own powerful belief in a remission, against the odds, is unfounded. Support could be viewed as being oversolicitous, and it could even remind an individual of his or her own inability to reciprocate. There is a subtlety in the communication of support, as much conveyed by the language of our bodies, the tone of our voices and the history of our relationships as by the content of what we say. "Unfortunately the 'transfer' of social support from helper to patient is so subtle, so hidden by cues, body language, and choice of phrase, that it is unclear in most measurements of support what messages are being sent and received" (Revenson, Wollman, and Felton 1983:1314). There is a clue in this analysis that suggests something at once to every psychotherapist and to every psychologically healthy parent. To whom is the message of caring unclear? It is probably not clear to the person who provides it either in a narcissistic way or solely as an expression of duty. It is probably least clear to the researcher, whose tools are often too rough to capture the nuances of a single exchange and too detailed to discover the long-term pattern. But genuine caring is perhaps quite frequently clear to the recipient, whether a patient or a child, and the "real thing" may be as important, or more important, than the precise tone or the precise match. Genuine caring is, in its own blundering way, more likely to provide a responsive match to the changing needs of any person than a computerized, selected combination of appropriate strokes.

We must be careful not to generalize too much from these studies, especially since they all deal only with psychological consequences of insufficient support. Yet the conclusion makes sense when applied to all forms of health. The benefit of this thing we have called social support appears, to us, not to come solely from its ability to ward off some particular stressful happening. Neither is the benefit determined entirely by whether one has received affection from a family member as opposed to appreciation from one's friend or work supervisor. Support cannot even be evaluated by the difference between the value of an intimate conversation and help with painting a fence or getting to the doctor. Rather, social support connotes all we mean by caring relationships among people. Our embeddedness in a continuing network of such relationships is perhaps what counts most. This secure place in a network has a profound affect upon how we think and how we feel about our surroundings, and particularly about how we affirm the value of ourselves. Consequently, we have defined social support with a psychological dimension going beyond the particular social, emotional, and material exchanges between people. This dimension means that we see ourselves as objects of continued caring and concern by others, for whom we also care. Although social support can affect our interpretation of specific events and our ability to cope in certain ways, its most powerful effect seems to be in the capacity for viewing ourselves as cared for, needed and worthy of the love of others. We must still ask, however, how social support can be so powerful? Why does such a psychological state help ward off illness?

PHYSICAL AND PSYCHOSOCIAL IMMUNITY

Social support is a general term. In relation to health, the concept is intended to provide some focus for the psychosocial processes that have been shown experimentally to influence susceptibility to some infections, to some neoplastic processes (unusual cell growths), and to some aspects of the humoral (glandular) and cell mediated immune response (Stein, Schiavi and Camerino 1978).

In other words, social support has some effect on those systems of the body most specialized to deal with the external challenges that cause illness. It is tempting to think we are hot on the trail of a miracle cure. Two pats on the back, one friendly smile, four hugs a day, and perhaps the proverbial apple will unleash a powerful master immune chemical that directs the charge against all intruders. If that master chemical or that special place in the nervous system can be found, are we not then close to a vaccine to protect us during those harsh days when the four hugs are just not coming? We would not wish to discourage the four hugs, nor the image of unleashing a powerful, inner defender. There is a measure of truth in the healing power of both the hugs and the image of powerful resistance. But not all hugs (or all forms of support) are equal. Nor are the body mechanisms for fighting disease so simple or so central. We are, though, on the trail of something exciting in understanding the magic of staying well. The trail will require us to look seriously at our understanding of the immune system, the stressors we face, and the psychological and social meanings of the concept of support.

An understanding of how supportive social exchanges may protect health arises in part from the increasing recognition among researchers from different disciplines of the relationships among social, psychological, and physiological determinants of health and disease (Lipowski 1977). In chapter 1, we hinted at a view of illness much broader than our common concept of a single physical ailment and much more dependent upon other people. But such a view of health is too general to help us understand the exact mechanism by which support relates to health. It is the more circumscribed line of inquiry regarding stress in the social environment and illness that helps place the question of supportive ties into the mainstream of interdisciplinary literature on health breakdown (Dohrenwend and Dohrenwend 1974; Mechanic 1976; Pelletier 1976).

The concern about stress in the social environment arises concurrently with a shift in incidence rates from communicable, lethal infections to stress-related illnesses. Dyphtheria, smallpox, and polio have been largely supplanted as the major hazards by heart ailments, cancer, accidents, and behavioral disorders. The latter are all clearly related to environmental stressors. In an attempt to understand the meanings of these patterns, the field of stress and illness has become a highly prolific one. Newspaper and journal articles and entire books have been written on the subject. Four points from all this study are sufficiently relevant to the issue of social support to warrant our attention: (1) the body's immune system has many separate parts and some key parts are subject to psychosocial influences; (2) psychosocial stressors, particularly as they relate to the self-concept, are of major importance to health; (3) social support networks may provide vitally needed protection for the self-concept; and (4) opportunities for social support are embedded in a socioeconomic context.

THE PSYCHOLOGICAL
SENSITIVITY OF THE IMMUNE SYSTEM

Though ill health was once viewed primarily as a matter of microbes, the holistic view has shifted our attention to a perspective emphasizing harmony and the constantly changing homeostatic balance among interacting systems of the person. The conception is vital rather than mechanical, assuming a spiritual or life force rather than solely considering a set of component organs. This view contrasts sharply with the idea that the goal of healthful living is freedom from tension. Rather, the vitalistic conception stresses that there is ample room for growth through challenge and response at every body level. Most important, the view stresses the relationships among the separate systems of the body, even the interactions between the person and the environment, rather than focusing upon the functions of a particular body part.

Social support presumably works its preventive effects through the person's immune system. The immune system is "a constantly vigilant sentinel dedicated to maintaining the integrity of the individual by discriminating between self and nonself and mediating between host and pathogen" (Ader 1980). It defends against foreign invaders such as bacteria, viruses, and chemical toxins, and it also takes on the neoplasms, those abnormal mutant cellular growths commonly grouped under the heading of cancer. The immune system has something in common with the nervous system. Both relate the individual organism to the world outside. Both systems are affected by experience and have mechanisms of memory. Both the nervous system and the immune system defend and adapt. Where the immune system responds to a potentially overbearing invasion of bacteria, the nervous system, through a variety of psychological defenses, protects us against disruptive levels of threatening information. Hence, overwhelming shame over failure, which might otherwise cause breakdown, can be reduced by projecting the blame to an external source. The two systems are each capable of overzealous defense, the nervous system neurotically protecting us from false fears, the immune system mistakenly rejecting some of our body parts and causing allergic or autoimmune reactions. Though many disease states are still poorly understood, there are medical theories relating the autoimmune response to diseases such as ulcerative colitis, multiple sclerosis, and arthritis (Solomon and Amkraut 1983).

The immune system fights back in three different ways. First, it can create or induce an immunity so that, even if we are exposed to a particular pathogenic agent, it will not affect us. Second, the immune system may elaborate or strengthen a particular defense so that our tolerance limits are greater. Vitamin C, for example, is claimed to heighten our resistence to germs associated with the common cold, presumably by such enhancement of tolerance levels. Third, the immune system may go to work by activating particular cells or substances that devour or otherwise remove the disease-causing agent.

The immune system itself is made up of complex factors focusing upon the activities of leukocytes in the blood, particularly those associated with B-lymphocytes which produce antibodies. Though some immune system cells are with us at birth, others only develop after we have been exposed to a particular foreign substance (antigen). In this way the immune system changes with experience. The B cells are joined by two other major actors in the system: T cells and macrophages. Macrophages are rather unspecific gobblers of foreign substances. They carry the signal of foreign attack (antigen) to the T cells, which then go into action. Some T cells attack the intruder directly. One substance these T cells release goes right to work attracting a bigger aggregation of macrophages to the area where they are needed. Some T cells (called helpers) can also stimulate more of the specific B-lymphocytes, and still others (called suppressors) work to control the proliferation of both B cells and other T cells. Without such controls, we might be overcome by our own white blood cells (leucocytes).

The immune system depends for its normal functions upon other systems of the body. In the normal process, specialized white blood cells are attracted to invading bacteria. The leucocytes engulf the bacteria and then release enzymes that destroy them. The efficiency of this system depends partly on the ability to discriminate what is unwanted bacteria, as well as on the ability to attract germs and attach to them. Here one can see the relation to other systems of the body. Cholesterol is a major component of the wall of the white blood cells. Too much cholesterol in the wall of the white blood cell reduces its ability to block the bacteria, meaning less resistance to disease. This situation is particularly serious for people who for reasons of age or sickness already have a lower resistance to disease. Cholesterol levels are affected largely by diet, although they can also be affected by life style and by stress. The importance of the link between this nutritional factor and disease resistance is suggested by a laboratory finding. In one study of cholesterol-fed laboratory animals, susceptability to infection was so much greater in the experimental group that the group had to be considerably enlarged because of the number dying during the experiment (Duwe, Fitch, and Ostwald 1981).

The immune system, in the case of tumor, is faced with a complex decision about what to destroy and what to leave alone. One particular antibody coats certain tumor cells, whereupon the macrophages attack them. Some T cells, known as killer cells, also attack tumors when they receive the appropriate signal. The NK (or natural killer) cells do not have to wait to be sensitized by a signal before attacking tumors. These natural killer cells are considered a first line of defense against cancer (Solomon and Amkraut 1983).

We are dealing with a system that has many checks and balances, many self-regulating or feedback mechanisms. Often, something that inhibits one part of the system actually enhances another part, and the immediate effects may be quite different from the long-term effects. The system is truly amazing. When we speak of the immune response, we are speaking, therefore, of a large number of separate but related activities designed to perform a highly complicated task. The very complexity of the system makes it sensitive to its connection with two other related systems of the body; the endocrine system and the central nervous system. It is through these relationships that we can begin to make sense of the effects of our thoughts and feelings toward other people. The entire subject, known as psychoneuroimmunology, is too new to be deeply understood in a brief abstract, but some exciting discoveries are coming from research in the area. Some parts of the immune system have been affected by hypnosis (Black, Humphrey, and Niven 1963), and Soviet scientists have performed experiments showing that classical Pavlovian conditioning can activate a portion of our immune system with a new and different signal than the one that naturally produces the response. This result means the immune system can learn not only from its physical encounter with germs but also from our experiences as people (Ader 1980; Talwar et al. 1975).

A remarkable scientific breakthrough in the field comes from the work of Janice Kiecolt-Glaser and her colleagues (Kiecolt-Glaser, Specher, et al. 1984) at Ohio State University. The findings are reminiscent of the first scientific identification of genes. After numerous studies of cross-bred fruit flies, and of chromosome structure, the gene was theoretically described as the entity responsible in inheritance. Its final identification in the laboratory provided the confirmatory convergence that makes scientists glow. Similarly, the findings of Kiecolt-Glaser and colleagues show social-psychological attributes to be linked to actual immune response at the cell level. The study comes after so many of our epidemiological and experimental findings suggested such an effect must truly be occurring. In one study, the group found that those with higher scores on a test of loneliness and those tested under a high stress condition tended to show blood samples with lower transformation of B-lymphocytes in response to a well-known (Epstein-Barr) virus. Natural killer cell activity was shown, in a separate study, to decrease among medical students under the stress of examinations, and to be typically lower for those medical students with higher scores on tests of loneliness and life stress (Kiecolt-Glaser, Ricker, et al. 1984; Kiecolt-Glaser, Garner, et al. 1984).

A quite different investigation, this time of psychiatric inpatients one day after their admission, showed those with higher loneliness scores to have significantly higher urinary cortisol levels, significantly lower levels of natural killer cell activity, and a poorer lymphocyte response in a test of immuno-competency. A related laboratory study in New South Wales, Australia, found a significant drop in one of the important T cell functions (dealing with the transformation of lymphocytes) six weeks after the death of a spouse (Bartrop et al. 1977). These studies show that the immune response is affected by stress and by social isolation, just as the greater body of epidemiological studies suggest.

The easiest way to make any sense of these effects on the immune system is to trace typical physical happenings during times of strong emotion. The messages from outside that signal "fear" or "anger" are passed on to the autonomic nervous system, immediately regulating a number of internal organs in preparation to flee or to strike out. Simultaneous glandular activity sends hormones through the bloodstream, elaborating the response and sending messages back to the nervous system. Sometimes immediately, but more frequently over time, these actions, transmitted by the nervous system and the endocrine system, affect the competence of our immune system (Besedovsky and Sorkin 1977).

The immune system is not stable, but rather is plastic and changes in its capacity to ward off various illnesses. Resistance is affected by a number of factors. Glucosteroids in the blood can depress the aggregation of white blood cells. They can reduce antibody production and limit the allergic response. The effect is indirect. The corticosteroids work not on the antibodies but on precursor cells, which then prevent antibody production from getting started (Solomon and Amkraut 1983). This fact is consistent with clinical observations about the potentially dangerous side effects of corticosteroid treatments—increasing susceptibility to a variety of illnesses (Bacter 1974; David, Greico, and Cushman 1973). The key point to remember is that hormonal treatments are but elaborations of substances already produced and discharged during natural endocrine activity. Levels of corticosteroids in our blood are, of course, affected by psychological experiences. Active mourning, clinical depression, separation, high levels of uncertainty, and breakdown of our usual psychological defenses have all been shown to affect steroid levels (Coe et al. 1978; Hafer et al. 1972; Hennessy et al. 1977; Katz et al. 1970; Sachar 1975; Wolff et al. 1964).

Although corticosteroids appear to be most important in transforming the effects of stress into lowered immune responses (a less competent disease resistance), other hormones have also been shown to be both responsive to stressful experience and capable of suppressing one or another part of the immune response (Stein et al. 1976). Occasionally, the effects are helpful. The action of T cells, for example, appears to depend on a hormone from the thymus gland. The hormonal effects are widely spread throughout diverse aspects of the immunological system. Hormones affect many of the same involuntary organ systems regulated by the autonomic nervous system. Patterned neural events, mediated by the hypothalamus, as well as metabolic activities relating to basic life processes such as the way the body utilizes glucose (particularly during times of arousal), will also have effects on portions of the immunological buffer. In an extensive review of the function of the hypothalamus in immune processes, Stein et al. (1978) note there is no single mediating factor in the immune response. Various processes, including the autonomic nervous system and neuroendocrine activity, participate.

The object here is not to reduce complex psycho-social events, including those associated with disruption of social support, to a simple physiological mechanism. Rather, we are obliged to recognize that the chain of physiological occurrences relevant to an individual's disease resistance is affected by the most central activating and integrating systems of the body: the hypothalamus, the autonomic nervous system, the reticular formation, and the pituitary and adrenal glands. Because the immunological system operates with so great a number of disparate but connected mechanisms, pharmacological assistance to disease control will apparently continue to be restricted to specific innoculation against particular infectious states. A more general immunological protection against stress-related breakdowns is likely to require an exploration into psychological and social factors. When we speak of the psychological and social attributes of an individual, we are examining factors more relevant to the state of the host than to the nature of the specific "bug" or stressor.

So much for our hopes of a miracle vaccine—but surely we did not expect the magic of good health to be revealed so simply. Perhaps we can find a form of social innoculation—a particular suit of psychological armor—that seems to fit best. For this search, we will have to ask how people handle the stresses of life.

A MATTER OF PERCEPTION

So far we have established that integration in a supportive network makes a difference in our ability to resist breakdown, and that social psychological factors affect the workings of the immune system. Now we are ready to examine these social psychological factors. This investigation entails an inquiry into the content of our own thoughts and feelings, asking more precisely what are these psychological processes that translate a social reality into a biochemical one.

To comprehend resistance to illness, it is critical to understand that many of the stressor events impairing our normal defenses are likely to be incorporated through the nervous system. Following this assumption, a major class of stressors begin as symbols (concepts, ideas, and perceptions) that go along with feelings and moods. Emotional changes occur hand in hand with the activity of the endocrine glands, which in turn affect the level of immunological function.

Just what are these symbolic stressors? They could be about any event we find disturbing. The illness of a close family member and the loss of jobs are common examples. Some of these stressor symbols have been listed as items on a scale designed to tell just how much stress one has experienced. Because symbols can be highly individual, the original scoring method, which assigned the same weight to a particular stressful life event for every person (Holmes and Rahe 1967), has been refined to incorporate a more subjective dimension (Chiriboga 1977). The work of Richard Lazarus and his colleagues has been instrumental in demonstrating the subjective psychological processes that determine the impact of various stressors. Basically, it is when a situation is *perceived* to be stressful that the pattern of stress reaction is likely to follow (Lazarus 1975a; Lazarus 1975b; Lazarus et al. 1965). When the stress reaction is extremely pronounced, and when extended beyond the normal periods of restorative homeostatic mechanisms, it is believed to lie at the heart of psychosomatic disorders. Some have argued that every illness has a psychosomatic component. Sustained stress reactions could then be central to the psychosomatic portion of all illness (Pelletier 1977).

The subjective factor in experiencing stressful life events was highlighted in one study of groups of people in the United States who had been displaced from their native cultures. These people had experienced drastic social change and major disruptions in interpersonal ties. For those who came through these changes and remained healthy, the investigator postulated a type of "emotional insulation" from the negative effects of stressful change. He recognized "a capacity to experience personal deprivation without a profound emotional or psychological response" (Hinkle 1974:24). One conclusion of this research is that people react to the meaning of information coming from the social environment and not necessarily to objective features that someone else might discern. This finding does not mean, of course, that being hit by a truck, by loss of a job, or by loss of a loved one are negligible facts that one can easily escape. Objective stressors are real, and they hurt. The matter, however, is one of balance. How we perceive what is happening can be a major factor in increasing, or decreasing, the likelihood that stressful circumstances will lead to a health breakdown.

To understand fully how caring relationships can make a difference in our resistance, we do need to take seriously the notion that people are active participants in their environments. Not only is the nature of stressful events subject to an internal appraisal process, but the process is itself affected by a continuous interplay between person and circumstances (Lazarus 1974). The differences in how formidable we perceive stressful circumstances to be reflects both our current assets for coping with the problem and some prior assets. The situation is like a deposit of love and respect put into an account during our early development and available to draw upon later. The more valued self-image can manage a wider range of stressors with grace, if current supportive resources are available. Stressors are upon everyone, though surely not equitably distributed by social class. The sum of our capacities for effectively dealing with them varies even more widely. This capacity has been called "resistance resources" (Antonovsky 1979).

It is the psychological nature of stressor events that makes the ways by which thought processes prolong the period of stress comprehensible. Understanding psychological handling of stressful events provides a means for unraveling the ways in which basic attitudes toward illness affect one's vulnerability to breakdown as well as recuperation from illness. These basic orientations, or coping styles, have been shown to relate to recovery from surgical procedures. One of the styles of coping that has been studied is denial of the problem. These studies show confusing results. Sometimes denial can be a positive factor in recovery, at other times it works against recovery (Cohen and Lazarus 1973; Janis 1958). What has emerged clearly from the studies is that persons do sufficiently better under the duress of illness when they believe they are still able to exercise a measure of control over their environments (Janis and Rodin 1979; Weiss 1972). Moreover, the ability to assign responsibility to oneself or to a dependable other person for what may happen, helps preclude outcomes unfavorable to physical and emotional health (Abramson, Seligman, and Teasdale 1978; Rodin 1980; Schultz and Hanusa 1978).[2]

Certain psychological factors, then, do relate to health maintenance. Is this path of investigation the way to understand the benefits of social support? Just what is so special to our psychological status about caring relationships with other people?

THE LINK TO SOCIAL SUPPORT

One way of understanding the functions of a sustained network of supportive others comes from a theory of cognitive tension. The theory of cognitive dissonance, as it is known in one of its popular forms, states that a condition of tension occurs in an individual when certain cognitive incongruities occur (Abelson 1958; Festinger 1957; Heider 1946). For example, assume you have purchased a gift for more than you can afford. Dissonance may be resolved by convincing yourself the gift is well deserved and will be greatly appreciated and reciprocated. Or, let us say that we believe ourselves to be kind. Some information from a source we consider reliable or valuable

---

[2]Medical beliefs in other cultures have often recognized the importance of attributing responsibility for health and illness. Chapter 7 contains a comparison with other cultural forms of healing.

tells us we have done something quite cruel. The resulting tension over these two incongruous pieces of information about ourselves can only be reduced if one or the other of the elements change. As human organisms, we strive to reduce tension of this type, therefore we quite naturally attempt to resolve the incongruent messages. In our last example, resolution might be attempted by translating the combined messages to, "Yes, I am basically kind, however, there are times when kindness is not appropriate," or, "yes, it was cruel but I was not truly responsible." This interpretation allows both the initial message and the second message to be "diluted" or understood in a tension-reducing way.

To understand how this mode of reducing cognitive disparity relates to social support, it will be helpful to examine the results of a psychological experiment. A group of male college students was given a task they believed to indicate "practical intelligence" and "social sensitivity." Each subject, sitting isolated from four other subjects, was led to believe that he alone was performing the task as the spokesperson for the other four. The avowed role of the other four subjects was to provide feedback, or criticism, to help the spokesperson improve his performance. If the eventual performance was judged the best among all the different groups that took part in the experiment, the entire group would be rewarded with a prize.

There was, however, some deception in the experiment. Although each of the young men had the opportunity to meet the others in his group at the start, direct communication was not possible, and the criticism was delivered to the spokesperson indirectly by the experimenter. Unbeknownst to the spokesperson, the experimenter was actually originating all the feedback supposedly coming from the four other participants. Though much of the feedback was positive or encouraging, one of the critics, as played by the experimenter, delivered harsh and abusive criticism of the subject's abilities on this sensitive task. The subjects, in this situation, ended up reducing the validity of the negative criticism by assuming the negative critic was either angry or stupid. This example illustrates that, where we are able to attribute negative behavior to negative sources, we do just fine. This action restores a balance that maintains the positive self in the face of harsh criticism.

There was one further wrinkle in the experiment, however. In half of the cases, the subject found himself in an experiment wherein one of the other subjects was his closest friend. When the harsh, negative critic was later revealed to be the best friend, the subject showed signs of tension, like sighs or blushing or nervous laughter. Also, the subject changed his explanation. In this circumstance, the negative critic was explained away as not understanding the task, as joking, or as both. Subjects managed to keep the image of the close friend positive by rationalizing the criticism. Such situations do cause tension, but typically the self-concept remains positive and the source of incongruity is resolved in a way that keeps the good friend also positive (Pilisuk 1968b).

The information one takes in has a function. People do not merely store perceptions, images, beliefs, and attitudes like a computer. Our cognitive processes have a basic purpose, one that may well be related to our health. This discussion brings us to a technique that has been used in the study of meaning.

Studies using a technique called the semantic differential describe the underlying dimensions of our many and varied concepts. The data from these studies show that the most important, first dimension of meaning is the evaluative dimension, translated as good-bad, loved-hated, positive-negative, liked-disliked. The most common attribute of meaning lies in this dimension of our adult language and thought. The distinction, however, probably also exists in the infant's most primitive perception of gratifying-ungratifying, edible-nonedible (Osgood and Tannenbaum 1955).

The basic evaluative dimension does not pertain to every last perception or thought we have, but it does apply to those we care most about: the people and concepts that are the objects of our strongest attitudes or deepest values. These "concepts with a charge" are not just stored in a file cabinet waiting to be used to identify something in the environment. Rather, they are grouped in special arrangements that separate the good from the bad, and that keep the concept of the self clearly attached to the good and away from the bad. In this way, the evolution of conscious thought clearly contributes to our survival. A concept of self, positive enough to be kept alive and surrounded by some closely attached and dependable others, is indeed a mechanism of obvious survival value.

It is possible to conceive of the various elements of cognition as satellites kept in concentric circles at various distances from the self-concept. Among the innermost circles are the cognitive elements involving significant others, or people with whom we are most emotionally intimate and who provide a stable and congruent feedback for our self-image. They may also include a few prized attributes of the self-image (Mead 1934; Pilisuk 1968b). Because we distort information incongruous to our self concepts and our central supports (Pilisuk 1968a), a positive symbol of each individual's life must be reaffirmed and protected by the presence of an enduring set of significant others. This reaffirmation and protection is the function of the support network.

DIFFERENCES IN PERCEIVING
STRESSORS AND SUPPORTS

Incongruities involving one's self-concept that do break through produce a higher degree of tension or anxiety, a basic threat to the individual

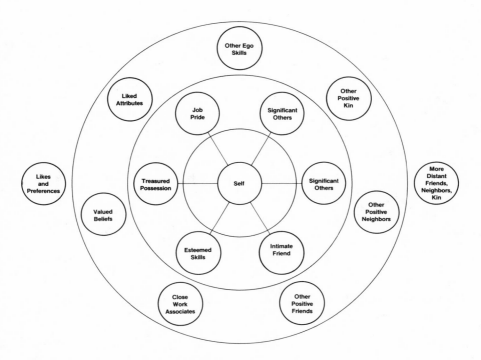

FIGURE 1. Adult Cognitive Buffer for Self-Protection

(Fairbairn 1952; Pilisuk 1962; Sullivan 1953). Certain stressors, therefore, damage the protective mechanisms provided by the buffering of significant others by threatening the highly individual symbols most central to a person's existence. Not all symbols are as close to our hearts as others, however. Some symbols change easily, some never. Also, some tensions from incongruous parts seem much more painful than others. Figure 1 shows the image of a cognitive system capable of protecting the self-concept. For the individual whose primitive images in early childhood did not involve stable and positive supports, the inner circle of highly positive, significant others is sometimes linked too closely with negative and tension-inducing predecessors. For such individuals, potential pain is greater, as is the need to distort information threatening the self.

   It is possible to experience a major change in your life and to consider yourself challenged rather than overwhelmed. These differences in the way we perceive ourselves likely affect how we feel and how our body responds to external stressors. One study distinguished people who had experienced

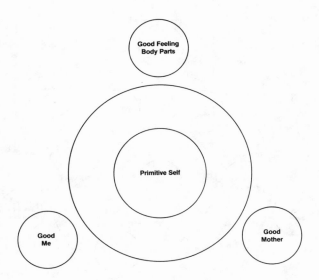

FIGURE 2. Infant's Cognitive Buffer

a large number of potentially stressful life events into two groups: those who saw themselves as challenged and those who saw themselves as over-whelmed. The two groups did not differ significantly on any of the major personality variables of the study. They did differ, however, on a rating of what is known as family mutuality. Those with closer, more reciprocal fam-ily ties were less likely to have related to the high level of stressors by feeling overwhelmed. Close, nonfamilial ties were also somewhat related to the likelihood that one would be challenged rather than overwhelmed. The findings support the concept of a protective buffer of intimates against ex-ternal stressors of life (Caplan 1964; Lowenthal, Thurnher, and Chiriboga 1975).

The same study found two other characteristics of the overwhelmed as opposed to the challenged group. The former were more frequently preoccupied with thoughts of death and were three times more likely to have experienced the loss of parents, either through death or divorce, dur-ing their own childhood or adolescence. Anxiety from unresolved, early experience appears to infect later experience, and the loss of closely at-tached individuals early in life often remains a reminder of the vulnerability of our caretakers and, ultimately, of ourselves. The potential power of these ghosts of very early experience is illustrated in a picture of the infant's cog-nitive buffer (Figure 2). Because this buffer is comprised solely of the good mother and rudimentary psychological and biological concepts of the self, we can see how vulnerable the infant is to negative experience.

FITTING SUPPORT INTO
THE DYSFUNCTION EQUATION

How are we to summarize the effects of social support on health? Surely such effects exist, most likely mediated by psychological processes. Certainly support can be a factor in our methods of coping with stressful circumstances. But here we get into more complex questions we have not yet resolved. What is effective coping? What circumstances are stressful? A brief look a these questions will help us to explain how our knowledge of social support to date fits into our understanding of the stress-illness connection.

External stress may be long-term, as in deprivation (Pearlin and Schooler 1978), may occur in daily hassles (Lazarus 1980), or may come about by sudden, catastrophic events (Chan 1977). The effects may be cumulative or separate and may be dependent on our own particular ways of coping with stressors. We may be adept at intrapsychic coping methods, manipulating in our minds the seriousness of the threat (Lazarus 1966; Moos 1979), and our ability to cope in this manner may well depend upon more enduring aspects of our character such as our ego-strength (Coelho, Hamburg, and Adams 1974; Haan 1977; Vaillant 1977). The intrapsychic or cognitive forms of coping are sometimes contrasted with behavioral coping—trying to take some action to deal with the stressful event (Billings and Moos 1981). Another way of looking at coping is to ask just where the coping process is aimed. Is it directed toward dealing with our problems or is it targeted toward handling the potentially overwhelming emotional consequences of the problem (Antonovsky 1973; Lazarus 1981). The effects of supportive people in one's life space may vary with the differences in how we cope.

In examining what is stressful, the most widely used instrument of study has been the Social Readjustment Rating Scale (Holmes and Rahe 1967), wherein individuals check which of a large number of events, from bereavement to job promotion, have occurred in the past year. With large samples, one typically finds that a large number of life changes are associated with more frequent illness—but not always (Andrews and Tennant 1978; Dohrenwend and Dohrenwend 1974). Many have pointed out that not all changes are equally taxing and that negative changes, such as the death of an intimate family member, are surely different in effect from positive changes such as job promotion or marriage (Mueller, Edwards, and Yarvis 1977; Sarason, Johnson, and Siegel 1978). Others have shown that the same external event may be perceived quite differently by different people (Lowenthal et al. 1975; Redfield and Stone 1979). Even after the types of people and the types of coping are straightened out, these differences in *perception* of stressful experiences will surely affect the way other people can be of help.

Although the help we need must be sensitive to our special view of the situation, it must also be sufficiently rich to deal with different harsh realities. Victims of a flood need something different from victims of imprisonment, illness, or a bad marriage. One study found that work-related stressors typically generated more problem-solving responses, while health-related stressors were likely to be met with attempts to alleviate the emotional response (Folkman and Lazarus 1980). In one of the more methodical and thorough studies of stress, coping, and supportive social resources, Billings and Moos (1981) found that the social resources an individual had were, indeed, factors in moderating the relationship between a preponderance of stressful life events and healthful functioning.

Obviously, any subject social scientists get their hands on can become quite complex. The bewildering variety of findings reflects the fact that we are studying a phenomenon in which individual ways of constructing experience make a great deal of difference in how stressed we feel, how supported we think we are, and how likely we are to show signs of health breakdown as a result. But all this scrutiny reveals an underlying basic concept. Social support affects us profoundly in our patterns of thought and behavior and in ways affecting our capacities for warding off illness. It is important, but not all-important, to our way of comprehension of the relationships between the stressors of life and our resistance to disease. Being embedded in a continuing network of basically supportive exchanges affects our cognitive system. The image of positive and durable others shelters the self-image from data that would be unduly threatening. In other words, being valued by a community of others contributes to being valued by oneself. The secure, positive, and cared for self helps restore equilibrium after destabilizing threats. Such restoration is the neural signal that helps preclude a failure in the immune system.

Using present knowledge, a schema for the relationship of social support to health maintenance has been summarized in a prevention equation. It is based primarily upon George Albee's formulation of the problem (Swift 1979).

$$\text{Incidence of Dysfunction} = \frac{\text{Stress} + \text{Constitutional Vulnerabilities}}{\text{Social Supports} + \text{Coping Skills} + \text{Competence}}$$

The formula recognizes social support as an important component among several unifying psychological concepts in the prevention of disorders.

SOCIAL SUPPORT: CONTROL
OVER HEALTH OR ILLNESS

Social support, we have argued, protects the self-concept, reduces psychic strain, and therefore guards against the destabilizing effects of sustained stress upon the immune system. This beneficial effect is enough to make us take notice, yet there is still another way that support affects health. Social support is also related to our sense of control over our well-being and to our ability to stick with healthful behavior patterns.

Our culture values activity, control over one's life, and a sense of mastery. These values, when we are ill, may help mobilize our minds and bodies to fight and to stay alive. They are not, of course, values that make it easy for us to experience increased dependence with any sense of dignity in our old age, nor are they characteristics that permit us to view our own deaths as part of a continuing process of the larger world and, therefore, a more acceptable outcome. To lack assertiveness is considered shameful, and extreme dependence is considered an unmitigated horror. Some psychologists believe people learn to be helpless, apathetic, and withdrawn by life experiences that provide little opportunity to learn mastery and control. Under such circumstances, the opposite is learned. This "learned helplessness" is a major problem behind clinical depression (Seligman 1975). Other symptoms may also be associated with a person's giving up or withdrawing in the face of a major environmental stressor. In one classic study, Langer and Rodin (1976) experimented in a nursing home by giving plants to two groups of residents under quite different conditions. In one group the residents were told they were competent to make their own decisions and that they were responsible for the care of the plants. The second group was told that the staff was responsible for the plant care. Despite having the same health status at the start of the study, the "responsible" group suffered only about half as many deaths as the other group during the eighteen months of the study. The results suggest that, beyond the mere presence of social relationships, there are some ties that enhance feelings of control, and there are some that do not.

Evidently, the ways we are treated by our networks, particularly as we grow older, can make a clear difference in our sense of control over our lives and in the degree to which we make use of our mental capacities. Support networks can also affect our health by influencing us in staying with a difficult regime of medical treatment, diet, or exercise. How social support affects compliance to medical practices can be illustrated by the treatment of chronic hemodialysis patients. Such patients require artificial means of filtering body wastes to compensate for defective or absent kidneys. The regime is also quite restricting, with severe limitations upon fluid intake and diet. Estimates of noncompliance among dialysis patients range from 13 percent (Borkman 1976) to 45 percent (De Nour and Czaczkes 1972; Haynes 1979) and result in deadly consequences. One survey of hemodialysis facilities estimated that 61 percent of patients' deaths were related to noncompliance (Abrams, Moore, and Westervelt 1971). Peter Burgher's careful study of the supportive networks of hemodialysis patients offers insight into the relevance of social support in sticking with a difficult task in personal health care. He found that a major factor characterizing those who observed the regime faithfully was their enmeshment in a supportive family network, while ties with health and medical personnel were typically not significant factors (Burgher 1981). Of forty-one different studies examining the conditions of compliance to a medical regime, thirty-four found social support to be a significant factor (Baekeland and Lundwall 1975; Haynes and Sackett 1974).[3]

Even in situations where no special behavioral routine is demanded, the social environment can help speed recovery. One review of thirty-four controlled studies showed that, on the average, surgical or coronary patients provided with information and/or emotional support during their medical crises, do better than patients receiving only ordinary care. In thirteen of these studies, the researchers used number of hospital days in post-surgery (or post–heart attack) as one indicator of outcome. They found that the supportive interventions, modest as they were in these studies, reduced the average hospital stay by approximately two days (Mumford, Schlesinger, and Glass 1982). Something in supportive social exchange seems to enhance the restorative and healing capacities of our bodies.

SOCIAL INEQUALITY IN SUPPORTIVE TIES AND HEALTH

The most broadly based studies regarding effects of the social environment on health extend to the consideration of social inequality as a major factor determining the ways in which the behaviors of certain groups affect the income, housing, nutrition, environmental quality, and medical access of others (Eisenberg 1973). The affluent simply have more and the poor have less of the basic resources necessary to remain healthy. Not only do poor people have fewer resources, they are also subject to more stressors.

The reportedly higher incidence of psychosis among the poor has been viewed as the direct result of a more stressful environment. Barbara and Bruce Dohrenwend (1974) offered an intriguing hypothesis to explain the findings on stress and mental illness in a study of midtown Manhattan.

---

[3]Six of the studies did not show a statistically significant relationship, and one study showed an inverse relationship.

Their argument was that situational stress causes emotional and behavioral responses often judged to be psychotic. Yet, such reactions may be no more than the response of normal persons to unusually stressful conditions. Counting these situational responses as if they were true psychoses results in overstating the incidence of long-term mental illness among the poor. But the causes are still more complex. Though there may be an exaggeration in our estimates of mental illness among poor people, what happens if the stressors do not go away, as is often the case in working-class life? Frequently the responses we are dealing with are reactions to chronic and long-term stressors—prolonged unemployment, inadequate housing, or poverty—all indicators of continuing threat to the individual's self-concept.

An illustration of the long-term nature of working-class duress is found in the stress of job loss. Susan Gore's study (1978) of working-class men found that the stress of unemployent often persists for more than a year, progressing from anticipation of being laid off, to actual job loss, to failure to find new work, and eventually to the stressors associated with a new job, new hours, relocation, and loss of contact with former colleagues. Other studies have confirmed this pattern, showing that after industrial plant closings there is a major and long-term disruption in the lives of the people affected that involves their mental state, their likelihood of illness, and the well-being of their families (Bluestone and Harrison 1982; Lawrence and Chown 1985).

Gore followed the consequences of two plant shutdowns to determine whether social support helps reduce the effects of unemployment upon health. In this sample of one-hundred stable, unemployed, married men, there were no differences between rural or urban groups in the length of time out of work or the amount of economic hardship; however, on the average, the rural unemployed showed a higher level of social support from family and friends. During the period of unemployment, the unsupported group (urban) showed significantly higher blood pressure elevations and more changes in cholesterol, illness symptoms, and mood than did the supported men. Either social support helped, or the lack of it hurt.

The study by Gore, however, raises a question. Some of the men who felt best supported through their period of unemployment were part of a close-knit ethnic community. We know that ethnic communities in this country have often maintained strong family ties. Studies of lower-class (Stack 1974) and middle-class Blacks (McAdoo 1979) show evidence of this family strength. Hispanic and Native American populations have retained extremely strong patterns of extended family affiliation. Yet, all these ethnic groups are overrepresented on most indications of sickness, have shorter life expectancies, and exhibit greater alcoholism. What is wrong with the protection offered by their social support?

There are two answers. The first is that, given the conditions faced by poorer segments of our minority communities, the appropriate question is not why have so many fallen ill, but rather why have so many remained well. It seems likely that social support has been a critical buffer in poor minority communities, yet not enough to withstand all the stressors. Second, we are convinced that social support is often undermined by the effects of broader environmental stressors. Poverty and inequality may sometimes affect the supportive interpersonal ties we have associated with health maintenance, as when unemployment precipitates family disintegration. One examination of the evidence relating both economic stressors *and* familial social supports to psychological disorder concluded that both factors—the stressors and the supports—are systematically distributed within socioeconomic classes (Liem and Liem 1978). It is as simple as that. If you are poor, you have more stress and less supportive resources. The viewpoint finds support in the assertion by C. Arden Miller, a former president of the American Public Health Association, that "For the vast majority of people in our society the life circumstances leading to poor health are not adopted as a matter of personal choice but are thrust upon people by the social and economic circumstances into which they are born" (1976:55). Miller notes that we find entire communities in the United States where the average level of hemoglobin in blood samples of children is at levels sufficiently low to warrant a diagnosis of anemia.

There are examples of highly supportive communities among rather poor subcultures, but anthropologists note that, with the introduction of Western values of individual success and with the decline of the family farm, the protective enclaves of kin and clan lose much of their effectiveness. Oscar Lewis notes that poverty often inflicts a set of cultural traits, such as emphasis on short-term gratification, fatalism, and present time orientation, on individuals. Such characteristics may interfere with the benefits of long-term familial ties (Lewis 1966a, 1966b). The point is made more strongly in Valentine's (1970) critique of the culture of poverty concept, in which he suggests that poverty, rather than creating a uniform culture, inhibits members of an existing culture from fully expressing the activities and relationships to which the culture gives meaning. Poverty, as we shall show in later chapters, can destroy natural patterns of support. Hence, Arden Miller's statement is as likely to apply to levels of support in the social environment as to hemoglobin levels in the internal environment. When viewed in this way, it is not possible to look upon social support as a phenomenon existing outside of its societal context.

The effects of poverty upon health are not, of course, limited to the disruption of important social ties. Many of the consequences of poverty upon health are largely independent of supportive social ties (except, perhaps, in the metaphysical sense of illuminating the interdependence of all humankind). The societal perspective is an important reminder that psychologically valuable concepts such as support networks, stress reduction, and coping still address but a limited portion of the field of preventive health.

So far, we have reviewed the evidence for social support in physical and mental health maintenance, examined the likely mediating mechanisms of such an association, and considered the societal context in which social support occurs. The discussion leads to the paradoxical conclusion that, though supportive, interpersonal relationships are important in health maintenance, the traditional sources for providing such support seem to be declining. A sense of affiliation or belonging has long been recognized as a basic human need (Maslow 1943; Murray 1938), yet the very social currents of careerism, autonomy, mobility, privacy, and achievement that disrupt our traditional roots and ties also make difficult the continuity of new bonds (Keyes 1973). We are led to ask, What are the available sources from which persons now seek supportive ties? and, What is the professional's role in relation to such sources?

In the third chapter, we will ask just how far blood-based groups go in meeting the supportive needs of people. Kinship, however, is not the only source of support. Where there is an absence of enduring, kin-based supportive networks, the isolated individual sometimes finds support from voluntary associations of persons with similar experiences or from certain neighbors who fulfill the function of natural helpers. These supportive associations, some established independently and others established with professional assistance, are now supplementing traditional, kin-based ties and providing new targets for preventive intervention.

Chapter 4 examines the potential of the nonkinship network for social support. Professional efforts through formal agencies are very important (despite inherent limitations) in the nurturance of naturally occurring supportive ties and in the establishment of new ones where needed. In Chapter 6, we will look at the professional's role and the place of social policy in creating support. Here, however, we have a concluding message about the implications of the relationship between health and support for the professional provider of human services.

UNRESOLVED ISSUES IN
ENHANCING SUPPORTIVE TIES

A knowledge of facilitative behaviors, actions likely to prove supportive or to assist people in maintaining group affiliations, is available in the professional literature. Empathetic listening, for example, is a frequently listed behavior. The impermanence of interpersonal ties, however, and the extent of social isolation reflect larger societal issues. Caring for other persons is not an immediately profitable activity. To add loving care into what is experienced by many as an unloving and uncaring society (Bronfenbrenner 1974; Slater 1976) is a task no less intricate than any yet faced by psychology or by the larger health field.

One major limitation is the unrecognized political aspect of the problem. Everyone is affected at times by loneliness or by a loss in their support networks, and thereby in immunological protection, as people leave or die and once strong bonds fade and wither. For the socially marginal individual, however, that state is chronic. For many of the permanent poor, for some of the elderly, for some of the disabled, and for many minorities the routine affronts from a noxious and sparse environment go beyond the buffering protection a close group of family and friends might offer. It is worth noting again that those factors among the disadvantaged that are the source of high levels of life stress are also factors leading to the breakdown of supportive ties. Job loss, for example, increases the strain of supporting a family and, hence, is frequently a factor in divorce. Similarly, one study of welfare recipients showed how poverty limits social participation by precluding expenditures for local transportation, for recreation, or even for minimal membership dues to local groups (Lebeaux 1971). In considering intentional, mutual support networks as a critical form of self-help in preventive medicine, one of the main threats to health is too easily excluded: the stressors associated with inequality. Working within this limitation, some benefits to health can still be realized by assisting people in developing or maintaining their social support networks—providing the complexities of the task are appreciated.

Probably both naturally occurring and contrived forms of social support will prove instrumental to health. When considering the development and nurturance of durable ties, professionals would be advised to raise several important issues. First, can we demonstrate the actual benefits of the supportive units we create for various at-risk populations? Research in this area is just beginning and must be encouraged. Second, can we avoid professional domination of the natural helping networks that are so vitally needed? Although professional assistance may be useful, the provision of social and emotional support is often a task best left to natural helpers.

Third, can we establish contact with and learn from those who know more than we do about social support? One source of information is the older generation, who has lived through times when supportive ties were a more naturally occurring component of people's lives. Additionally, minority communities such as small Chicano towns or urban Chinatowns have maintained a sense of familial, tribal, or ethnic cohesion in spite of the pressures of assimilation. These communities contain a wealth of information about naturally occurring social support networks.

Fourth, can ways be found for people to be compensated for helping groups provide deeper and more enduring emotional bonds? Such work was mentioned in the report by the President's Task Force in Mental Health. There is, to date, no category for this service on any existing pre-paid health insurance program; yet it is a task that requires knowledge, sensitivity, and experience, and one that may be more vital to our health than some of the highly technological diagnostic and treatment efforts now receiving extensive compensation.

Finally, we must specify a question for people working in the human services to ask themselves. Are we professionals able to apply our understanding of social networks to ourselves? In so doing, we may be able to escape our own isolation as professionals—the isolation that sometimes forces us to separate our findings from our practice and from social policy, and ourselves from other helping professionals. If we cannot model the benefits of working with supportive networks, then we are not likely to influence others with our findings. What is worse, without such support in our own lives, our own health and well-being may suffer. Somewhere in our approach to our own work we must find ways to create warm and caring environments. The settings in which we work may be as important as the objectives of our work—nurturing life-sustaining networks of social support.

3
THE FAMILY
AND CARING

Writing about "The World We Have Lost," Peter Laslett describes an appeal by the bakers of London to the royal authorities in the year 1619 for permission to raise the price of bread. The appeal from one of the bakers contains a carefully detailed description of his costs. These include expenditures for the care of each member of a large family, who were, in fact, the baker's work force. It included, as well, the costs of maintaining a handful of unrelated apprentices, maids, and handymen who also lived as family members and worked on the baker's small homestead and who were expected to marry into the family. This circumscribed group of individuals, unchanging in composition from year to year, lived and worked together as one family unit. From time to time a family member would travel into the heart of London to deliver bread or visit the marketplace; but, most days this little family band provided, without forethought, all meaningful personal exchanges for one another.

This chapter has been adapted from a paper by M. Pilisuk and S. H. Parks, Social support and family stress, *Marriage and Family Review*, 1983, 6(1–2), 137–156. Haworth Press, Inc., 28 East 22 Street, New York, N.Y. 10010.

Not all these exchanges were positive. Wives sometimes remained in abusive families, for they had nowhere else to go, and many children were forced into early and tedious labor, robbing them of childhood. For better or for worse, however, the family homestead was the group in which personal relationships took place. The homestead was the family, the community, and the world for its members. Something of this family of old has been lost—that much is clear. What remains of the family, however, is less clear.

What is this thing we call family and what is its place in providing social support, in protecting us from loneliness? In times not so long past, we were able to make more assumptions about families. Sometimes a marriage was interrupted by the early death of a spouse, occasionally by divorce. But by and large, there were far fewer marital separations and far fewer households with only one adult member. The nuclear family was typically large, with an abundance of siblings, and it was more permanent. It was also embedded in an extended family, then understood somewhat better by its members than now. There was the wife's family and the husband's family, and typically this clan included aunts and uncles, nephews and nieces, and cousins and grandparents who lived close by. This family network was not always present, but it was common enough to allow us to assume that the family unit, nuclear and extended, was the prime provider of social support—the place where people got and gave the products of social interaction. The family exchanged financial help, help with daily chores, care for babies, or sick people, or frail old people. It convened for celebrations of birthdays, holidays, and vacations and interacted in the varied ways we mean by love. Choices, however, were few. The options for incorporating changes into families were restricted by the strong expectations of other kin members. To take a kin member into the family was the essence of truly caring. Not to take in a kin member was unthinkable.

The kinship network was not always a protective nest. The early death of a parent, lack of treatment facilities for mentally disturbed kin, and unquestioned physical abuse by some patriarchial households all created disruptions in the family norm for which there was no hope of remedy. This family of the preindustrial era in many cases departed from the norm of a safe intimate network. But the norm did exist, and the typical family then was different than the family of today. In *A Little Commonwealth,* a study of the preindustrial community of Plymouth, Demos described the family unit as being

> . . . joined to other institutions and other purposes in an intricate web of interconnections. It did not stand out in any special way from adjacent parts of the social backdrop; it acquired no distinctive aura of emotional or ideological

significance. Its importance, while impossible to doubt, was more assumed than understood—was indeed, so basic and so automatic as to be almost invisible. Family and community, private and public life, formed part of the same moral equation. The one supported the other, and they became in a sense indistinguishable. (1970:186)

In the nineteenth century, following the social upheaval of the industrial revolution, the American home became idealized as a retreat from the harsh realities of the industrial society (Poster 1978). This idealization included a vision of perfect love, companionship, and moral regeneration (Jeffrey 1972). With the economic center changing from the home to the marketplace, there also came a change in the feeling of connectedness by family members to the community at large. The world of work became the basic connection to the community, separated from the world of home and family (Reiss 1971).

Progressively, the division of work and home/family, or public and private realms, further isolated the family from the community and created separate sex roles within the family. Men (fathers) worked away from the home, while the home and care for the children became the exclusive responsibility of women (mothers). This pattern additionally affected sex role behaviors—and hence family interactions—because men, who worked in the larger community for pay, retained primary legal and economic power over women, who worked in the home for their keep.

Conditions in the larger community were stressful. The working environment was, particularly at the beginning of industrialization, harsh and alienating. Even the proportionally few entrepreneurs in nonlabor positions were living through the excitement and stress of creating new rules, forging a new way of interacting personally and economically in the world. The home, not part of this realm, became more and more separate—a safe haven to which escape was promised at the end of a long, arduous day. Isolation of the home unit from the larger community, separation of sex roles into the public and private realms, and unequal distribution of power all combined to promote a particular idealization of the family (Skolnick and Skolnick 1971). The ideal family had a loving, caring, homemaker mother whose domestic skills included keeping her family well fed, cleanly clothed, feeling cared for, and in contact with other family members. The ideal father was a good provider, an authority figure, and a nonalcoholic who dealt with the distant world of work and came home to build shelves, provide discipline, and be taken care of. Most importantly, the family was idealized as a safe place.

Cultural anthropologists have long made a distinction between the "ideal culture" and the behavioral patterns that are actually are the norm.

One anthropologist (Harris 1968) has suggested there is an inverted relationship between commitment to an ideal in word and commitment in deed. He postulated that a certain idea may be strengthened by the very failure of people to abide by it. According to this logic, the more impossible it is for individuals to maintain the ideal family as a protective environment, safe from the competitive, success-oriented industrial world, the more firmly entrenched that ideal becomes. This process of entrenchment is described by Skolnick (1973) with a four-part syllogism: (1) society needs stable adults to survive; (2) stable adults are produced by warm, harmonious, stable families; (3) society is surviving; so (4) families *must* be warm, stable, and harmonious. For a family to be otherwise would be shameful deviance.

THE CHANGING FAMILY

The emergence of the study of new family forms is due in large part to feminist scholars. These scholars have examined the actual roles of women in families, adding to a historical precedent that focused almost exclusively upon the work roles and economic conditions affecting men. The earlier perspective viewed the family—and women—as being primarily ancillary to a man's world (Fairchilds 1976; Jordanova 1981; Tilly and Scott 1975). The newer perspective has permitted the study of families to address the roles and relationships among women, whose centrality to the family as a unit is apparent.

The American social and economic structures have evolved in ways that affected family structure. Upward mobility in socioeconomic status demanded literal mobility in geography. As families moved away from farms and into cities, neighborhood networks were substituted for kinship networks. Neighbors, however, moved on, repeating the mobility cycle, and those ties were broken. The family was changing: who constituted "family" changed, and the needs of its members changed. Ways in which families related to the larger community changed and sex roles changed as women became more influential in the economic sector. Family historians disagree on the reasons for this historical shift. Edward Shorter (1975) argues, from examining data on illegitimate birth increases in the late eighteenth and early nineteenth centuries, that new freedoms were expressed by women, resulting in unplanned pregnancies. This position is challenged by Marxist family historians who consider the changing economy (which required working-class women to enter the outside world) to be responsible. Working women and men were not adequately compensated to establish marriages and households. Some delayed marriage and others found themselves unable to provide for their children (Tilly and Scott 1978). Changing attitudes are difficult to prove by analyzing historical data. Depending on the perspective taken, many interpretations of the same records can be posited. Of importance to our point here is that change did occur. What did not change was the internalized, idealized image of what a family *should* be, and what it *should* do.

The stereotypic nuclear family, as an ideal, probably reached its peak of acceptance after the Second World War. People longed to return to normality. Families temporarily separated by fathers in military service or by night shifts in defense plants, desperately wished to resume lives that had been interrupted, and young people were eager to get on with marriage and careers. They were ready to become financially secure, to purchase homes, and to raise families. The good life, amidst postwar prosperity, seemed within reach of more Americans than ever before. Perhaps tranquility has its price. A nation, possessed with the virtues of "making it" on an individual basis, paid for its willingness to conform.

The "silent generation" of young people yearning for post war security sought a happy family life and the security of a steady, upwardly mobile job in a large corporation (Whyte 1956). People motivated by their own advancement are easily manipulated and ready to succumb to popular suspicions of outsiders, to those whose needs were not being met, or to those who would rock the boat. The ideal family became a medium for political apathy, prejudice, and the acceptance of gross injustice. Senator Joseph McCarthy's politics of fear and hatred became a symbol of the politics born from this foundation and representing this era.

Little wonder, then, that the youth generation of the 1960s, only one decade later, saw hypocrisy in an adult world so wrapped up in conformity as to be unable even to indulge the fruits of their own successes, no less to share these successes with those less fortunate. The explosion was inevitable, and the political and cultural disparities brought to light in the 1960s shook society at every level. The family was hit hardest of all by a generation critical not only of their parents, but of the very means by which their parents' maintained themselves. The family itself was looked upon as a repressive institution (Freidenberg 1971). Nothing could have opened the wounds more than the unpopular war in Viet Nam, and a great cynicism, crystalized by the Watergate crisis but reflected everywhere, was born. The view was that established institutions just could not be counted upon (Conger 1981).

What followed was the inward search of the "me" generation. The search was an attempt to find meaning within a social order that offered few guideposts to mark the way. We looked to our feelings to tell us what was real and pursued "our own thing," hoping to recreate worth in a life that was our own and independent of a social-political order that seemed not to be working. We experimented with means to care for ourselves: with health foods, with jogging, with meditation and Zen, and with hosts of activities for managing the stress of life. Families often impeded this search and were left behind. Beyond the symbols of nonconforming T-shirts, there was substantial change in openly acknowledged sexuality. People experimented with new roles in the work world. Women, particularly from the middle class, moved into positions once the exclusive province of men. People generally put a great deal of energy into the pursuit of careers. Marriages often had to be delayed or even abandoned to permit greater attention to the personal career or personal indulgence. For many, the personal search, however liberating of oppressive constraints and unhealthy habits of living, also lead to a preoccupation with the alleviation of stress and to an endless, unfulfilled search for contact (Frank 1979).

The family, shorn of the glitter of its ideal forms, seemed to experience a lessening of attachments across geographic distances and across the generations. Change itself—and locating a community that supported that change (even if it meant severing family and kin ties)—was valued by the new culture. For those who left the family, new supportive circles, however tenuous, could be found. For those who remained, the old values, still strongly embraced, were also irrevocably altered.

The ideal family was also altered by the changing role of women. A path that demands respect for the potential of each woman—a path from which there can really be no turning—has led to a revolutionary change in sex roles. Young women today, contrary to their sisters one decade and more older, accept as given their rights to jobs formerly available only to their male peers. It is estimated that by 1990 only one in four wives will fit into the unemployed homemaker role. This fact has an impact on family structure that, like the stone thrown into a pool of water, causes an even larger reaction in the environment around it. Changes ranging from intimate, personal relations between couples to the nation's very economic structure all become necessary to incorporate the changes in family structure. In tanden with women's changing roles, the 1980s have seen some men selecting roles that express concerns for the family—of homemaking and parenting—and the trend will probably continue (Ross, Mirowsky, and Ulbrich 1983). The joy men can find in parenting coupled with the extremely difficult economic constraints of the decade may conspire to encourage more men and women to balance their lives with family concerns and work-world concerns. Should this pattern continue over several generations, the old sex roles and structure of the family—and even more so the idealized family—could become part of history. Its new form would barely resemble the American family of the nineteenth and twentieth centuries.

There is an apparent contradiction in this pattern of increased sharing of parental functions between mothers and fathers and in the finding that young men of today are listing family life as less important than they did a decade before (Regan and Roland, in press). Michael Lamb's work on the changing role of fathers helps explain. First, the change in fathering is not a general phenomenon. While some fathers have become more involved with their children in recent years, the increase has been modest. Mothers still spend substantially more time than fathers interacting with their children and are more available to their children than fathers, even when both parents are working outside the home. Fathers are more likely to "help out when they can (or when it is convenient)" (Lamb, in press). Still, male parenting as an ideal is clearly present in the culture, and its potential impact is great.

In 1980, 73 percent of the United States' population lived in households containing a married couple—down from 82 percent ten years earlier. There were, however, substantial increases in the percentage of people living in single parent families and in the number of people living alone (*Washington Post* 1982). Nationally, the changes have been greatest in the San Francisco-Oakland area and in the greater Washington D.C. area. In these places, fertility rates, which have been dropping across the country, are lowest, and the number of one-person households and nonkin households are greatest. The two areas lead a change occurring more slowing in many areas of the country (Swan 1982). These demographic changes do not tell us whether there has been a shift in the psychological importance of family ties. They do tell us that a shift is occurring in the composition of households, with the traditional married couple and children becoming a less pervasive form. In a similar way, the 20 percent of the United States' population changing residence each year does not not tell us that extended kinship ties are less important, only that some of them are probably more distant than before. These demographic changes, however, reflect human decisions that do have an impact upon the functions of the family.

The condition of the contemporary American family continues to be a matter of hot debate, verbalized in language reflectng deeply held values and strong emotions. Has the family actually declined in importance? Is the extended family surviving the mobility of this decade? Are the changes in the family for the better or for the worse? The "family" is discussed at length on radio talk shows, addressed in television situation comedies, and is the topic of articles in all women's magazines. Opinions on the condition of the family range from Bronfenbrenner's (1970) somber prediction of serious problems for American society if adults do not reinvolve themselves in the lives of children, to David Cooper's enthusiastic welcome of the decline of the family as we know it today (1970).

Rather than plunge into this debate we will discuss two related issues that bear upon the family as a support system. First, do people still belong in a meaningful way to families, or is there a growing group of people untied and unsupported by any family ties of kinship? Second, and critical to the issues before us, is the contemporary family a viable support group, able to provide the nurturant care needed by its members? To answer these questions, we will need a working definition of the family—a matter more difficult than meets the eye, especially with changes of historical importance still occurring. It will be useful to backtrack a bit to this struggle to define the family. The issues raised, even in defining the term, show how hard it is to distinguish what the family is from what we would like it to be.

DEFINING THE "IDEAL" AND "REAL" FAMILY

The *Universal Lexicon* of 1735 (reported in Berkner 1972) defined the family as a "number of persons subject to the power and authority of the head of the household either by nature or by law." "Nature" in this meaning referred to children, and "law" referred to wife and servants. Today's definitions are not usually phrased in the language of possession common to eighteenth-century writers, but for many Americans the understanding of family still centers around legally defined responsibility. Currently, in America and in Europe, there are tremendous variations in styles of family life; yet, when we speak of "family," we often assume we are talking about the same thing. For this reason, liberals can view child care as supportive to the needs of the family, while conservatives, see the family as aided by measures to keep women in household roles. To some, family includes any persons living in a supportive, long-term relationship under the same roof as one economic and consumer unit. To others, the meaning of family is limited to father, mother, and biological children. When those children reach adulthood and leave home, more families are created: the original family, which now has only two members, and other family units comprised of the adult child, a spouse, and *their* children. Additional definitions exist that include grandparents or kin not living in the same household, or that exclude any household member not tied by blood. Anthropological studies of kinship consider the contemporary family as one wherein heredity is recognized through both maternal and paternal lines. The pattern of residence is neolocal (or strangely assigned to neither kinship line), and monogamous, permanent marriage is still the ideally recognized form. The changed contemporary American families, however, may be unlike any other cultural forms.

G. P. Murdock, a pioneer in family studies and author of what might be considered the classical approach, described the nuclear family as a universal social group. "Whether as the sole prevailing form of the family or as the basic unit from which more complex familial forms are compounded, it exists as a distinct and strongly functional group in known society" (1949:23). This traditional concept of the family also strongly supported the existence of the extended family as the ideal in most societies of the world. Then came a time of tremendous social change. Mobility and subsequent changing family relationships created new individual and family needs that had not been expressed before. Indeed, the changing economic structure with an expanding middle class and the ethic of upward mobility, radically altered many interactions among family members.

The family models that could function supportively were changing, and the ways in which people traditionally sought caring relationships and self-validation changed also. Building new models is not easy. Particularly in fundamental interactions between family members, we fall back upon our experiences, and we repeat patterns familiar to us. One good example of this repetition occurs in child rearing. Almost everyone can think of some event in their childhood involving a parent that they solemnly vowed never to do to *their* child; and, most parents can think of some interaction they have had with a child after which they were shocked by the realilzation they were repeating a pattern they promised themselves they would never duplicate. Conversely, most people can remember the comfort and cared for feeling of some act, some family pattern or ritual, that they consciously determine to continue in their own families. Most people can also think of times when, in relating to their child or remembering an event from their childhood, they were flooded with a sense that things *should not* be this way, or this is how it *should* be.

Perhaps more often in child rearing than in other cultural practices, we find evidence of a "cultural lag" that makes society less adaptable to the tasks of molding individuals to rapidly changing technologies (Mead 1953); hence, we can understand how important continuity and "rightness" in family patterns is to most people. In times of upheaval or tremendous social change, clinging to a belief in a standard—in the "normal"—is sometimes the most productive way to get by. It is sometimes the only way to ensure survival. Only the most highly individual, the most creative, and possibly the least social among us are able to move their expectations away from those of the larger society.

Changes in family norms and roles have no necessarily positive or negative values associated with them, except when held against a standard that defines them as deviant. The classical definition of the family firmly established a standard, or a norm, by which deviations could be measured. Clearly, the definition of a problem depends upon what is defined as normal.

Ideas of what is normal in the family have had incredible impact on society. Laws are based on what is considered normal. An example, which has only in this decade begun to change, is the assumption that children should live with their mothers when parents divorce. Only in cases of extreme incapacity on the part of the mother have courts traditionally consented to place the child with the father. This practice was based on the very practical understanding that, in most cases, the mother had been the primary parenting figure for the child, because the father was absent most of the day for occupational reasons. The assumption of mother-present, father-absent households stemmed from the traditional definition of the family, in which the work of women (bearing, nursing, and rearing children; preservation and preparation of food; and maintenance of the family home) was centered by necessity in the home. This definition, in turn, was necessarily predicated upon an understood definition of "home."

We therefore have laws to govern social behavior. Values about "good" and "bad" behavior stem from our cultural understanding of how far a behavior deviates from the standard or the norm. When the standard reflects an idealization that is not reality, we wind up with a legal institution that perpetuates an ideal state that does not actually exist. Often, this split between the ideal and the real is not observed consciously. As conscientious members of society, we strive to work toward what we believe is the way things *should* be, and we are not even aware that our sense of *should* might be predicated upon a model that no longer exists, if indeed it ever did.

What is conscious is dis-ease: a discomfort that the old way of doing things—the patterns fallen back on as a resource—do not work because too much has changed. Change is painful. It means giving up understandings of a lifetime and replacing them with something else. Even when the second understanding seems better, easier, necessary, or unavoidable, a loss has occurred in giving up an old pattern. The family, the direct center of each person's psychological network and the direct center of the social context of America, has changed in composition, ideology, and function. Because a valued ideal is lost, pain occurs with this change.

Family roles are still assumed by many to be rooted in biology and, therefore, to be outside the historical process (Goode 1964). Clearly, however, the nature of the family depends upon the circumstances shaping its members. Poverty modifies the roles of family members in order to meet immediate needs for survival. In all social classes, when illness or accident leaves a family member disabled, the roles of other family members must modify to accommodate the changes. Of necessity, children take on responsibilities, and therefore experiences, that make their family life different from that in other families.

In pluralist American culture, religious and ethical standards and customs differ from family to family, from cultural community to community. All this variation modifies the experiences of family members and, therefore, the structure of the family. Some children are reared by grandparents, as are most of the other children in their neighborhood. Some families temporarily house children of kin or friends, children who, for whatever reasons, cannot comfortably "fit in" with their own nuclear family. These relationships are sometimes informal, temporary, and conducted with the expectation that the visiting child will act by the new house rules and will return home when it seems appropriate. On occasion, the second family becomes a new nuclear family for the child—an arrangement that may or may not be formally sanctioned by law. Legal sanction, lagging behind social practice, fails to address several contemporary forms of family structure, including homosexual and multiple-parenting families.

Although understanding the differences among us, we persist with a cultural sense of what a family *should* be doing. For some people, this ideal lingers as an uneasy, vague sense of dissatisfaction with mates for not being or not doing something that is not quite definable. For women, the ideal might linger as guilt when making the decision to return to work after the birth of a child, or when deciding issues of marriage, divorce, or even of entering friendship or love relationships with other adults. For men, it might present itself as insecurity in the multiple roles of husband/father/worker, or it may contribute to feelings of entrapment because of felt responsibility.

This lingering sense of the *should* is a legacy from our real history as an evolving culture and from our idealized history that created definitions of family relationships very difficult, if not impossible, to actualize. These relationships were possibly never really as commonly practiced as we believe.

PERSPECTIVES IN THE STUDY OF THE FAMILY

Early studies of the family defined the objects of study in traditional terms, thereby perpetuating the myth of the family as being the husband, who holds a job in the larger community, his wife, a homemaker, and their two or more children. Differing forms were either ignored or referred to as "broken families." The idealization generally included concepts of upward mobility and of striving for home ownership.

When scholars design research, a precise definition in concrete terms (or operationalization) of the objects of study is essential to ensure that each unit being observed is treated equally. This definition helps reduce research bias. In the past, the use of the traditional definition for family necessarily eliminated any alternative family structures from the study. The myth of the traditional family was therefore reinforced by virtue of the number of studies describing the traditional family model and other "deviating" forms. This problem has been addressed by current researchers, who attempt to look at the *function* of families rather than the structure alone.

The common failures of family function have made family therapies an important vehicle for the study of the family. Providing self-validating and corrective communication to its members lies at the heart of family systems therapy. In fact, one of the major breakthroughs in our contemporary understanding of the family came from the work of the family system theorists. The family system pioneers were psychotherapists, many of whom worked with schizophrenic patients and their families. They found that many of the bizarre symptoms that made no apparent sense on an individual basis did make sense when viewed in relation to the family. One individual's symptoms served a balancing function, so to speak, sometimes preserving the stability of the rest of the family. The systems approach introduced an appreciation of family dynamics that departed from the view that psychotherapy was essentially an operation performed upon the minds of individuals. Rather, individuals were viewed as enacting, in their thoughts, feelings, and behavior, the dynamic, balancing roles permissible within a system of familial exchanges. Once such a system of exchanges had been applied to the pathology-inducing family, applying the system concept to the normal family also became useful. This view enabled us to recognize the importance of familial role expectations in understanding individual functioning. Now we face the need for a still more radical departure in order to understand the interdependence between the family and the community, the family and society.

One method that evolved to study family processes was to observe the actual functioning of families in their social context. In other words, by identifying what things family members do for one another and what activities take place under the jurisdiction of the family, a new definition of family would evolve. The emphasis upon who actually performs specific functions leads, in turn, to a review of the functions that the family, as a whole, is serving for the larger society. Thus we can identify the particular societal framework that guided the study. An example of this type of study is McIntosh's (1979) Marxist analysis of the family as the locus of activities essential to the reproduction of capitalism. The purpose of the family, therefore, was to reproduce and perpetuate the ideology of capitalism. The work of still another Marxist, Herbert Marcuse (1968), found the family's emotional nurturance to be a critical function that must be protected against depersonalizing economic forces. Some social feminists, who see capitalism as a male-created and dominated enterprise, consider the structure and the emotional function of the family to be to perpetuate paternalism—which shapes both contemporary capitalism and socialist cultural forms (Mitchell 1972).

A contrasting study is exemplified by Goode (1964), whose sociobiological approach identified the family as being the only significant social institution charged with transforming a biological organism into a human being. Viewed from this perspective, "family" can only be defined in terms of the presence and absence of sex roles predetermined by biology. Another orientation offered by R. D. Laing (1967), a psychoanalyst, sees the family as a "protection racket" in which mutual protection is present as a means to restrain our potentials for violence.

Seemingly, then, the family can be a source of pathology or of support. It might be where we develop a self, or where we find protection from ourselves. It could be the contribution of socialized individuals to a social order, a protective buffer against that order, a tool of the state or the organization, or a place of belonging and warmth in face of a cold, larger society. Each of these perspectives, however, must address an underlying and common reality: families have shown a remarkable persistence. Whatever change it has undergone, the family is a prime focus for any look at caring relationships. When analyzing families, the continuing human need for love, belonging, and acceptance must be addressed, either directly or indirectly. Demographic research studies show that structures and functions of families vary greatly and that the needs of individuals within those structures also vary (Guttentag and Secord 1983). However, the basic needs for caring and belonging seem to be understood by whatever model of study, as needs appropriately addressed by the family (Guttentag and Secord 1983). We contend, though, that these needs are not adequately met by the family alone.

THE FAMILY AS CAREGIVER

In former times, whether through the nuclear family, the extended family, or clan bonds, kinship provided the main source of support. These kinship ties have proven surprisingly durable. Massive migrations from other continents to North America and from rural areas to the cities disrupted some of these bonds, but the cord of kinship ties has shown great elasticity. More children still live in families with two parents than in any other arrangement (Visher and Visher 1979). Most adults live in communities where they maintain one or more contacts with a living parent or other close relatives (Sussman 1965; Troll 1971). Most elderly people are able to name at least one living relative who resides close by and would care for them if need be (Kulys and Tobin 1980). Studies show that the extended family has been maintained in urban as well as in rural America (Litwak 1960a, 1960b; Litwak and Szelenyi 1969; Skolnick 1973; Sussman and Burchinal 1962). A particular form of three-generation family involving both fictive and blood kin has continued to thrive in the black community (Stack 1974), and, in the Chicano community, extended family ties have remained particularly strong (Sena-Rivera 1980). Research by Claude Fischer and his associates, based upon survey data, provides an excellent example of the studies demonstrating that most people are retaining contacts with their families, and that these contacts involve significant social exchanges (Fischer et al. 1977). The extended family in the United States obviously survives, but the adequacy of its support functions is more difficult to determine.

Survey data has the advantage of being truly representative of the population being studied. Such data, however, cannot establish fine gradations in the meanings of people's attachments to one another. The surveys do not and cannot clearly determine the quality or the intensity of support in relations. For this reason, the more subjective, more intuitive views of social psychiatrists (Caplan 1974; Frank 1979) sometimes appear to be seeing a different picture—diminishing family and community ties. Actually, the views are of different aspects of the same reality. Although family ties and local social interaction obviously persist for most people, their permanence and their quality may be diminishing.

The adequacy of the family's support function also depends upon the challenges it must face. Mobility is one such challenge. In past centuries, geographic mobility resulted from the search for more fruitful or less oppressive environments. The pattern began by sending a familial envoy to explore the new setting. Others in the immediate and the extended family followed after the initial exploration of the new environment. Professional mobility, however, introduces the concept of marketability, wherein one moves, at any time, to pursue the offer that promises the best career advancement. Multiple career lines within the extended family, and even within the nuclear family, add a major factor to kinship separation and, therefore, reduce the supportive exchanges kin are able to provide. Wives and husbands are separated by the failure of communities to offer good career opportunities for both of them. Day laborers, and particularly farm workers, have long experienced household disruptions when following the movement of factories or the seasons of planting and harvesting. Economic and psychological uncertainties add to the strains imposed by vocational mobility. Under such pressures, how adequate is the nuclear family as a source of support?

FAMILY SUPPORT AND THE CHILD
One perspective on the adequacy of familial support may be gleaned from an examination of the supportive needs of children. Most children live in a family household with two parents. A large and perhaps growing number, estimated at 17 percent of all children under eighteen years of age, live with a single parent, and an additional 13 percent live in reconstituted families (Colvin, Greenwood, and Hansen 1981; Visher and Visher 1979). The changing role of women has brought larger numbers of women

into the work force, but the social system has not responded to this fact by providing alternatives for nurturing its youngest citizens. In 1984 at least 59 percent of mothers of school aged children worked outside the home. Forty-three percent of married mothers with children under the age of six worked outside the home (Langway et al. 1980). Though studies show that children of working mothers can fare quite well (Hoffman 1974), adequate resources for the child's care must be made available or problems will follow (Lambert et al. 1972). It is estimated that more than 2 million children between seven and thirteen return home from school to households with no adult present (Langway et al. 1980). There is often a serious gap in their nurturance and guidance.

Under some circumstances, private day-care options are available. Some families live among kin, one or two of whom serve as caregivers. Some communities function much like extended families and provide or exchange child care among neighbors. The problems in finding and paying for quality child care are, however, enormous. Although 7 million children live with parents employed outside the home, public, licensed day-care facilities are available for only 1.6 million (Colvin, Greenwood, and Hansen 1981). Poverty is common among working mothers: 51 percent of the women in single-parent families live below the poverty line (Verzaro and Hennon 1980), and seven out of ten people receiving food stamps are female (Stallard, Ehrenreich, and Sklar 1983; United States Department of Commerce, Bureau of the Census 1985).

Although the changing status of men and women has left gaps in the care of children, the forces that have created this situation are not entirely negative. The traditional family has been a major source of victimization, as exemplified by the physical abuse of some women by their mates. Moreover, studies show that the married woman who works outside the home demonstrates more positive psychological adjustment than the full-time homemaker (Baruch, Barnett, and Rivers 1984). In conclusion, adequate care for members of the family may depend, in part, upon resources outside the immediate family itself.

Child care is not likely to become a primary concern for most fathers in the immediate future. Studies comparing college men in the 1980s with their cohorts a decade earlier show a declining priority for the values of marriage and family, while women continue to plan for a family as well as a career (Regan and Roland, in press). This finding suggests that women's commitment to family tasks will continue, even though they are also continuing to add career tasks to their lives. It also implies that men, whose priorities are not family-oriented will, by and large, not be committed to modifying the traditional model of husband/father/worker to which they have been socialized. Faced with inadequate public child care, the extended family is now often called upon to give more to the developing child at the very time when fewer of its adult female members are available, in either a geographic, an economic, or a pyschological sense.

The social supports developed by association with the kin network as a whole appear to be critical to the family's well-being. An available parent or sibling in town at the time of childbirth can provide the trusted relief necessary to avoid the isolation and post partum depression of the mother, frequently observed during the infant's first three months. Particularly when the infant is unusually difficult to handle, the support received by the mother from kinfolk and friends appears critical to the development of the crucial bonding relationship between mother and infant (Crockenberg 1981). We now know that the social stress of poverty combined with its economic stresses are factors predicting the likelihood of child abuse and maltreatment (Garbarino 1976). Aberrant treatment of children, even in the face of the stresses of poverty, is somewhat alleviated by an adequate support system.

Two studies, for example, found that mothers who reported having support in the area of childrearing (babysitting, discussions on child rearing problems) were less dominating, emotionally warmer, and more perceptive to the needs of their children than were mothers who lacked this support from their social networks (Belle 1982; Longfellow 1979). Isolation is not healthy and tends to magnify the stresses existing in the family unit. When extended kin are near, however, these relatives are resources to the stressed family. They provide not only emergency assistance, but they also help the developing child. Contact with grandparents has been shown to be a factor in the development of the child's ability to recognize the needs of others (pro-social behavior) (Bryant in press).

In examining each of the contributions the extended family can make, we find the issue is not so much whether the nuclear or extended family continues to survive, but rather, which of the surviving forms of family life show a capacity to provide the needed supports during the prenatal or early childhood periods. It is the great difference in the availability of supportiveness provided by kinship ties that gives reason for concern.

The deficient side of nurturance within families has attracted the attention of some researchers who have examined just what forms of support are, or are not, being provided by family ties. Bronfenbrenner (1974), a leading authority in the study of children and families, despairs at the high degree of estrangement prevalent between children and adults. The lives of couples, as well as of single parents, do not always accommodate the tasks of parenting. For example, in one study, fathers' interactions with their one-year-old infants occurred only 2.7 times per day and lasted an average of thirty-seven seconds (Bronfenbrenner 1974). Reasons for this startling piece of data are complex, but two explanations emerge. Men have traditionally been socialized to feel that child care is not their responsibility. Additionally, they experience intense social pressure to define their role as parent in terms of their role as provider.

The examination of the supportive needs of dependent children and of their frequently stressed parents reveals that ties with kin lack the supportive resources for effective socialization (Broeck 1974; Bronfenbrenner 1977; Cochran and Brassard 1979). Many parents and children do not have even miminally functional ties with extended family, and the resources within the family unit are not adequate to meet the demands made by children. Similar gaps in nurturant functions become apparent when we examine the needs of the elderly.

FAMILY SUPPORT FOR OLDER PEOPLE

Whether because supportive public services have been insufficient or because of cultural traditions, the evidence continues to suggest that family ties are extremely important in the lives of the elderly. The reliance on family help—particularly at times of acute illness—shows that the bonds of kinship are not easy to erase (Cantor 1979; Rosenmayr and Köckeis 1970; Shanas 1979; Troll, Miller, and Atchley 1979). Spouses are the most frequently mentioned source of assistance for elderly persons who are ill or housebound (Shanas 1979). Adult children, living either with their parents or outside the home, provide the next greatest amount of such assistance and are the largest category of assistance for elderly women.

Ties to kin become particularly important in times of crisis. Most elderly adults name close relatives when they are asked who would be responsible for them in a crisis (Kulys and Tobin 1980). This reliance becomes significant when we understand that approximately 10 percent of elderly are without a geographically or emotionally close relative (Shanas 1979). Of further significance, many elderly are unsure whether the individual they named as being responsible in times of crisis would actually come through for them. One study, which interviewed relatives who had been named as responsible in a crisis, found that some of those people were surprised, disinterested, or even annoyed by the choice (Kulys and Tobin 1980). Since network size typically declines with age (Kahn and Antonucci 1980; Stueve and Fischer 1978), supporting the elderly partner who is taking care of an ill spouse is formidable (Fengler and Goodrich 1979). A large number of elderly, particularly men, succumb within months following the death of a spouse (Parkes 1972). That finding is even more striking when we consider the studies that demonstrate the value of a single confidant or supportive tie in mitigating the stressful effects of bereavement (Lowenthal and Haven

1968). Many men in our society lack even one intimate relationship other than a spouse, and are left with exceedingly few supportive resources when that spouse dies.

Family size and social roles are both factors limiting the support available for family members all along the age continuum. The number of elderly has risen rapidly; so also has the number of very old and surviving but frail elderly. Adults, themselves retired and quite aware of growing older, are finding they are responsible for caring for an elderly parent. Persons of child-bearing age during the Great Depression tended to limit the size of their families, and the population had a higher incidence of never-married persons (Treas 1977). Therefore, there are presently fewer kin available in the pool of caretakers. Also, more of the offspring are past middle age, and more of the women are committed to careers and work outside the home. As a result of this lack of suitable caretakers, too large a number of frail elderly live in institutional settings or alone. Particularly where poverty is an issue, nursing and rest homes have been unsatisfactory, and living alone has been in inexpensive and isolated, single-room occupancy hotels. The pattern is even continuing: the baby boom generation has contributed another group of late-married families with few children, and of unmarried people. They will become the next large group of old people with few family members concerned with their care.

In developed countries, formal institutions have gradually taken over many of the functions once belonging uniquely to the family (Hawkes 1978). Longer life, more education, and better standards of living add to the definition of needs so that broader support has become a necessity (Rosenmayr 1977). The number of social services provided is well known, but their adequacy in meeting the economic, social, and health needs of individuals is questionable. The social security office, senior nutrition program, day health clinic, and senior citizens' centers do not reach all elders who need them and cannot provide fully for some they do reach. The conclusion that some people are falling through the cracks in their supportive systems is evidenced by the extremely prevalent use of psychoactive drugs by older adults (Brecher 1972; Green 1978) and by the fact that one-fourth of all suicides in the United States are by persons aged sixty-five or older (Butler 1975). These warning indicators for the elderly are matched by conditions in the young family. The high incidence of child abuse and delinquency provide striking examples.

Among the elderly, as among children, there is a substantial subset of individuals with needs for supportive assistance that are not being met either by kinship networks, by friendship networks, or by association with formal service organizations.

FAMILY SUPPORT AT STRESSFUL TIMES

The very old and the very young are perhaps the most obvious casualties of an inadequate network of supportive affiliation. There are, however, other life transition times and other disruptive life circumstances that tax the resources of the typical kin network. Marital separation is one example, and a common one. Two percent of all United States marriages terminate each year, and the actual number of divorces in any given year has reached half the annual number of marriages (Bloom, Asher, and White 1978). The human costs are obvious from the finding that marital separations are associated with higher rates of alcoholism, traffic accidents, admission to psychiatric facilities, homicides, and disease mortality generally (Bloom, Asher, and White 1978). The adverse effects upon supportive care for children have also been noted, as have the reciprocal effects problem children have upon their divorced parents (Hetherington, Cox, and Cox 1977).

The family may or may not provide support for the member who has just been through a divorce. One study shows that people receive significantly less help during divorce when other members of the family are also experiencing important life events or when the family disapproves of the divorce (Kitson, Moir, and Mason 1982). Like sustained illness, divorce often taxes family support beyond its resources; and, in a circular fashion, the absence of support can contribute to future separation and future health problems.

Stress upon the nuclear family, which culminates in marital disruption for some, exists at a somewhat lower threshold within a larger number of nuclear family households and individuals. Many of the contributing tensions are from persistent environmental stressors such as job loss, unemployment, underemployment, discrimination, stressful working conditions, natural disasters, and excessive social conflict.

The concept of endemic stress has been coined to describe the pervasive social strains affecting large numbers of people through an interactive mechanism. This stress, born in an atmosphere of scarcity and uncertainty, is a generalized feeling that something is wrong. Endemic stress, then, is not only the stress an individual experiences directly, but is also the stress experienced by others. The stress-induced behavior of one person provides an increasing source of stress for others, culminatng in an accelerating pattern of endemic stress. In harsh economic times, for example, people experience not only the stresses of their own immediate family's economic position, but also the shared stress of a neighbor's inability to meet a mortgage payment. An entire household shares the impact of a neighbor whose food stamp allocations are uncertain. The suicide or heart attack of a distant relative following a business failure contributes to a foreboding atmosphere, eventually shared and enhanced by all the person's daily contacts (Fried 1982).

The amount of social support available to most individuals may be adequate to help them through short-term hassles and pressures; yet, these same sources may prove inadequate to deal with needs requiring intensive support over an extended time period. The management of illness provides an example of the limits of social support. Sickness of short duration is typically met by mobilization of the immediate family. Chronic illness, however, coupled with fear and uncertainty about the future, may require greater economic and psychological resources than many kin are able to provide.

The family stress in this case often falls upon the wife. One study showed that the wife in an intact household received little help in caring for the needs of a frail or mentally impaired person living at home. The spouse of an impaired person is, in most caases, not provided with much physical or emotional support. Tragically, the family in this case provides for one dependent member by exhausting or depleting the life of another one (Poulshock, Deimling, and Silverston 1982).

Just as there are limits to the resources of family, there are also limits in the number of available, close family ties. A substantial number of individuals, unmarried by choice, have accommodated with fair success to their life demands. Such people, however, do best if they are young, educated, well employed, attractive and healthy. Their adjustment depends upon their market value, and, as a group, they are at high risk following stressful live events because of their low level of familial support.

By examining broader social forces, we will be able to see the changing set of challenges and strains confronting the family's resources for giving. We will also see the changing values that underlie the family's capacity for nurturance. One value that really makes a difference is that of achieving individual success.

RUGGED INDIVIDUALISM AND SUPPORTIVE FAMILIES

The need for a stable family in a cohesive community is inconsistent with both the myths and the realities of autonomous, competitive, individual achievement fostered by the socioeconomic order. Our media cultivate the image, for women as well as for men, of the lone hero. The automated and specialized workplace has never been promoted, by management or by labor unions, as a place that esteems the value of each contributing cooperator to a mutually valued task. Rather, the workplace, like the school environment, has become a source for only the more transient forms of support. For most men, the absence of a companion other than a spouse has become a reality. For many women, the absence of relationships that validate her as an individual outside the role of mother, wife, homemaker, and employee is also a reality. Lacking a network of self-validating relationships, sex—or more likely the pursuit of sex—has become a filler against anomic loneliness. Sexual contact has become the prototype of all interactions. Its supportive value lies in the encounter, not in the enduring relationship. Feelings of the moment become a more cherished because continued feelings of relatedness, while present, are less deep and less secure.

Competitive industrial development has changed the roles within the family. When men held dominant and exclusive roles in the economic workforce, the assigned but often unappreciated role left to women was that of builder of supportive familial networks. Postcollege and professional mobility introduced the era of the portable nuclear family, the woman's role becoming one of coping with moves made for the good of the company or the husband's career. The industrial system now has openings for many women who leave the role of primary family caregiver and join men in the role of the worker, pursuing an often ephemeral success. Lack of fulfillment for the isolated suburban homemaker was indeed a maddening development. Entry into the pressures of the full-time, competitive work world is not only difficult, it divides the energy many women spend in caregiving functions for the family, thereby altering patterns of nurturance. It has sometimes left visible gaps.

This narrative is not meant to echo a nostalgia for an old-style nuclear family, in which women maintained the exclusive roles of housewife, caregiver, and nurturer. Suburban living places serious limitations on women as homemakers. Women are apparently more sensitive than men to the arrangements of their living settings (Nordstrom in press). Many suburban women who remain home live in physical environments designed in ways that preclude communal sharing, creating isolation from neighbors and from general community participation.

For some women, entry into the work world or returning to school has been a critical experience in self-definition. This experience occurs despite the fact that reentry poses its own set of problems—approaching new, stressful situations and adding one more demanding set of role obligations rather than redefining existing roles.

In one suburban setting in Adelaide, Australia, a special community project, based upon developing a number of natural support groups among homemakers, resulted in sharing chores, active political participation in community affairs, demands for better neighborhood facilities, and more active development of friendships (Egar and Sarkissian in press). These successful changes in the lives of suburban homemakers suggest that the existing suburban arrangements left a great deal to be desired, particularly for the psychological well-being of women. Still, our original point is also true. For most women who escaped the stifling and isolated suburban household, the alternative was work, often at low pay, and frequently without alternative or supplemental supports to compensate the household for the nurturance not traditionally offered by any other source. In those cases where no alternative help was available, a gap was left in the nurturance of other family members. Obviously, not only women can fill this function; rather, the point is that, unless someone provides this nurturance, an important measure of caring is lost. To recover it, we will have to look into nontraditional households, to more androgenous roles for both men and women and to new institutions that add supportive resources to an increasing variety of family forms.

It is possible to object to our analysis so far, to insist that we are speaking of only one trend in family relationships—a trend characterized by high rates of divorce, by a lessening of the difference in traditional male-female roles, and by a weakening of old family values. Perhaps lack of support is related to the liberal outlook that arose in the 1960s and the social order is now reverting to a more traditional, more conservative view of the "proper" role of family. It might even be argued that an unfettered free enterprise system will lead not only to a stronger economy but to a revitalization of the family as a provider of care.

It should be pointed out that yearning to go back to old ways (whether the old patterns are imagined or real) is not a matter of shared agreement among Americans. Though the 1980s have ushered in a period of fiscal conservatism and caution about spending, this attitude should not, according to public opinion polls, be confused with a general desire to go back. Public opinion specialist Daniel Yankelovich writes:

"The sweeping changes in marriage, family life and the relationship to children fill many people with sadness and nostalgia. But while some people, when we survey them, claim in the abstract that they want to return to the family life of the past, when it comes to specifics, only one out of five has any hankering to go back to traditional standards of sexual relationships, to the spick-and-span housekeeping norms of the past or to the male monopoly on working outside the home. Americans long for the warmth and closeness they associate with family life in earlier decades, but not if it means going back to the old rules" (1981:29).

For some people, however, financial and political conservatism are one with the restoration of the idealized family. The philosophy is, alas, honored more in belief than in practice.

The newer, conservative philosophy is exemplified in booming "sun belt" economies like Houston, Texas (Viviano 1982). In contrast to the heavily unionized industrial cities of the East and Midwest, the sun belt cities of Miami, Atlanta, Dallas/Ft. Worth, Anaheim, and San Diego have been strong centers of support for the conservative credo that places great faith in individual enterprise and a return to traditional family values. Economic growth has occurred there, even while large sectors of the Midwest and the East were facing economic decline. This growth has created a shift of power, wealth, and influence to the southern and western sections of the country, a shift that occurred over a short period of time. The effects upon family life have not been particularly positive. The 8.2 divorces per 1,000 marriages each year found in Dallas/Fort Worth and in Houston are the highest figures for metropolitan areas in the United States. In fact, of the cities mentioned above, all had divorce rates of 6 per 1,000 or higher. The rates are far in excess of those found in eastern cities, even after controlling for larger Catholic populations in the East. Other signs of distress in these areas include exceptionally high crime rates in Florida cities and a suicide rate three times the national average in San Diego.

Where lies the culprit in this disparity between beliefs and reality about the benefits of a nostalgic family? One insight comes from a representative of a Houston Family Service Center, who noted that the fierce competition for money and the emphasis upon careerism were exacting heavy tolls on family life at every economic level. Texas has one of the more successful resettlement programs for Indo-Chinese refugees—successful, that is, in employment figures and in income. In contrast to the Vietnamese refugees in San Francisco, however, who remain dependent upon public assistance and who cling together in strong traditional families, the families of Houston refugees are falling apart. Pauline Van Tho, a placement counselor with Houston Catholic Charities summarized the conflict: "Americans have been good to us—they are wonderful people. But the constant struggle to get ahead hurts, and it hurts our families the most" (Viviano 1982:9).

Here we are reminded that competitive, individual striving calls for a denial of our interdependence. Pressures upon the family reflect the pressures upon individuals never to give without calculating the return benefits—an attitude destructive not only to the family but to all longterm relationships.

Today, the protective web of supportive familial ties has many gaps. Those who have traditionally relied upon the nurturant care provided by full-time homemakers are now likely to experience a deficiency in caring. Elderly parents or dependent children (or husbands) are prime candidates. Women whose roles are multiple and who try to sustain the classic role of supportive caretaker are another group for whom the available supportive resources are often too skimpy. Finally, all of us at times of sustained stress are likely to find family networks unable to fill the gap.

Our thesis is, first, that most people have maintained ties with their kin but that, on the whole, there are fewer such ties and they are less intimate than in past generations. Second, the need for enduring supportive ties has remained, and voluntary supportive relationships outside the family have become important to many people, largely as an aid to problems caused by mobility, life transition, and personal autonomous development. In comparison with kinship ties, though, extrafamilial ties, despite some important exceptions, are often transitory.

Transitory or permanent, the many forms of close ties that go beyond the boundaries of blood relationships are important. What families cannot provide alone can sometimes be found by a more diversified set of connections among people—some quite close and strong, some weak and distant, but nonetheless significant.

SUPPORTIVE FUNCTIONS OF STRONG AND WEAK TIES

Sociologists distinguish the properties of *gemeinshaft*, the quality of relationships in small, continuing face to face groups, from *gesellshaft* qualities of more transitory and impersonal interactions. Gerald Caplan (1974) and Jerome Frank (1979) are among several psychiatrists and social critics who have taken a dim view of the amount of *gemeinschaft* protection available in modern industrial society. Small, dense networks, with frequent interactions, associated mainly with the family, are the main social forms capable of protecting individuals from the confusing feedback and disorder of modern life. They see the family as overly taxed and inadequately assisted in its function as a supportive buffer. Other social theorists have argued that the same complexity from which Caplan would have us protected is the very vitalilty of urban life, connecting the individual to the mainstream of civilization (Sennett 1970a). In fact, isolated, middle-class, suburban families are viewed by this latter theory as being oppressive and restrictive to their members (Sennett 1970b). Caplan's emphasis upon primary groups, though, is quite effective when he examines the functions they provide for the individual. These functions include consistent communication, clear expectations, supportive assistance with tasks, evaluation of day-to-day behavior, and rewards for daily behavior (Caplan 1974). He might also have added continuity of relationships over time and assistance in coping with threats from the larger environment to self-esteem.

Several studies pointing to the presence of family ties as buffers against health breakdown suggest that a small, densely connected network of intimate ties remains critical to individual well-being (Cassell and Tyroler 1961; Lasch 1978; Phillips 1975; Stout 1964). These studies have been summarized in chapter 2. Such close ties, however important, may nevertheless be insufficient for certain types of psycho-social transition. Job loss is a circumstance for which the dense, kinship-dominated network can typically provide consolation, but not reassurance or assistance in locating a new job—there are just too few jobs available on family farms or in other family businesses. To branch out, to find more disparate opportunities, requires a more disparate network. Bereavement provides still another example of the limits of small, family-life networks. The family can be consoling and when its assistance is hampered by psychological or physical distance, a small, supportive, mutual help group can be of similar value. But for eventual movement into new areas of commitment, whether it be finding new colleagues or a new spouse, a larger network of weaker ties may be critical (Granovetter 1973; Parkes 1972).

Sociologists describe the close, intimate, family-type group in special ways. They call it is a dense network, meaning that the people with whom one individual interacts are all known to one another. They say also that the types of interactions between individuals are multiple and varied, meaning not only exchanges of money, or of interests, or of emotional problems, but all types of personal exchanges. The dense and varied network is more like the small-town family of old, often thought of as providing well for the needs of its members.

Yet there are studies suggesting that *low* density families and friendship networks with less versatile ties may be better able to help a person cope with certain problems. One study examined the sources available to assist two groups of middle-aged women. One group consisted of widows, the second was composed of women returning to school. The study lends support to the value, for both groups, of having weaker ties. The types of help people sought were analyzed. The women able to receive cognitive guidance (e.g., advice, explanation, and information) from someone outside their immediate family were better able to cope with their problems (Hirsch 1980). Although initial solace may have been offered by a few close ties, recently bereaved women apparently needed something else to assist their coping with a transition in role. In another study, a group of women who were victims of violence at home received little support from the couples' close-knit networks of people who knew them well. The woman could find support, however, from independent ties of her own. Apparently, coping with a serious, internal family conflict, or with an important life transition, typically requires a set of associations beyond the close circle of family supports.

Our conclusion must be that social support requires a variety of sources, including but not restricted to the family, to meet the diversity of individual needs.

SOCIAL SUPPORT: THE EXTRA-FAMILIAL CONTEXT

We have defined social support as a set of exchanges that provide individuals with material and physical assistance, social contact, and emotional sharing, as well as with the sense that they are the continuing focus of concern by others (Pilisuk and Parks 1981). The importance of this support has been shown most clearly by the health consequences of persons lacking adequate support. The continuity and vitality of the nuclear and the immediate extended family remains the single, most important social factor in continuing supportive relationships. But the supportive needs of family members often exceed the capacities of small kin groups. This inadequacy reflects competing societal pressures, internalized within the person, for individual success in the broader society. The family is affected in two ways. Not only are its members in need of more diverse forms of support, but its members are more often preoccupied with pursuits that compete with the support they can offer to other members of their immediate family. In consequence, the family is pressed. It is less certain to be a source of satisfaction and more frequently subject to disruption. With familial support less sufficient, it becomes necessary to review the diverse forms of nonfamilial support that have arisen. These new forms must be seen not only as supports to the individual but as needed relief from the strains and demands placed upon the family.

Mobility, individualistic and competitive career goals, and fears of making emotional commitments have contributed to discontinuities in the lives of individuals and in the ways families function for their members and for society. Revolutionary changes are taking place in natural helping outside the traditional family, in the form of an amazing variety of friendships, natural helpers, and mutual help groups. These, along with the many formal public services available to families, are part of the contemporary family's ability to function.

We know more about families and the individuals in them than we do about their contexts. When we do study the effects of the context on the person, it is usually to find the effects of a solo attribute, such as mothers reading to their children, or participation in a Head Start program upon reading ability. Of major importance to our well-being, however, is the interaction of different settings. Like the relationship of notes and music, the harmony or conflict of the context of our lives shapes the individual.

One project involving multiple contexts was designed to improve the school performance of low-income, minority students in the elementary grades (reported in Bronfenbrenner 1974). Thirty neighborhood mothers visited every home with a child in the study. The child's parents were enlisted in several activities. They were asked to listen to their children read, to give praise, and to ensure a quiet study time not conflicting with the child's favorite television program. Children in the kindergarten and first grade were given books to take home and buttons to wear saying, "Please read to me." Fathers were recruited to be library storytellers. Each family was given a child's dictionary. At a time set aside for the kids to do homework, the parents met to discuss common problems. High school business students provided clerical aid for teachers, who also benefited from an on-the-job program designed to make them aware of environmental factors affecting the child in the classroom. A number of adult guests with skilled jobs came to the classrooms to tell how their elementary school subjects had been helpful to them. The program was successful, both in improving the reading scores of the children and in promoting the satisfaction of the parents. This study prompted Urie Bronfenbrenner to conclude, "The developmental potential of child rearing is increased as a function of the number of supportive links between the setting and other contexts involving the child or persons responsible for his or her care" (1974:848).

Bronfenbrenner argues that the family does not exist in a vacuum. The family's potential to provide a rewarding environment for any of its members, of any age, depends upon its connections and upon the compatible forms of nurturance and support its members can find outside the family. Too often the family has been rather isolated from the big schools, the big hospitals, and the big shopping centers. Social institutions operating on a smaller scale might offer more opportunity for direct interaction and shared responsibility. The family is often omitted from attempts to solve problems of street crime or substance abuse, and the larger institutions are frequently viewed as adversaries. The family is even unwelcome in most mental health rehabilitation programs. Where there are special problems, such as chronic illness, disability, frail elders, emotional disturbance, or physical handicap, the clear need—rarely met—is for the family and a small-sized, personally oriented, well-managed human service organization to work cooperatively.

Typically, the family household of today is able to provide sufficient support for its members only through its connections with a larger pool of caring people. A nuclear family may be isolated from kin or closely embedded in a larger extended family. It may be geographically alone or set in a cohesive net of community ties. These larger contexts will make a difference both to intact and to disrupted families. The situations are described in Figure 3.

Figure 3 pictures the pattern of variation in the supportive contexts available to the nuclear family and to family members. The intact family, well connected to its circle of extended kin and to the community, is represented by diagram a. Diagram b illustrates a recently separated individual

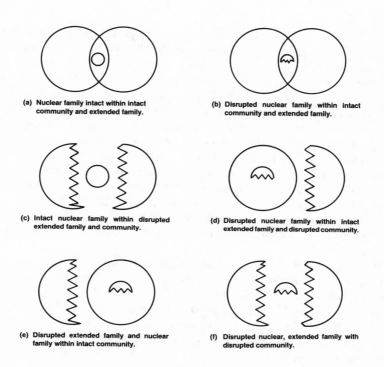

FIGURE 3. Familial and community resources for support of the nuclear family. Reprinted with permission from Pilisuk, M., and Parks, S. H. (1983). Social support and family stress. *Journal of Marriage and Family Review, 6*(1–2), 137–156. Haworth Press, Inc. 28 East 22 Street, New York, N.Y. 10010.

or family who has the range of supports necessary to deal with the stressful circumstances. Diagram c represents the newly relocated nuclear family in a strange environment. Its potential for necessary support will depend upon reweaving social ties. Diagrams d, e, and f all show the disrupted nuclear family or isolated individual with inadequate support, either from the extended family, from the community, or from both.

Single mothers in one study made different use of networks (outside the home) than married mothers. The single mothers made more demands that were essentially one-way or nonreciprocal. The needs were more typically immediate and pressing, such as emergency care for a sick child or a discussion of personal problems. But meeting such demands drains resources from other people in the network and thereby limits their availability; hence, a complementary set of formal service providers as well as informal helpers may be necessary for these mothers (Cochran and Brassard 1979). The supportive assistance needed by either formal or informal service providers, therefore, will vary with the nature of the deficit.

Informal networks of friends or voluntary support groups, and formal agency services are two sources of social support that complement family ties. A community setting that furnishes these additional supports provides the context necessary for families to meet the supportive needs of their members. Other nonkinship forms of informal support have also come into being. Human services have come to view network building as one of their important functions. To the extent that such nonkinship forces can be incorporated as normal aids to the supportive functions of actual kinship, we see the potential for a new concept of the family. The new family will be understood to include the principle contexts that make it work. The providers of child care or hospice care may then be considered part of the family network.

Whoever the members are, and whatever their ties to one another, a family retains some major responsibilities for meeting basic emotional needs, sexuality, rearing children, and domestic and economic functions such as acquiring and preparing food. Studies of the family might be most adequately designed by pursuing a view of the *connectedness* of family members with one another and with the community in which they live. This connection between the family and its surrounding ties increases our understanding of which needs are met, how they are met, and how that intercommunication relates with the larger community. This view integrates the concept of family into a network including other family organizations, institutions, and community life.

The sad irony of the current nostalgia for the idealized family is that such nostalgia is used to justify reductions in the very programs that are most needed by families struggling to care for their members. Just as we are understanding the need to establish more personal contacts between service programs and family members, we are witnessing unprecedented reductions in maternal and child health care, in aid for the disabled, and in funding for programs providing child care. Programs to prevent adolescent pregnancy, to reduce family violence, to provide food and legal services for poor families, and to allow homemaker service and heating allowances for the elderly and disabled are all being reduced. None of these programs can substitute for the family, and none of them are automatically sufficient for creating a supportive environment for families to flourish. Without them, however, we force our poorer families to become desparate. Where such programs do function well, they help make our neighborhoods and our institutions an inseparable part of our family support system.

The local YMCA, the senior center, the playground, the neighborhood tavern, the church or synagogue, the nutrition program, social security, and the job market are now part of our understanding of family. So also are child care, single-parent support groups, the helpful neighbor, the kidney dialysis group, and the affirmative action counselor. The distant relative or unrelated student joining a household, the homosexual couple on the next block, foster parents, and board-and-care home operators are all part of this family context. The family is not the self-contained and idealized group of old, for when all is said and done, family is more than a set of blood ties. It is a state of mind that recognizes the very special feelings of caring and continuity that we hold for certain people, and it is the recognition in our cultural beliefs and our social institutions that such caring is of value.

> "Ultimately, the future of individual families, whatever their form, will depend on the future of the *human* family, on the degree to which we are able collectively to view ourselves as our brother's and sister's, and above all, our children's keepers—*all* our children. And we should do so, not for sentimental reasons, not even out of a feeling of moral obligation, but simply, because, in John Donne's words, "No man is an island, entire of itself," because in the most profound sense we are, as he says, a "part of the main," a part of each other, sharing, when all is said and done, the basic hopes and dreams, and a common final destiny" (Conger 1981:1484).

Families are different now. We still seem to be there for our kin members, and we still seem to need what our kinship has to offer. How families function to meet every need, however, has changed. Some students of the American family express deep concern for the coming generations, and some express gratitude and excitement at the prospect of a newer, a more effective family structure for the generations to come; but most people are aware that the old model of the family is changing.

What does this change mean for our continuing needs for validation, for enduring love relationships, and for feelings of belonging? To answer this question, we will have to examine the world of new ties, weak and strong, temporary and permanent, formal and casual, that are part of the contemporary community.

4
THE CHOSEN TIES
OF FRIENDSHIP

How the needs of people living in today's postindustrial society are met and are not met by modern families has been studied many times (Bronfenbrenner 1974; Pilisuk and Parks 1983; Sussman 1965). We have learned that even contemporary, mobile social beings remain tied to family members in very primary ways, that is, in ways so basic to the self-concept they are not fully conscious. To observe our families is to see directly the continued importance of our long-term social ties. Despite some evidence to the contrary, such as violent criminal behavior and institutionalized isolation, a stranger to our planet would readily ascribe to us a need for affiliation with others. Most individuals appear to be quite competent at pursuing love and a sense of belonging in a variety of natural, unplanned ways. We seem to strive for balance in relationships, both giving and receiving the love and belonging basic to our humanity.

Despite remarkable differences in the types of families in various societies, there remains at least one central common function: providing the infant and young child with basic sustenance and protection and, in supportive families, loving acceptance as a person. Families, regardless of their culturally defined patterns, respond to the need to be loved, to be touched and cared for, and therefore, to be connected with important others. This connectedness is the most basic lesson a family teaches. It addresses a fundamental human condition and need.

Cultural stereotypes tempt people to believe that every individual has experienced the unqualified love and caring of a family. This is clearly not the case, however. Not all people are enmeshed in a network of caring kin. In fact, for many, the most basic physical and emotional needs are not met through family ties or family-like networks. For these individuals, there is potential for serious harm (Steele 1971). Some people leave discordant, unsupportive, or dangerous families with deep wounds that they carry throughout their lifetimes, often passing on their pain to their children. Others are able to leave negative family experiences behind, incorporating valuable lessons to guide their actions and interactions in the future. The difference in these two methods of coping appears to depend upon who, other than family, is available to provide support for the individual (Miller and Lefcourt 1983; Pilisuk and Parks 1983).

Regardless of the degree of acceptance provided by families, it is a developmental necessity for all people to alter the ties binding them to the family of childhood before they can become competent adults (Andrews and Withey 1976). The change may be less dramatic in societies where one is born, lives, and dies among the same group of kin in the same locale. In modern society the acquired ties of friendship can be critical to this process. These changing networks, extending beyond family ties, proceed continuously throughout childhood with relationships with friends and other important people, as well as with family members. Through these associations, identities apart from our kin network are developed (Blos 1962; Csikszentmihalyi and Larson 1984). This identity helps us define the values we place upon others in the larger society.

The social network, as students of culture note, is partially ascribed and partially achieved (Boussevain and Mitchell 1973). Kin represent ascribed networks; of them, we have no choice. To describe all of a kin network, we include consanguinous, or blood, kin and some kin achieved or chosen by marriage, affinal kin. Most in-law ties are simultaneously ascribed and achieved. Once affinal ties are achieved, they are ascribed by law and custom (Keesing 1975). Friendship networks are predominantly achieved, although they, too, are ascriptive in that social and environmental factors strongly influence their selection (Salzinger 1982). Much human behavior, as Kurt Lewin noted, is interaction of the person with the context, and the environmental context of our lives is created in large part by the people surrounding us (Lewin 1946). In a fundamental sense, therefore, "the individual and the social network continually create and recreate each other" (Salzinger 1982). From this point of view, our friendship networks are substantially more important to us than we may recognize.

What is lacking in kin networks can be balanced with friendships. Ties of friendship are particularly important to the ways we allow ourselves to be taken care of emotionally by others (Lee 1980). Friends help determine the view of oneself as an integral part of a network of people who care about us and for whom we, in turn, care. The ties ordained by birth in a family are inevitably augmented by ties that are chosen, thereby expanding the linkages to the surrounding community. The ties that bind us to the family and the social order are learned in infancy and developed throughout the entire life cycle. These bonds are the very interdependent strengths necessary to provide healthfulness during the stresses and changes that occur throughout the course of a lifetime. The rules for making those connections are a legacy, passed on to our children in the hope that they will have the necessary skills for achieving mental and physical healthfulness through connection with others.

FRIENDSHIP PATTERNS IN CHILDHOOD

Friendship is particularly important in childhood. Friends are safe people around whom to explore a new facet of personality which might not be accepted in the familiarity of family expectations. Friends also allow children to break dependent relationships with their parents and kin. Children share secrets with a best friend instead of confidences with mother, or find a comrade for daring adventures instead of listening to the wisdom of age and experience offered so freely by parents, grandparents, and siblings. Relationships within kinship networks are reinforced by the presence and pressures of numerous others. Through friends, a separation from family can be achieved (Forrest 1984).

Friendship formation is a universal human development, evidenced by the fact that by the age of three, children in all societies have developed friendship patterns (DuBois 1974). Children at this age who do not have actual peer relationships often compensate with fantasy friends, who can remain in their lives for several years (Reisman 1979). Two-year-old Jennifer, with no siblings and with peer relationships limited to eight weekly hours of nursery school, created a friend named Serkey. Serkey became a companion during long afternoons and also became responsible for various naughty activities, such as drawing on the wall or washing clothes in the toilet. She listened silently to scoldings from her young friend, learned to be brave in the doctor's office, and was a comfort when the bedroom was too dark at night. Serkey remained a special friend for nearly three years, until Jennifer went to kindergarten. By this time, the child was ready to substitute relationships with real children for her imaginary one. Eight years later, however, Serkey still remained a treasured memory—a special friend.

Friends for the very young are quite openly instrumental (Asher and Gottman 1981; Bell 1981; Bigelow 1977; Rubin 1980). "I like Sue because she has a red fire truck," is a common type of response when young children are asked about their friends. They appear to find friends, make friends, and become a friend in easy, natural ways. One preschooler asks another, "Will you play with me?" and the answer may be "Yes." Each child continues his or her activity, although now they continue their separate activities alongside each other. Developmentalists call this situation "parallel play" (Bigelow 1977; Dickens and Perlman 1981; Youniss 1980). The answer, however, might as easily be "No," and, although the friend-seeker might persist a bit, the rules of the game are clear: whoever wants a friend or playmate asks for one, and the potential friend may accept or decline.

During adolescence, friends become the child's most important standards (Bell 1981; Dickens and Perlman 1981). During this time, learning about life as an independent individual is a primary objective, the "second individuation process" (Blau 1967). The developmental task at this time in life is to learn a bewildering variety of familial, social, and vocational roles (Allport 1962; Harris 1964; Stevens-Long 1979). To accomplish this assignment, adolescents must first be able to perceive and understand the critical issues they face. Their task is no less than to make sense of the world they have inherited. Second, they must address their role in that world at a time when changes in technology and social systems are occurring at unprecedented rates, continually changing the rules for successful personal definition and social adjustment.

Our culture places great value upon independence. We speak approvingly of independence training, never of training for interdependence. Ideologically, we encourage independence to the extreme, so that notions of what is "mentally healthy" emphasize assertion and independence and regard dependency as "pathological." Indeed, measures of moral development (Kohlberg 1969) place adolescent boys on a higher level of development because they identify more with the larger world, whereas female identity is tied with relationships and interdependence (Gilligan 1982). Teachers and parents typically encourage independent behavior in the early years. By the time most children reach adolescence, they have learned to inhibit the dependent patterns of childhood in order to please adults (Mussen, Conger, and Kagan 1969). They have not, however, perfected the independent patterns necessary to be completely functioning adults, nor are they allowed to exercise the independence they have been taught to seek.

The social system actually inhibits independence with compulsory secondary education and the structure of higher education, laws relating to child labor, and legal and moral restrictions on sexual behavior. Achieving independence becomes culturally blocked and this inconsistency results in anxiety and conflict for adolescents (Harris 1964; Mussen, Conger and Kagan 1969). At this time, adolescents turn to their peers. They develop friendships that take on meanings of enormous proportion, as they turn to each other for companionship and guidance through the maze of tasks and responsibilities thrust upon them by the external world. Placed in a situation with no chance of personal income and no sanctioned social role other than student in an educational system not always relevant to a young person's needs, teenagers—male or female—typically invest a good deal of effort in being with, and like, their friends. Whether the friendship focuses upon tossing a football or a frisbee, rehearsing a drama production, listening to or playing music, or hanging out in the shopping malls, the attachments are a major part of the distinction of self from family that our society requires (Bettleheim 1965). The social structures used to create responsible adults often ignore the teenager's actual circumstances—unless he or she is in trouble—but do provide a strong message that places prime value upon success. Typically, however, the quest for friendships at this age is more dominant than the drive for individual success. What takes place within these friendships allows young people, beginning their paths to adulthood, to break the ties of emotional dependence upon their families while remaining in a network that continues many of the kinship functions without the same restrictions.

ADULT FRIENDSHIPS

In a previous chapter, the theory of attachment was applied not only to infants and children but, in differing ways, to people of all ages. Friendship also occurs throughout the life span, changing in form from child to adult, on through life cycle, although the importance of friendship to older persons has not always been noticed. Friendships, which may be critical to the well-being of older people who have suffered losses in family ties, have been inadequately examined by social theorists. Adult associations are relatively more controlled by gender, social class, economics, and nonfamily concerns than are the friendships of children (Axelrod 1956; Bell and Boat 1957; Bonacich 1967; Verbrugge 1977). In circumstances of special need, they display a critical importance.

Most social life for people past infancy occurs with friends. One study found that 91 percent of people over sixty-five-years of age see emotionally supportive friends on a daily basis (Troll, Miller, and Atchley 1979). This number seems surprisingly high—it is not significantly lower than the 94 percent of adolescents who see their friends "all the time." This finding reminds us once again of the need for balance between time spent alone, time giving to others, and time receiving support from others. Old age, however, is also a time of diminishing resources, as old friends die or become infirm and less available. Our own studies of older people show great differences in the number of close friends and the amount of contact with them. In general, wider friendship networks among older people are associated with satisfactory income and with better health (Pilisuk, Montgomery, and Parks 1985).

Diminishing healthfulness in old age brings with it increased dependence upon the ties that inherently imply obligation (Cohen and Sokolovsky 1980). Sometimes ill health becomes so serious that formerly independent individuals are no longer able—or are seen as being unable—to live alone and make decisions on their own regarding the complexities of money, food purchase and preparation, and other daily tasks. At this time, the ties of kinship generally take over as a first line of defense, even where friends are present (Kivett 1985; Lee 1980; Verdon 1981).

We have need for strong ties with families, beginning with our infancy when we are dependent on the nuturing of others and continuing, as the cycle unfolds, to the time when we are dependent once again on caring assistance from others. What takes place in the middle? How do contemporary adults ensure their place in a supportive, nurturing network throughout their lives?

GENDER DIFFERENCES IN FRIENDSHIPS

The Friends of Women. The traditions associated with the social role of housewife and mother have much to do with the pattern of friendship among women. Before 1750, prior to the industrial revolution, the home was the central place of occupation, and all members of the household engaged in both housekeeping tasks and the family's special economic activity. Child care, working arrangements, and the form of payment for the product all shaped women's lives (Jordanova 1981). The care of children or households were not matters given very direct attention.

The introduction of factories, first fueled by the labor of children, then by women, and finally by men, separated the workplace from the home. Ideologically, the role of housewife was created, replete with images that women were frail, domestic, emotional, and unsuited for the economic workplace. Socialist feminists theorize that this process was a way of drawing a distinction between the working and the merchant (middle) classes (Oakley 1974). Education and religion reinforced the concept of the woman as the perfect wife, mother, and housekeeper. The household was in the private domain, and the workplace was public. Households had no regulations, for better or worse, controlling the working conditions. The role demanded economic dependence and offered no opportunity for either a change in job or protest against unsupportable working conditions. It had little structured contact with other adults except as a consumer (Jephcott,

Seear, and Smith 1962). The image of the woman as consumer, in fact, still persists in contemporary advertising.

The contacts women made in the course of schooling or housekeeping chores were by nature noncompetitive and cooperative. Of course, a mate had to be found, so some competition existed for the young, unmarried woman with other possible contenders for the same man. For the most part, however, the contacts women had with one another provided opportunity for noncompetitive sharing of experience. Today, contacts between women are still dominated by child rearing, by concern for the health of the family, by family gatherings, by household decor, and by the sharing of personal problems. Although women's roles have been judged by society to be of lesser value ("only a housewife"), the permission for genuine contact, indeed the acceptance of the need for friendships to help maintain contact with the external world, has been granted to women (Lopata 1973; Oakley 1974).

For many women, the capacity for friendship has remained or grown even stronger with increased movement into employment outside the home. The skills of making and nurturing noncompetitive connections have come with women into the labor market. Traditionally, those skills have been utilized in "server" roles to men, as in coffee preparation and greeting guests or clients. Incrementally, however, skills that deal with maintaining a family network have become acknowledged in large organizations. The Japanese experience is illuminating.

In the mid-1970s, the American marketplace began to take serious notice of the management style used in Japanese manufacturing firms. "Japanese Management Style Out-Produces US," the headlines told Americans. The innovative production methods used emphasized, among other things, cooperative participation over competition. Large, Japanese manufacturing plants were paying attention to the family structure by providing child care facilities within the plant, by formulating a policy of hiring both the husband and the wife, and by sponsoring social activities to foster friendships among plant employees.[1] Companies competed with one another for the honor of using and recognizing the largest number of worker suggestions to improve working conditions and, thereby, production. This "innovation" in management—that of recognizing and utilizing the skills of making and keeping connections—is indigenous to the traditional role of American women. It is a skill our society ignores and devalues at great risk.

---

[1] See chapter 7 for a fuller account of the support environment of the salaried Japanese worker.

Under stressful circumstances, friendships can display a critical importance (Jones, Freeman, and Goswick 1981; Miller and Lefcourt 1983; Peplau and Perlman 1982). During the loss experienced by divorce, for example, friendship can make the difference between anguish, acceptance, or hopefulness. Nonsupportive friends during this time, particularly friends with whom close emotional bonds have existed in the past, make adjustment following divorce more difficult. Divorcing couples must make a community and a psychic rending at the same time. People are both members of a community, and they are individuals with their own ego-centered views of divorce (Epstein 1974). There is therefore a need for new roles and a new vision of who the individual is under the changed circumstances. This new vision is necessary for both the individual and for his or her friends. Supportive, self-validating, and confirming friendships are of particular importance during such changes (Blau 1981). Frienship becomes yet more important when ties with kin are strained because of divorce (Candy 1978).

There are gender differences in how one adjusts to the loss of intimate relationships (Brown, Harris, and Copeland 1977; Fischer 1982; Habif and Lahey 1980; Peplau and Perlman 1982; Sandler and Lakey 1982). The grief experienced by men and women on the dissolution of a relationship as central as marriage is profound. Women, however, identify more with their roles as wives and mothers than do men to their roles as husbands and fathers. To be female in this culture has traditionally meant not being self-sufficient. Women are, therefore, traditionally less individuated than are men and are, alternatively, more strongly tied to others (Gilligan 1979). Indeed, researchers have found that depression among women is inextricably linked with the loss of emotional relatedness (Sharf 1980). During divorce, women not only bear their own grief at the loss of a formerly important relationship, plus their loss of the identity as wives—and indeed as community members—but they also bear the discomfort and disapproval of society's view of them as somehow inappropriate, or soiled. This sense of irrevocable loss can shatter the basic sense of self, altering a woman's fundamental identification. Because her web of associations is altered, she must become reacquainted with who she is and how she relates with the larger social environment.

To adjust to divorce, then, a woman must go beyond grieving for a lost relationship, a lost romantic dream, and must develop a new identification of herself as an individual separate from the husband she no longer has. The friends she has and her skills in connecting with people in an emotionally supportive way are her resources. Although divorce frequently means economic hardship, women are more likely to have had friendship patterns that included sharing emotional concerns. Consequently, they are more likely to have an available network of support during their grief and adjustment. Those who have had such support have proven to be more effective with their children following the separation (Hetherington, Cox, and Cox 1977).

Clearly, of course, not all women have this support, for typically, it is the support of an independent circle of friends rather than close family ties or "couple" friends that provides the needed reassurance (Hirsch 1980). Women's accommodation to divorce is one example of the value of a diverse type of social network in a social order presenting frequent disruption of such ties.

Once again, however, the caution for balance in all things becomes apparent. Exchange theory states that individuals strive for equity or balance in interaction, that is, that the gains made through the interaction are equal for everyone (Homans 1961; Thibaut and Kelley 1959; Walster, Berscheid, and Walster 1973; Walster, Walster, and Berscheid 1978). Recent research has shown that among older women, social relationships marked by inequity were unsatisfactory to the point that the women experiencing them recorded significantly lower morale than did women in equitable friendships (Roberto and Scott 1984–1985). This result held true whether the woman was underbenefited or overbenefited. Based upon evidence that women structure and prefer noncompetitive relationship models, one is tempted to hypothesize that this finding would be more true for women than for men (Gilligan 1981; Kohlberg and Kramer 1969; Lever 1976; Maccoby and Jacklin 1974; J. B. Miller, 1976). Inadequate research at this time makes that hypothesis impossible to verify, however. The need for further research on male and female adult friendship patterns and social interactions is apparent, for new findings could have significant impact on future human services.

Friendships Among Men. Loyal and caring friendships among men are sufficiently rare to make them the stuff of dramatic and touching movies. Even in films of male friendship, the associations have unlikely beginnings. In *The Defiant Ones,* two escaped prisoners, a black man and a white man, are chained together, symbolizing the even stronger tie that was to emerge. *Midnight Cowboy* had a self-styled male prostitute and a street hustler develop an attachment that went beyond the selfish needs of either of them.

Men have few friends. Even among men educated in human and social needs, when asked to name those closest to them—the people with whom they are emotionally connected—men most often name their mates and are unable to name anyone else (Cowan and Cowan 1985). Males in our culture have been taught to define themselves socially as security objects, the source of support for their families' needs, for the consumerism of their families, and themselves. Future hopes must always be balanced against immediate needs and outstanding bills. Men are always part of the hustle, usually within the law, to get ahead. They are never to be fully relaxed and never fully trusted—a serious handicap for enduring friendships. This "psychology of scarcity" (England 1980; Fried 1982) means the provider is never secure, never able to know how much is enough. In this context, all social contact becomes an arena for potential economic gain.

Some men, however, have buddies. A buddy is someone who shares an activity: a tennis, poker, or hunting partner, a fellow team member. Buddies talk about work or sports or politics. They exchange jokes and advice about car problems. The companionship is real, and the "buddy" form of friendship has meaning, but it can lack emotional support and connection. It is not conducive to addressing dimensions of loneliness other than the need for superficial social contact.

Whatever else, men must be successful. Success is competitive. To be good is not to perform with enjoyment or even with skill. It is to make the A-team, to get the lead part, to make good grades, to land a good job, and to earn competitive awards. The lesson, starting earlier and reinforced more frequently for males than for females, is that they must surpass others. The standard of how well one must do is not a standard of excellence, but of competitive ascendance. This competitiveness is illustrated by our fascination for prizes, awards, and recognition. They are tokens of doing better, of being better than those around us. Competition makes establishing a trusting friendship, from which support might grow, unlikely.

Sociologist Erving Goffman states, "In an important sense there is only one completely unblushing male in America: a young, married, white, urban, northern, heterosexual Protestant father of college education, fully employed, of good complexion, weight and height, and with recent record in sports" (1968:153). Men are taught to compare themselves against this mode and they usually find themselves falling uncomfortably short of the standard, in one way or another.

Our social system teaches little girls to compete for success through objectification of their bodies: beauty and the power it brings will be the path to success for her as a woman. We teach little boys to compete for success through their objectification as security objects: be a winner so you will grow up a winner in life, defined by your ability to provide an income for your family. Interdependence is valued only insofar as it is necessary for the attainment of these gender-defined goals. For men, the perpetuation of the "old boy system" provides both access to those in power and a clear definition of who has power and who does not.

SOCIAL TIES: SOME UNRESOLVED ISSUES

So much of the human experience is taken up in striving for connections. Children, with uninhibited ease, supplement reality with fantasy to meet their needs. Others of us form friendships through shared activities, organizations, work, and through involvement in neighborhood and community issues and activities. This process of connection takes place in an environmental context, each new tie influencing the development of a unique pattern of friendships that build upon each other.

Friendships are made by acts of individual or mutual choice and are products of chance encounters. Both the choices and the chances are reflections of other forces. Friendships, like family patterns, are influenced by the social and economic environment, which is itself influenced by the expectations and patterns accepted in the culture. The reverse is also true: cultural patterns are dependent on the society's social and economic structure, which is both shaped by and shapes family connections and interactions within and beyond these family networks. Connections form multidimensional webs, linking the individual with the larger culture and the economic system with family and kin ties, like a ribbon woven in and out the warp and woof of an environment. Different types of friendship found throughout society are as much a product of the social networks and the environment of the individuals involved as of individual needs or desires. Social networks, according to one researcher, are simultaneously within and beyond the control of each member.

"When two people become friends, within some environmental constraints, they are "freely" choosing one another and therefore are creating their respective social networks. However, they are unlikely to have commensurate control over whether or not their new friend knows their old friends or over their new friends choice of friends. This has two implications. First, they cannot control the degree of connectedness within their immediate networks, and second, they cannot control the configuration of relationships in their friend's networks. In fact their "free choices" have linked them to a larger system which they cannot control, and which will significantly affect their lives" (Salzinger 1982:119).

How, then, do people in today's society satisfy their needs for belonging when their networks are marked by change and when traditional kinship ties are no longer in place? Beneath differences in personal circumstances, a need for intimacy and for connection persists. For this reason, people continue to marry and choose parenthood, develop close and enduring friendships, seek out less intimate relationships with acquaintances, and sometimes form unique types of "family" (Erikson 1964, 1968; Levinson 1978). The connections so made dispel the loneliness experienced by many people.

With so many diverse options for acquiring ties by choice, it seems paradoxical that so many people are lonely. We will next examine some of the reasons for loneliness among people and discuss the theory and practical experience of friendship as a means for reducing these feelings. Then we will look at giving and receiving in our social ties. What do we receive in exchange for addressing the supportive needs of others? Is the exchange always a fair one, justifying our efforts in sustaining a friendship?

THEORIES OF FRIENDSHIP AND LONELINESS

Throughout history, philosophers and poets have addressed friendship and loneliness. Much religious tradition is built upon the urge people have to connect—with God or some ultimate, individual purpose or goal. Freud considered religious feelings to be our own created beliefs, used to comfort us from residual feelings of our lost omnipotence or the lost omnipotence of our parents (Freud 1930). For the infant, all basic needs are met as if by magic, but we soon outgrow our protective cocoons. By virtue of our own developmental patterns, we become, among other things, lonely. Friendship provides one means by which people can reduce feelings of loneliness and anomie. Otto Rank, student, friend, and critic of Sigmund Freud, argued (1932) that loneliness is an inevitable consequence of being born. He believed, however, that the sense of aloneness is balanced by an equally inevitable urge for independence. The struggle to reduce isolation by connecting with others forms only half the equation. The balanced human, in this model, seeks to live and experience three related dimensions: loneliness, friendship, and independence.

We can understand the difficulty in our efforts to define friendship by reviewing the concept in history. In Plato's *Dialogue Lysis,* Socrates struggled with the problem of how people become friends (Reisman 1979). How can bad persons enter relationships that are good? Could, Socrates puzzled, something bad come of something good? How, too, can a good person become the friend of a bad person? Throughout the essay, Socrates attempts to understand why people become friends, concluding that, although not very profound, one basis of friendship is similarity. The dialogue concludes with the observation that the friendship between two apparently dissimilar friends might be based upon certain characteristics of each that are not readily apparent to the observer. Socrates, therefore, came just short of considering a particular category of friendship. Centuries later, social psychologist Ted Newcomb (1961), studying the acquaintance process, found persons to be first attracted to others they believe to be like themselves. Among people who remain friends, however, similarities become apparent as the friendship grows.

Aristotle, in *Nicomachean Ethics,* outlined types, or categories, of friendships, all of which are predicated upon relationships between people who do not wish each other harm. Aristotle noted that in friendships of *utility,* people prefer those who respond to their middle-range qualities: not persons who praise all they do or criticize all they do. They want persons useful to themselves, so that each might gain from the relationship. Friendships based on *pleasure,* the second kind of friendship, center around sharing activities and other pleasant diversions. Aristotle's third friendship type was friendship based on *virtue.* This friendship occurs when two friends love one another because they recognize each other's goodness. This definition became, as history progressed, the prototype of the ideal friendship (Jones 1981).

Ralph Waldo Emerson, in more recent Western history, wrote of less ideal friendships. In his essay, "Friendship," the first element in friendship was free expression and open sharing of thoughts without concern. His second element of friendship was mutuality of tenderness. That feeling, however, was clearly secondary to the safe exchange of ideas. Emerson's view of friendship was based on intellectual stimulation and discourse and did not address friendship as a function of emotional companionship, as something that prevents loneliness. Loneliness, to Emerson, is existential— a fundamental human condition expressed by the poet's lines, "When it comes right down to it, each of us is entirely alone." This loneliness is universal and unrelated to aloneness—that is, its "cure" is found in the spiritual realm, not necessarily through joining a club or "going out to meet people."

Current studies of loneliness come primarily from the cultural wing of the psychoanalytic tradition. Karen Horney, Harry Stack Sullivan, and Erich Fromm (1937; 1953; and 1947, respectively) all address the basic needs of seeking and engaging in satisfying interpersonal interactions. The studies from this perspective outline the dangers of disturbed human relationships and associate the lack of competent interaction skills with mental illness. But these theorists and those who have followed them continue to disagree regarding the reason and "cure" for loneliness. Some believe that human love—or the capacity for the emotion itself—is the answer for curbing individual loneliness. These theorists believe loneliness is the manifestation of an unhealthy ego state (Hammer 1972; Moustakas 1972, 1975), having components of fear, depression, alienation, and guilt. Loneliness is seen somewhat like an illness from which the individual eventually recovers (Brennan and Auslander 1979; Diamant and Windholz 1981; Peplau and Perlman 1982). From these theories came therapies to enhance the individual's ability to love, as a way to reduce acute self-awareness of aloneness and vulnerability (Hammer 1972). Such therapies focused upon the individual and, simplistically stated, placed both the cause and the cure for the condition into the realm of individual responsibility. The individual, in turn, was seen as competent to affect ego changes that would allow enhancement of his or her ability to love and to accept others, thereby reducing the sense of loneliness. In the process, the individual forms friendships.

Themes of loneliness—ranging from the sacred to the profane—are pervasive in poetry, literature, and musical lyrics. In her pioneering work using survey data, Weiss (1973) found feelings of loneliness to be commonly reported, as did Lopata (1973) when examining the demographics of the older person. Much of the present research on this elusive subject has examined loneliness in relation to intimacy and the individual's ability to form intimate relationships (Cutrona 1982; Davis 1976; Dohrenwend and Dohrenwend 1974; Jones 1981; Miller and Lefcourt 1982; Peplau and Perlman 1982). A second but closely related approach to loneliness looks at it from a cognitive and emotional perspective (Jones 1982; Jones, Freemon, and Goswick 1981; Jones, Hobbs, and Hockenburg 1982; Miller and Lefcourt 1983; Russell, Peplau, and Ferguson 1978; Young 1981).

A third approach to the study of loneliness might be called the societal perspective. This view locates the individual within a social, political and economic structure and, thereby, examines loneliness at a different level of abstraction. The approach has evolved somewhat indirectly from network analysis research. That tool and the perspective it assumes (see chapter 6) places the individual in an intricate web of social and community ties, then of economic and political ties as well (Minkler and Estes 1984; Roberto and Scott 1984–1985; Stokes 1983). By using this approach, loneliness becomes associated with competition and drives for power, along with concomitant feelings of powerlessness and victimization. Its cure is intrinsically embedded in the larger social context, because it is the inevitable result of the sense of vulnerability. In this view of loneliness, only by addressing the political realities that shape the individual's personal and family circumstances can he or she find peace and connection with the environment (Jones 1982; Lopata 1973).

One particularly compelling theory identifies four major dimensions of loneliness (Sadler and Johnson 1980). *Cosmic* loneliness refers to one's relation to God or some ultimate destiny. The dimension concerns itself with major philosophical ideas of finality and ultimacy of self, and is similar to Emerson's loneliness, discussed previously. The "divided self" concept, apparent in the writings of Karl Jung (1966) and William James (1950), represents this cosmic loneliness. At the death of a loved person, most people experience cosmic loneliness as they attempt to sort out some of life's meanings. The experience of this form of loneliness can be healing as well as painful, for it forces on one a period of awareness of the ultimacy of life. Helena Znaniecki Lopata's research on widows in America (1973) quotes women's experience of cosmic loneliness: "I miss my husband; I am lonesome. I'm alone all the time. . . . Now there is just me" (1973:69). Workshops on death and dying address cosmic loneliness particularly well by providing a safe and supportive environment to explore feelings of disconnection with the universe.

Cultural loneliness refers to one's relationship with changed cultural patterns affecting our systems of meaning. This dimension might describe the particular kind of loneliness experienced by some elderly people, who describe the world as being incomprehensibly different to them now than when they felt a part of it. It expresses a particular relationship to the world marked by a sense of powerlessness and insecurity. Cultural loneliness is not by any means exclusive to lonely elderly. It is also intimately related to Macy's concept of despair, described in chapter 1, in which the doubt and anxiety generated by a highly technical society seemingly bent upon self-destruction is expressed as intense loneliness. It is this cultural form of loneliness that also forces people into revivalistic cults bent upon turning away the evil forces of change and returning to a period remembered as better. The Peyote cult among the Navajos and the Ghost Dance religion among Plains Indians promised to roll back the tides of time and territory to a setting in which the reciprocal relationships among people, their work, beliefs, and tribal allegiances made sense (Aberle and Stewart 1957; Mead 1932). Similarly, a long period of affluent and modern occupation by American soldiers in Melanesia, followed by the post–World War II withdrawal, brought in a period of Cargo Cults. These religious orders promised the return of Christ upon large ships. The ships would also bring radios and other material trappings of the West, as well as opportunities to work for pay—all of which had suddenly disappeared (Mead 1953). People see one another all the time. But only the cultural and personal meanings attached to these encounters define their value. When the cultural meanings change, as they did in the case just mentioned, or as they did for the Russian aristocracy depicted in Chekhov's "Cherry Orchard," we are both confused and lonely.

The third and fourth loneliness dimensions, *social* and *interpersonal*, are related to enduring relationships of the self to others in an organized pattern, and these dimensions are the ones most commonly the focus of research. Social loneliness refers to the feeling that one's membership in community of individuals is threatened or lost. The group or community is still there, but the individual feels trapped or separated from it. Social loneliness is triggered when radical alterations are made in the network. Change in social patterns because of retirement exemplifies this form of loneliness.

Interpersonal loneliness is the self-awareness generated when a special relationship within that community or network is broken or threatened. The loneliness of a widow whose social position and friendships were dependent upon her husband's work position describes this form of loneliness (Lopata 1973).

Both the social and the interpersonal dimensions create an awareness that something is acutely lacking in one's personal world. These dimensions are experienced, for example, as empty nest syndrome, or are felt when a relationship with a lover is severed. They are perhaps the dimensions of loneliness that can be most immediately redressed under most circumstances (Conner, Power, and Bultena 1979; Peplau and Perlman 1982). They come from a sense of disconnection and can be mended by attention to making connections: with kin, friends, or even the community at large. It takes, however, good health and a certain amount of money to participate in the community, be it attending church or political forums, lunching with former work friends, or becoming active in a club or special interest organization. The poor, the physically or mentally handicapped, the isolated— all can suffer social and interpersonal loneliness to a debilitating extent and be virtually unable to take action on their own to reduce this sense. Sadler and Johnson's theory (1980) proposes that loneliness on any one of these dimensions occurs frequently during one's lifetime and, for the most part, is dealt with on an individual level. When more than one dimension is experienced simultaneously, however, overload is likely, and it can become impossible for the person to cope with it individually.

Whether caused by an existential state bestowed at birth or the product of dissolution, rapid change, or personal loss, loneliness in some form is rarely far away. For this reason, we select mates, form relationships, develop friendships, and create organizations and groups to meet our many needs. Perhaps, from the existential viewpoint, these actions are taken to flee from a basic aloneness; or, perhaps ties are developed and maintained because, on some level, we are already connected with others and the ties are mere manifestations of that connection.

These theories of loneliness respond to the question of why we seek friendship at all. Just what social ties are sought and what motivates people to continue them is addressed by another line of thought—the theory of social exchange.

THE EXCHANGE THEORY OF FRIENDSHIP

How do people become friends? What happens during a social interaction that results in feelings of friendliness between two people, or among several people? The concept of exchange theory helps explain some of the questions surrounding the actual process of building friendships.

The best known of the behavioral psychologists, B. F. Skinner (1953), conducted experimental animal research on how behavior patterns are created or learned. In one study, he fed corn to pigeons who happened to peck at a target in a cage. By feeding the animals when they touched the target, their target-pecking behavior was increased. Skinner named this process "operant conditioning" and, from this experiment and others like it, evolved a set of concepts regarding conditioned behavior that can be generalized to human interactions.

"Shaping" behavior through reinforcement may work in more than one direction. The behavior of the laboratory rat that learns to discriminate the correct symbol is being shaped by the student who places the reinforcing food pellet behind that door. The student's behavior, however, is also being shaped by the rat's response. The student comes to the laboratory when the rat is hungry, replaces the eaten pellet with another, and records each success on the laboratory report that determines his or her grade. The observation of this symbiosis in interactions between people gave rise to the theory of social exchange.

Fundamentally, the exchange theory for humans involves an interactive exchange between two persons that affects the behavior of both parties. If, for example, my behavior antagonizes the person with whom I am interacting, that person will probably let me know by, let us say, ignoring me. If this action bothers me and if I value my interaction with that person, I will modify my behavior until I receive from the other person the attention I seek. In this type of interaction, the exchange occurs because of mutual determination on the part of both parties to continue the interaction. If my behavior were so obnoxious that the other party became completely uninterested in continuing the interaction, the response to my behavior would probably be so extreme I would recognize that no changes I was able or willing to make would improve the interaction.

Exchange theory related to friendship formation grew out of its application to small group analysis. In small groups, the interactions among group members can be charted in terms of exchanges between the less powerful members and the more powerful members. Studies conducted by psychologists Schachter, Festinger, Back, and others have generated a series of propositions regarding behavior in small groups, including ideas about the cost and benefit of behaviors, the development of group cohesion, and the concept and analysis of reciprocity in group processes (Back 1951; Festinger, Schacter, and Back, 1950; Schacter 1951). Two general kinds of reinforcing activity were distinguished: symbolic behavior (such as social approval) and activity (Festinger, Schacter, and Back 1950), studied as frequency or interaction of communication (whether verbal or nonverbal). Once reinforcing behavior was defined, group interactions could be systematically analyzed for content to understand the process of group interaction. According to the theory, the relationships that continue are always those that provide a balanced exchange between the parties involved.

Sociologist George Homans was one of the first to apply small group theory to interactions between two individuals (Homans 1961). He saw interaction as being based on exchange and, indeed, as being dependent upon the reciprocal nature of the interactions. Exchange theory appears to describe a natural human condition, as evidenced by our language. "I found our meeting very rewarding," "I got a good deal out of her," and "Talking with him really takes it out of me" are a few examples of the exchange nature of our personal interactions. We make these exchanges naturally, often unconsciously and unaware of the process. Each individual in a dyadic interaction emits behavior reinforced to some degree by the other. Each person has options for which behavior to use, and each behavior has inherent costs and benefits.

As friendships form, the behavior presented by one party is accepted by another in mutually rewarding ways. Sara has been sick with the flu, miserable and wanting comfort. She runs into Bob, who asks how she is. Rather than replying with the acceptable "fine, thank you," she tells him how awful she has felt, how high her temperature was, and how long she has felt ill. One of several things might now happen. Bob might have an aversion to sickness and really wish she were not telling him all the details about her bout with the flu. If so, he might act bored and cut her story off, he might even walk away, or possibly he will allow her to finish and then abruptly (if politely) leave. Possibly however, Bob will feel valued because Sara was willing to confide in him how she really felt just then. If so, his response would be sympathetic, to let her know he is concerned about her and that he appreciates her confidence in him. Bob's nurturing response will then meet Sara's need for comfort, and she will respond to Bob in some way, perhaps with a grateful smile, which validates his comforting behavior toward her. Both parties of the exchange have benefited, and future exchanges, regardless of how small and insignificant from the perspective of an observer, will contain an understanding of the initial, mutually supportive exchange between them. These nonmaterial exchanges are based on ideas of fair play, cultural codes, and norms identifying appropriate behavior. All these factors influence the nature of social exchange (Bengtson, and Dowd 1980–1981).

Exchange theory also contains a concept of value, or how much an exchange is worth to a given member of the exchange. Behaviors highly valued by the receiving party are returned, if not in like kind, in intrinsic value. Sociologist George Simmel explored at length the concept of reciprocity in culture. Social equilibrium and cohesion could not exist, he theorized, without the "reciprocity of service and return service," and "all contacts among [people] rest on the schema of giving and returning the equivalence" (Simmel 1950). This reciprocity is important, too, among pairs of friends. Interactions create friendships when they are mutually rewarding. Once friendship is established between two people, affection becomes a powerful value, and behaviors are modified and encouraged by that value.

From exchange theory, the answer to Socrates' question of how a good person could befriend a bad one becomes more apparent: the behaviors, or interactions, worked out between the "good" and the "bad" persons are mutually supportive. Perhaps the behaviors seen by the "good" person or the "bad" person are only positive, or perhaps the "good" person enjoys the position of moral superiority felt by association with the "bad" person. Whatever the trade-offs, if friendship indeed exists, it supports and validates some aspect of each person in the relationship.

Altruistic behavior poses a problem for exchange theory (Bauman, Cialdini, and Kenrick 1981; Severy 1974; Wispe 1972). Do we ever do something for others with no hope of getting something in return? The exchange theorist says no, that there is always a subtle return that reinforces the giving. This return could be as subtle as the verification of one's own self-concept as a helping or good person. The return might come much later and, therefore, be hard to see at the time. Perhaps, at this level, social exchange becomes too subtle to really help explain anything. It surely seems that people are capable of long periods of giving, of caring, and of forgiving with little visible return for their efforts. People act in this way for their children, for their elderly parents, for someone they love, and sometimes for a total stranger. Although one could say the giver is gaining by reducing guilt or by chalking up brownie points in a personal log of self-justification, the argument seems too strained.

Sometimes giving is to someone who will never return the kindness. In some societies, a gift is never directly repaid but rather passed on to someone else. At times, the gift passes to one who has died or to one unable to understand (Hamill 1973). Sometimes the tangible return comes not to the giver but to the ancestors of the person who has provided the care or concern. Seemingly, we extend our human concerns and our love not only for reciprocation, but also because we are expressing our nature as an interdependent species. We sometimes care without looking back at the balance ledger. Some cultures are surely better able to tap this potential than others; but the potential to care deeply about the well-being of others is probably as basic as our social nature and does not have to be reduced to an expression of more selfish needs.

FRIENDSHIPS AND THE COMPETITIVE MARKETPLACE

We have looked at the process of having or being friends and have examined the development of friendships through the life cycle. We turned to the study of loneliness to learn more about the how and why of friendship matters, and turned to the theory of social exchange to illustrate the major scientific paradigm used to explain relationships of choice. This search led to the conclusion that friendship means more than making arrangements between two freely negotiating persons.

A wholly different set of concepts about friendships and loneliness stems from a social or environmental perspective. Such theorists look at the context in which people live for answers to why we feel alone and why we form friendships. The roots of our vulnerability, this environmental perspective argues, are embedded in the broader social context in which we live (Henry 1980). To understand the limited scripts available for action as friends—or even to appreciate the potential of new forms of friendship—it will be useful to look back in history to the marketplace origins of the present patterns of friendship and loneliness.

It is difficult to imagine the forms of loneliness found in European society before the Renaissance. In feudal society, most people were peasants or serfs who worked the land of the aristocracy and were dependent upon the beneficence of the lord of the estate. Life was hard, but psychologically it was accepted as the way things were. Illiterate peasants did not assume they had the capacity to improve their lot, and their religion reinforced acceptance of their status. Their admiration of the aristocracy and the church that governed them gave legitimacy to their condition. Scarcity sometimes bred competition among peasants, but more typically their relationships were natural outgrowths of the small working communities in which they lived. There was little privacy and no real hope for economic advancement. Though the lords were sometimes engaged in far-off warfare, the peasants knew little of life beyond the confines of their nearest village (Stearns 1977, 1983). Under these circumstances, friendship, like kinship, was no specially chosen or arranged tie. It was an outgrowth of the circumstances provided by life in relatively isolated settings. God provided companions just as He provided the land to be tilled.

After the rise of rudimentary village literacy and the building of roads, the sense of tranquility provided by a distant, objectified royal gentry was diminished. For the growing class of entrepreneurs and artisans, the market became a center of life where people met and dealt with strangers. Effective dealings provided a ladder to economic achievement through one's own efforts. The marketplace provided a bigger pool of contacts, with opportunities for a greater variety of connections to other people (Stearns 1977).

Some of the major beliefs of modern society have evolved from the early markets. The idea that rule is not divine but rather accountable developed at that time. So, also, the concept that hard work can lead to success and to salvation and the idea that the labor of people, just like any product, is for sale for a price grew from these mercantile beginnings. If people could leave their place of origin to explore, to trap for furs, to find better opportunities, then friendships could also become achievements, and loneliness, a sign of failure to achieve them. "We live our lives in the context of a complicated and extensive self-world network of relationships. The experience of loneliness conveys a message to us that something is wrong in the network" (Sadler and Johnson 1980:38).

The marketplace has now become more complex. The guiding belief that anyone can play is still widespread and taught to us by our schools and by the media. The Horatio Alger myth is fanned by stories like that of Charles Percy, who rose from modest origins to be president of Bell and Howell at age twenty-seven and, later, to become a United States senator. We assume that success brings an affluent life of popularity, which we mistake for a good life with meaningful relationships, and we hold doggedly to the myth that the opportunity for such success still exists.

Actual opportunities in the new marketplace are quite restricted. William Domhoff's classic *Who Rules America?* (1967) clearly shows how the concentration of elite power extends to special elite schools and country clubs, protecting elites from friendships with those less fortunate. Today, many people are afloat like dots on the ocean in the modern marketplace. A few strong swimmers push ahead, some linking together, and building rafts to search for calmer waters. In the game of success, however, there are in reality few players. Large and impersonal corporate entities vie through mergers and oligapoly. Like individual people, these giants have developed interconnecting networks. The corporate connections are made of overlapping board memberships and financial control crossing national boundaries, tying corporations to government agencies—indeed, to the very agencies created to monitor their activity.

International corporate networks, like the great universities and research centers, insure the supply of technology and technically trained persons. They own, both directly and through advertising, the media, which mirrors back to us images of opportunities that no longer exist (Wilensky 1974). In an economy with fewer opportunities for ordinary people to advance, and with a government that allows fewer opportunities to participate in issues of transcendent importance, we place increased dependence on our image of success: the value of possessions, of time spent working over time spent parenting, or of competition for better jobs. These priorities affect the quality of our friendships, for we are unwilling to risk the material for the intangible.

In a variation on the theme of social etiology for loneliness and anomie, Jules Henry (1980) suggests that Americans' conflicting positions of today are related to the temporary oppulence created by war production. Americans' feelings of vulnerability to foreign invasion and foreign enemies is converted into temporary periods of economic prosperity by the military-industrial complex. We therefore keep our economy active by investing in a war economy and grow "fat with fear": a fear of vulnerability, which in circular fashion feeds us, but which is also carried into our psyches and affects our abilities to form friendships and linkages with others.

Denying our vulnerability through prosperity and massive defense spending has components of both structural reality and psychological reality—that is to say, the result of the social context is a psychological reality. This psychological reality takes form in our children. Studies of young children in the United States show that many more of them are aware of the threat of nuclear war than we would have imagined. More than 50 percent of children believe they or their families will perish in such a war. Few children have faith in the ability of today's adults to change this fate (Escalona 1982; Mack 1982; Schwebel 1982). Although the topic is rarely discussed with parents or teachers, its implication appears to be profound. If there is no tomorrow, for what purpose do we make long-term commitments to other people? The lesson is to live for today. The synergism of environment and culture is illustrated once again by this model: as the war economy grows and prospers, we become increasingly removed from the decision making. We become increasingly alienated from control of our social context, and our fears make us vulnerable. From this emotion develops a mentality that precludes long-term and binding commitments.

Individual reality occurs in a context. The context includes the mighty and the impersonal, from personal resources and circumstances to national and international politics and economies. The effects of the social context can be seen in one of the methods we used to show how personal support networks can be described. Picture a set of concentric circles with ties to family and friends placed in different rings around the self at the center. To give that image a greater reality, imagine those concentric circles as expanding ripples around a stone in the water. The pattern is rarely a pure one, since the ripples surely overlap with ripples cast by other individual stones, some creating a much larger splash than ours. Each merging pattern floats not in a still tub, then, but rather on an ocean of moving waters. The ripple of our stone describes the lifetime of our personal network. Its place and its meaning are a product of its surroundings.

CHANGING PATTERNS:
INTENTIONAL SUPPORTIVE TIES

Friendships develop on individual, one-to-one bases, and they also occur through associations with all kinds of groups. In the last fifteen years, we have witnessed a rapid rise in the number of groups specially designed to provide support, to help or heal in some way. It is important to ask again what kind of loneliness these varieties of chosen ties protect against? How, too, do each of these different forms of friendship operate, and what is their meaning in the larger society? Several contemporary forms of friendship will be discussed in this section, and we will review their meaning in the context of society as a whole.

Some friendships take place in a group context. Some groups come together specifically to provide support for one another, either in a self-help context, as in Alcoholics Anonymous or writers' groups, or for strictly supportive functions, in the style of the coffee klatch (Katz and Bender 1976a).

Voluntary groups have been traditionally viewed as supplemental to the kin-based family group, the most reliable basis for continued social support. With higher mobility rates and less permanent marriage patterns than in previous generations, however, special, new forms of social groups have arisen in the United States. These newer forms have self-consciously considered the provision of social support to be among their aims. The differences among groups and the diversity of needs and expectations for social support present some difficulty in studying these associations. The groups can, however, be of great importance to the health and well-being of participants.

Individuals lacking supportive ties are vulnerable to a wide variety of physical and behavioral disturbances. It is just these deficiencies in supportive ties that the new groups address. Although relatively few voluntary groups consider their purpose to be health maintenance, their potential value in disease prevention adds to their more obvious service in combating loneliness and increasing a sense of belonging among their participants.

The number and variety of new social forms related to providing social support is bewildering. Labels describing different groups have been developed from the perspective of the human service provider (Froland et al. 1979; Schoen 1977) who has developed descriptions as well for the more generic form of social support groups, the self-help groups (Gartner and Reissman 1974; Katz and Bender 1976a). Because so many support groups exist (estimated at over 6 million in the United States alone), the social scientist may assume something about them is meeting the differing needs of their many members. But how can this elusive "something" be pinned down, be described in a way that tells us more about the people in these groups, and their reasons for belonging?

Groups can be described on several different levels. Structural dimensions of a group refer to the format for the group's setup: the characteristics of the members, the relation of the group to other institutions or groups, the focus or purpose, the rules and style of proceeding, and the spatial proximity or dispersion of group members. Though the structural dimensions are part of the design of the group, functional factors such as group intimacy, supportiveness, and the number of different helping exchanges that occur are outcomes of the structure and must also be considered. To study these groups completely, it would be necessary to define each element of structure and function. For our purposes, it shall be quite sufficient to describe some different types of groups and their meanings and functions for some of the people in them.

One form of group known as the *intentional extended family* is a group of people who have come together to duplicate a clan or a naturally occurring extended family. These groups are generally multigenerational, as are natural extended families, and their activities tend to be similar to that shared by kin: celebrating birthdays, holidays, and special events marking the lives of members, and sharing recreational activities (Atkinson 1971; Newcomber 1972; Pringle 1974). Some extended family groups are residential—that is, they live together under the same roof, joining smaller families into one larger one. These families not only share celebrations and special events, but also household tasks, child rearing, economic survival, and general day-to-day problem solving.

Some people, in search of alternative life styles, form residential extended families to help get by economically, yet still pursue trades such as writing, cabinetry, art, drama, or music. By pooling resources, these families are better able to provide stability and security for their children and themselves. What is given up in nuclear independence is gained in being able to share responsibilities, activities, joys, and problems.

Several church groups and private groups have taken a lead in bringing people together in forming an extended family of choice. Whatever their origin, extended families provide for their members a caring continuity of friendship that includes persons of different ages. In the fast-paced, highly mobile society in which we live, this conscious duplication of a kin network fills a void which many people feel for motherly advice and sisterly or brotherly affection and interaction. A couple in one experimental family noted that, in its absence, their children would never have gotten to know well any adults other than their parents. The group manages to reduce the isolation of some nuclear families and has proven to be an acceptable substitute, for many, for absent kin networks. An intentional extended family has the added benefit of being able to select for its membership people who are mutually supportive.

Some people create extended families without consciously applying the concept of kin to them. Karen, a single, forty-year-old professional woman, "adopted" families with children for whom she made birthday presents and cakes and with whom she shared special events. Because of her close friendships with nuclear families, she was better able to address her nurturing, mothering needs, as well as to share in the experience of family life. She became, like an aunt and sister, a cherished member of her intentional extended families. In previous, less mobile generations, Karen would most probably be surrounded by a network of blood kin for whom the role of unmarried aunt would be her only choice. The role would have allowed her to remain embedded in a family network, but it was also very prescriptive and provided fewer personal options than are available to Karen in the 1980s.

Friendships, it seems, can be supplemental to existing life circumstances. Groups of supportive friends can make the difference in successfully changing undesirable patterns, such as overeating or, more seriously, child or spouse abuse. Abusive families are often distinguished by extreme isolation, and it sometimes takes the intervention of professionals to break into the pattern of isolation before changes can take place. Mental health programs designed to intervene in abusive family patterns often require by court order support group meeting attendance (Pilisuk and Parks 1980). Once the isolation, the feeling of being completely alone with a shameful secret, has been broken, people are able to receive input from professionals and peers and learn new patterns of behavior.

Support groups mark a turning point in social history. In whatever forms they take, they speak to the need to take friendships more seriously, to create intentionally the types of relationships that, in the course of busy lives, do not seem to be arriving on their own.

THE GIFT OF FRIENDSHIP
A chosen tie is an investment. From children's playmates and teen romances to confidants, from running partners to support groups—each bond represents the interdependence that is our nature. The marvel is that these friendships emerge in heavily automated bureaucracies, on street corners and in preliterate, kin-based settings. In communist, capitalist, and nonaligned countries, people have been able to find playmates and soul mates in which to invest the gift of friendship.

We have argued that much of the interaction among friends can be predicted and understood by the theory of social exchange. To a remarkable degree, we do not either give or get, but merely exchange the pleasures, assistance, recognition, and rewards of social contact. But we have also noted that the exchange may not always occur just between two individuals, nor is reciprocation always predictable within a lifetime. Rather, friendship extends the balance sheet so that giving or receiving sometimes occurs with no clear exchange benefit other than to make this world a more caring place.

There is, of course, a collective return on this investment: millions of individuals who conserve energy or recycle wastes contribute to an ecology that will be kinder to them as well as to others. In the same way, the warmth, concern and caring that our friendships embody, constitute a social environment that will provide safe help from a stranger in an emergency. It will also provide friendly support from a trusted source, just when most needed. Friendship, like kinship, fights to emerge against the more individualistic and competitive values of Western society. Where it succeeds, the interdependent nature of humanity is given expression.

5
THE MEASURE
OF CARING

Love is not a prominent topic in the indices of textbooks on general psychology. Neither are topics of caring, friendship, relationships, or interdependence. In part, this neglect is because our culture emphasizes other concerns, such as learning, achievement, independence, and development; but this emphasis is not the only reason for the omission. Many psychologists and other social scientists, who have given a good bit of thought to problems of love in the lives of their clients or in their own personal lives, have elected to study something else. To study a phenomenon scientifically almost always implies an attempt to measure it. Caring relationships and social ties may be important, but can they be measured?

If such relationships are as important as we have implied, the effort is surely worth a try. Moreover, the attempt has recently been substantially boosted for two reasons. The first is that social support has become, within a short historical period, a highly visible and popular idea (Caplan 1974;

This chapter has been adapted from two papers by M. Pilisuk and S. H. Parks: The place of network analysis in the study of supportive social associations, *Basic and Applied Social Psychology*, 1981, *2*(2), 121–135; and Support networks: The measure of caring, *Academic Psychology Bulletin* in press.

Cassell 1976; Cobb 1976; Gottlieb 1981; Katz and Bender 1976a). If professional people are to see to it that this very special commodity gets delivered to where it will do the most good, and if they wish to demonstrate their effectiveness in facilitating this delivery, then the need to measure supportive actions becomes critical. Fortunately, this boost in the market for a more measurable notion of social support, has been accomplished by an awakening of interest in developing just such a measure. The interest stems from a recently flourishing idea in the social sciences called *network analysis*.

Network analysis has an interesting, perhaps unusual, history. Anthropologists, when visiting a culture new to them, have a tremendous choice of things to notice—from bones and artifacts to languages or marriage patterns, from child-rearing practices to ways of reckoning kinship. To make sense of the society under study, they often look for certain structural arrangements—households, villages, clans, or tribes, for example— that serve certain functions, like raising children or producing food, that the society must accomplish if it is to survive. In the social sciences generally, these structures are often taken as the starting point. Small groups, families, colleges, communities, tribes, corporations, unions, communes, cities, and nations are studied. In each instance, attention is placed first upon the social entity itself. However, some ever-changing social entities, like a friendship circle, can be slippery to pin down. When a different culture is studied, numerous social entities meaningful to people in the culture are not particularly visible to the outsider. Many inferences about the social units of the particular culture can turn out to be decidedly wrong because of the assumptions we carry with us. In some societies, for example, the father does not regularly live in the same household with his wife or children. This arrangement might appear to be a fragmented family, but in such societies the mother's brother plays the major male parenting role and the father is busy with obligations to his sister and to her children. Whether some fraternal order with a changing roster of members is a largely fictional organization or a major force in the lives of its participants is a matter the unskilled ethnographer could easily misdiagnose.

If we were able to hold off our study of the social unit and begin with a study, not of social entities, but of actual interactions among people, then the inferences we make are more likely to be free of our own cultural biases. That process is precisely what network analysis tries to do. It provides a way to study social reality primarily through its transactions.

Network analysis borrows from mathematical graph theory, but it does not typically use complicated mathematical formulations. Rather, it starts with an assumption that any individual can be represented as a dot on a sheet of paper and that any exchange between people can be represented by a line connecting two dots. In this way, we can start with a set of individuals and record who is linked by an exchange to whom. The starting point could also be a single individual, with the linkages plotted outward. The depicted network will have a certain shape (or structure). It might, for example, describe a group of five people in which each person in the group is linked to every possible other person. Then again, all communication could be either to or from the leader, with none of the other members linked—a more traditionally authoritarian structure. Could these simple graphs be of value? We believe they can, because these rudimentary maps of linkages provide building blocks for mapping somewhat more complex patterns of exchange.

The first task in plotting an individual's network of social ties is to describe just who is in the net and how these people are linked. Network mapping is illustrated with a method Carolyn Attneave created to help individuals describe their own personal networks (Figure 4). The personal network map differs from a family tree in that it includes not only all the immediate family and other kinfolk but also friends, neighbors, and work associates. It may even include storekeepers or professional people important in one's life.

Creating a personal network map begins with four lists. The first list is of members in your household. The second is of people with whom you have significant emotional ties. The third and fourth lists are of casual relationships and distant relationships. Each person named is represented by a number and a symbol to distinguish males from females. Each numbered symbol is then transferred to one of the four circular tiers on the network map. Figure 4 shows an unfilled personal network map. To better understand the concept and its visual impact, it might be useful to complete a personal network map of your own.

Networks vary greatly in their overall size as well as in the number of really close people. They differ in the proportion of kin to nonkin and in the number of negative relationships. Once the symbols (typically squares and circles) are put on the map, lines are drawn connecting all the people who have a connection with each other. With all such lines drawn, it is possible to spot any person who serves as a central connection to others. The map will also clearly show any important cliques in the network, and whether they are closed groups or are linked by one person to others.

Personal maps can be affected by many things: by moving, by deaths or departures, and by certain milestone events like marriages, births, graduations, or divorces. A major illness or even a change in lifestyle often brings a change to the network. For this reason, the personal network map is often completed several times, for example, as you are today, as you were at some earlier time, and even as you would ideally like your network to be.

Plotting a network map is a personal experience. The one, common

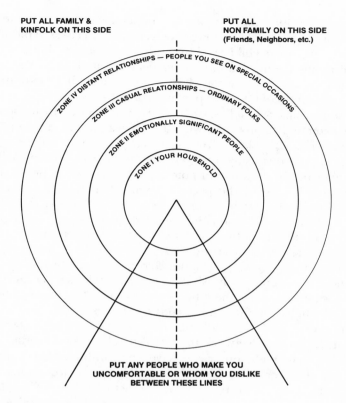

FIGURE 4. Personal Network Map
Reprinted with permission from Carolyn Attneave, Department of Psychology, University of Washington, 1978. Distributed by Boston Family Institute, 55 Williston Road, Brookline, Mass. 02146.

insight provided by any of these maps is that we are not alone and that our connection to other people can be measured. This measurement extends even to the type of connection and to the shape of the web of interconnection. The measurement has in fact, led to research.

THE PROMISE OF NETWORK ANALYSIS FOR RESEARCH

Two early studies established the usefulness of the network approach in research. One application was used in studying the actual exchange network among family members (Bott 1957), and a second was used to describe the types of interactions and associations in small, Norwegian fishing villages (Barnes 1954).

In marital or other family relationships, a major portion of interaction reflects social class. People in lower socioeconomic classes typically treat their spouses and their children differently than their middle-class counterparts. But this feeling leaves a good deal of family interaction unexplained since, within every social class, some families have extensive and frequent supportive communications and some have little such communication. In some nuclear families, each spouse is more heavily involved with his or her extended family than with the nuclear unit, yet other nuclear families are relatively isolated from external contacts. Elizabeth Bott described family relations using a ratio of the number of links actually used to the number of links that could potentially be plotted. A dense network was one in which most of the possible connections were actually linked. When the wife and the husband were each connected to separate and dense networks, then their marital relations tended to show a highly segregated pattern of communication, that is, there were more topics between wife and husband considered off limits (Bott 1957).

Barnes, an anthropologist, conducted a study of fishing villages in which some of the interrelationships could be explained by kinship ties, others by social class, and others by work groups. This range of ties gave people some choice in their interactions. The use of network analysis proved specifically useful in studying the ties that crosscut the boundaries of different social units. Network analysis also helped reveal certain aspects of interaction that might otherwise have gone unnoticed. For example, Barnes noted that person A might have had separate acquaintances with person B and person C, but the relationship between B and C could affect the A-B tie (Barnes 1972). Ties in which one person communicated with another only through a third party were depicted much more clearly by a graph of the network containing directional arrows.

Since these earlier studies, there have been many others, all moving us closer to measuring some very sensitive aspects of social interaction. For the social scientist, the concept of networks introduces an alternative way of looking at social units, be they family, village, workplace, or power elite. Network theory uses as its starting point the transactions occurring among individuals rather than the unit itself. From this view, a social support network is but a special network map in which the transactions are all in the form of supportive ties or caring exchanges among a set of individuals. For the student of larger society, social network analysis provides a tool for studying social relationships in a changing social scene. Rather than using a family, neighborhood, or organizational workplace as the unit of analysis, an individual can be selected and theoretically extracted from all social units, but not from personal interactions. The particular web of interrelationships extricated by this exercise can then be plotted.

The result is a personal network map of Jane Doe much like the one illustrated earlier. Of course, it is possible to start with a family or a household, even an organization or an entire community, and begin the plotting of ties within the unit between its members and those of other families, organizations, or communities. The method also permits the representation of some individuals in the unit only in a technical sense and not very much a part of its ongoing activity, while other individuals, not formally a part of the group, are shown to be actually playing a quite central role. No matter where the measurement begins, social scientists are free to select only the precise types of exchanges, or links, of interest to them. In this book, we have a particular interest in applying network analysis to the exchange of social support. The idea of a social support network is both a tool for the study of varying patterns of social ties and a commentary on the variability, the impermanence, and the frequent deficiencies in supportive ties.

The discovery (and supporting evidence) that supportive ties are important to health has been described in chapter 2. Successful systems of social support somehow foster good health, protect against physical and mental breakdown, provide helpful feedback that encourages health-related behaviors, and provide useful resources to cope with stressful circumstances (Cassell 1976; Cobb 1976; Cobb and Erbe 1978; Hammer 1981; Pilisuk and Froland 1978).

Wellman (1980) has argued that the rash of interest in studying this health-support relationship has sometimes led to confusion rather than to clarity. Some of this research, according to Wellman,

> has weakened and distorted the analysis of social support by oversimplifying the nature of ties and networks. This is because when we declare ahead of time that a set of ties constitute a "support system," we presume in advance precisely that which we want to leave open for study. In order to study the conditions under which individuals do get support, we must allow for the possibility that many of the ties are not necessarily supportive (Wellman 1980:172).

Wellman's claim that network analysis moves us closer to a real measurement of supportive exchange is based upon several arguments. First, he argues that, if we start by only studying support systems (the places an individual gets support), we miss an important resource. Support or caring are only some of the exchanges that occur in a person's network. The larger network could reveal other important sources of exchange. This network increases the pool of persons possibly available for future support. The analysis of networks reveals the pool of potential supportive caregivers, individuals who share no common group with the person but may, nonetheless, be important ties.

Second, Wellman argues that the network approach changes the focus from what the individual is getting to the broader social context. That context includes many exchanges among large numbers of people, some supportive, some neutral, some quite negative. The context, it is argued, helps us to understand the particulars. One individual, for example, may be an important caregiver to another; but, if the former person is embedded in a network with many other competing and demanding obligations, the prognosis for the relationship, or for the stress level of the individuals involved, may be foreboding. This revelation is certainly nothing new for single, working parents or for part-time caretakers of an elderly, disabled relative.

Wellman's third argument is that network analysis contains some specific, descriptive terms that oblige us to notice the variations among types of relationships. These definitions and clarifying terms may be important, for surely the study of caring relationships requires that we ask some rather specific questions, such as: What gets exchanged? How often? Does it go two ways or in one direction only? How strong is the bond?

Network analysis may encourage us to take special notice of the fact that social exchange is a two-way street. Whether the exchange is considerate caring, the spread of rumor, or the exercise of power, the use of networks to trace the pattern of interaction will sensitize us to the fact that people are not merely the recipients of either information or supportive care, but are the originators and providers as well. In a broader sociological sense, people are more than the products of the social interactions coming to them. They are also the sources of interaction, influencing others even as they are being influenced (Boussevain and Mitchell 1973).

Fourth, Wellman argues that network analysis is a way of linking the study of interpersonal ties to the study of large-scale phenomena. The kind of networks available in a small, rural village within a traditional society are quite different from those found in a modern city where so many of our connections are with large, bureaucratic institutions. In fact, one of the most important observations about true caring relationships between people is that they are greatly affected by the economic relationships possible in a society, by larger social values emphasized in our mass media, and by events such as war or recession. Try as we might, love between two people can be only imperfectly understood without an appreciation of the social forces that either promote caring or hinder it.

There is some risk in introducing network analysis into our way of thinking. Exchanges between people seem obvious, natural, and already understood. What value is gained by adding an abstract set of terms—a jargon—to describe these most basic and commonplace aspects of social life? Perhaps, simply because the phenomenon is so much a part of us, the formal, descriptive categories can help tune us in to the patterns we are likely to take for granted and that pass unnoticed. At any rate, let us walk through some of the terms.

THE VOCABULARY OF NETWORKS

Network analysis describes not only the *pattern* of linkages among individuals but also the actual exchanges that define ties between people. It is therefore sometimes related to *exchange* theory (discussed previously), which assumes individuals strive to maximize their rewards and minimize costs. In a two-person interaction, both people reward and punish each other. The rewards, or mutual reinforcements, continue the relationship. To sustain interaction in the exchange theory view, therefore, some balance or fair exchange is required, just as in economic transactions. Both Homans (1961) and Thibaut and Kelley (1959) have applied exchange theory in explaining why individuals join, leave, or remain in groups, matters of great relevance to social support networks. The assumptions of exchange theory, however, become unduly restricting when supportive transactions are examined using network analysis. In fact, in the previous chapter we argued that true human interdependence, involving lasting concerns for one another, is not a matter of equalizing the costs and gains of short-term exchanges. True caring assumes that the ledger recording caring exchanges will balance for the human family across the generations and with many people rather than exclusively between two persons on a short-term, tit-for-tat basis. The following concepts, therefore, do not make use of economic or reinforcement paradigms.

The main terms used to describe linkages between individuals are varied slightly in the network analysis literature. An analysis of social links, though, must include determination of the *structural* qualities of the network map (size, composition, accessibility, density, and structural stability), as well as the *functional and interactional* qualities (intimacy, multiplexity, symmetry) (Pilisuk and Froland 1978).

The structure of a network refers less to what goes on between the interconnected individuals and more to the shape of the net. *Size* is measured by the number of individuals bounded by the network. This measurement may include remote individuals, contacted infrequently and only by letter or phone, as well as those in closer contact. *Composition* (sometimes referred to as source) is often described in ratios, such as the number of kin to the number of voluntary associations or the number of work to nonwork exchanges. *Homogeneity* by race, income, age, or sex is also a factor in composition, as is the *dispersion* or variety of sources from which members come.

The importance of network composition is suggested in the old adage, "It isn't what you know but who you know that counts."

Some structural properties are illustrated in Figure 5. The figure pictures the network of a middle-class woman at age thirty-five, and again, at age seventy-five. It conveys an important fact about the size of networks available for interpersonal caring and about the variety of sources available within the network. It also describes changes in the network over time. Typically, in our society, older people have smaller networks with less varied sources of contacts (Pilisuk and Parks 1983). In chapter 3, we noted that modern families are having increasing difficulty providing sufficient care for their elderly members; yet other sources are often inadequate to make up the difference. In chapter 7, we will take a closer look at the support networks of older people in other cultures. In this chapter, we are content to show that network analysis makes some important observations about elders' support structure. The point is illustrated by Robert Kahn's metaphor of the convoy. Each individual moves through the life cycle surrounded by a set of significant other people, related through the giving or receiving of support. This convoy of significant others changes throughout the life cycle (Kahn 1978). These changing convoys are illustrated in Figure 5.

Accessibility (or reachability) deals with the ease of making a direct connection within the network. The switchboard and the telephone answering machine add steps to the communication linkage between two people. Geographical distance and the number of intermediaries one must go through before reaching people in the network are also two factors in accessibility. Geography becomes important when some of our closest attachements are suddenly uprooted and removed. The number of intermediaries is a factor in the frustration we feel when dealing with large organizations, where no one in charge is ever available.

Density is a structural characteristic describing the degree to which two individuals linked to one another are also linked to other members of the network. Rural, family-based society is more typically characterized by dense networks. Also, studies of the power elite in the United States show them to have a remarkable number of mutual and interconnected ties (Domhoff 1967; Perrucci and Pilisuk 1970). Groups with a higher density typically exert greater influence over the behavior of their members. *Clustering* is related to density, since it describes the degree to which separate cliques exist within the network. In the teenage years of striving for identity, a particular clique of friends often becomes a dominating and exclusive social force. Finally, *structural stability* deals with changes in the structure of the network over time. This concept is particularly important for viewing losses and gains within the unit resulting from death, marriage, or changes in residence and employment.

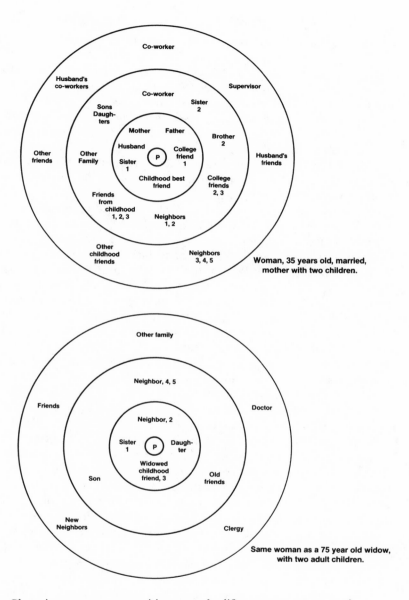

FIGURE 5. Changing convoy composition over the life course: one woman's convoy at two different points in her life cycle.

With permission from Kahn, R. L., and Antonucci, T. (1980). Convoys over the life course: Attachment, roles, and social support. In P. B. Baltes and O. G. Brim, Jr. (eds.), *Life-span development and behavior*, p. 277. N.Y.: Academic Press.

Functional and interactional concepts describe the actual links between pairs of individuals in the network. Interactional variables describe aspects of the communication pattern, while functional variables describe the linkages according to the potential tasks or roles—support, information, power, etc.—certain links provide for the individual. The two categories are not entirely distinct and are combined here.

Frequency (of contact) and *friendship duration* are obvious and, also, obviously important. Our own research on the personal networks of former mental patients now living in board and care facilities shows some very limited networks. Some residents had only infrequent contacts and no enduring friendships (Pilisuk and Parks 1983). *Mode* of contact refers to the method by which communication is made. Telephone calls, mail, and personal contact are all *modes*. Although direct personal contact has a special quality, modern family mobility has made the telephone an important link. Here we must be reminded that each mode of contact has its costs and that poverty restricts certain modes. Face-to-face participation in a community group, such as the Girl Scouts, may require fares for local transportation, something typically out of reach of the family on welfare. Also, the suggestion on television advertisements for people of all ages to "Reach out and touch someone" is not easily done for the large number of poor Americans, often older people, who cannot afford a phone.

The concept of *mode* is a reminder of the importance of written communication to people otherwise forgotten. During wartime, brainwashing techniques included the interception of personal mail from the outside to prisoners of war. In fact, for people in prison and for older people in more isolated nursing homes, some contact from outside the institution (even by monthly letter) is of far greater importance then can be imagined by those of us often bombarded by mail, phone, or personal contacts.

Intimacy refers to the closeness or centrality of the exchange to the individual. Intimate exchanges may be physical or psychological. The Native American concept of touching includes more than physical contact; it addresses the degree of inner engagement with others and with the larger environment (Storm 1972). In modern society, physical contact has lost much of its playful and nurturant quality and has become regarded as either sexual or nonexistent. Even sexuality can vary from a most intimate, mutual sharing to an act of disdain. Intimacy involves that empathetic ability to make one's own boundaries less restrictive in order to step into the shoes of another, thereby to be engaged with another person in ways that touch the self and renew it.

Multiplexity indicates the diversity of relationships. It is the number of different types of exchanges (financial, emotional, recreational, etc.) crossing a link. To better understand the multiplexity concept it may help to think of just how many different items can be exchanged between two people. The number is enormous. Even if we restrict the view to those that have to do with caring or support, the number of possible exchanges is still a challenge to the imagination. Sometimes the exchange is tangible, like a ride to the airport or the preparation of a birthday cake. Sometimes it is informational—highway directions or advice on your job interview. Sometimes it is merely having a partner with whom to share dinner, a game of cards or tennis, or the day's events. Other exchanges provide reassurance: "Just call me if you need help," or "You can do it, baby." Still other supportive experiences involve our deepest emotional feelings. "Hooray, you passed," or "I share your grief." Some exchanges are indirect: "The ramp is built. You can visit the group in your wheelchair." "I mentioned you to the boss and there may be a position." Each of these many functions is important in its own right. Conceivably, each need could be filled from an entirely different source, but many of our richer and more enduring relationships are multiple, that is, they include diverse types of exchanges. These relationships have the quality of versatility. Complex, versatile relationships are important to our adjustment, so much so that we romanticize them in their absence. The romantic ideal has always been to meet someone who fulfills every need. Unfortunately, no one can meet all the needs of another, and many potentially good relationships are lost because of such unrealistic expectations.

Symmetry (also called "directness" by Barnes (1969) addresses reciprocity and mutual participation in the exchange. Here, who gives and who receives, who initiates and who responds, is examined. Reciprocity can be critical to the value of a relationship for a child or any dependent person. There are times, with a seriously ill or dying person, that the symmetry of the relationship is hard to find. It is in this sense that we understand the idea of interdependence, unbounded by time or space. Perhaps, on some level, reciprocation is there, as a lesson in our vulnerability and mortality or to teach us about our capacities to care.

Finally, *functional stability* refers to changes in how the network is used. It describes the loss or reestablishment of contacts and the expectation that they will continue to be of functional value. Even the major points of entry/exit in a network structure—birth and death—are less critical instabilities when the network as a whole has functional stability in who takes care of what, and for whom.

The concepts described so far are summarized in Table 1. In this table, we have separated the conceptual definition, that is, the functional expression of each term, from the measurable index used in actual assessment. The various indices are sometimes found to be empirically related. We can observe that highly dense networks, with frequent and enduring relation-

TABLE 1. *Network Analysis Concepts as Functional and Measurable Descriptions of Supportive Association*

	TERM	FUNCTIONAL EXPRESSION	MEASURABLE INDEX
STRUCTURAL FACTORS	COMPOSITION OR SOURCE	Categories of individuals comprising the supportive association, or category or source of supportive function to the individual in the supportive association (e.g., kin, friends, coworkers, etc.)	Ratios of kin to friends, neighbors to kin, etc.; further defined as ratios of close kin to close friends, etc.
	ACCESSIBILITY	Ease with which any member of the supportive unit can be reached (e.g., primary or secondary associations) for the supportive function of an individual or overall for the group.	Level of association (e.g., number of kin-1, meaning kin directly connecting with individual; number of kin-2, or kin connecting with someone who connects directly to individual, etc.)
	DENSITY	Degree to which all members in the association are linked to one another.	Ratio of average number of interconnections per individual per group, divided by the total number of people in the group.
	CLUSTER	Degree to which members in the association form cliques.	Number of high density subgroups connected by singular or loose ties.
	STABILITY	Degree to which group structure changes over a period of time.	Sum of the changes in composition, accessibility, density, and cluster factors, taken over time.
FUNCTIONAL OR INTERACTIONAL FACTORS	FREQUENCY	Number of supportive transactions occurring per tie.	Actual number of transactions per connection and across single linkages.
	DURATION	Degree to which supportive interaction changes or remains the same over time.	Period of time during which transactions recur over the same linkages.
	MODE	Means or type of transaction; for example, personal exchange, telephone conversation, or letters.	Levels of exchange: number of primary (personal contact); secondary (telephone contact); and tertiary (letter or third party) transactions.
	INTIMACY	Centrality to the individual of the exchange.	Subjective ranking of closeness, most often based on frequency, duration, and mode of interaction.
	MULTIPLEXITY	The number of different types of exchange, either per individual, or per larger association.	Actual number of different types of exchange across a linkage.
	SYMMETRY	The reciprocity and mutual participation in exchanges.	Ratio of directed transaction of A to B and B to A.
	STABILITY	The loss or reestablishment of contacts, and the expectations that they will continue to be of functional value.	Composite index of changes in frequency, duration, mode, intimacy, and multiplexity over time.

Reprinted with permission from Pilisuk, M. and Parks, S. H. (1981). The place of network analysis in the study of supportive social associations. *Basic and Applied Social Psychology, 2*(2), 131–135.

ships, for example, often provide a basis for intimate exchanges. But this correlation is not always the case. Sometimes the close knit family exists apart from trusted friends or confidants. Therein lies the value of this set of constructs. They provide a method for differentiating the connections linking people and for examining various networks made visible by patterns in these linkages. Moreover, the single framework with quantifiable terms permits comparisons of various social units.

When used in research, the network idea reminds us that people are not separate islands. We could choose to view people as a bundle of needs and beliefs and their relationships as no more or less than ways to meet these needs and to affirm beliefs. But we would surely be missing something. Kurt Lewin, the founder of field theory, created a whole school of psychological thought based upon understanding the psychological properties of our environment. His students went on to study the settings in which young children spend their days. Later, Urie Bronfenbrenner's (1977) ecological approach again showed the critical importance of settings to human development. Some community psychologists have marked their distinction from clinical psychologists by just such concerns about the environment (Sarason 1976). Networks are the social or human part of environmental settings. What they tell us about caring relationships will depend upon just how much such caring is inevitably linked in these broad webs of human interconnections. Networks encompass membership in professional associations as well as in families and friendship circles. They include exchanges of money and power as well as affection. The better we identify the various networks in society, the better will be our chances of determining the relationship of such networks to the requirements of a caring society.

The practical value of the descriptive terms in demonstrating what occurs in connections among human beings can be illustrated in many ways. Here we wish to show their potential use for studying just five particular issues of importance to the understanding of social support networks:

1. Can network analysis actually uncover an underlying structure of linkages not visible when observing identifiable social units?
2. Can such underlying networks be uncovered where the medium of contact is supportive interaction?
3. Can the types of supportive ties be quantified to permit intergroup comparison?
4. Can the totality of supportive associations be plotted to establish where the gaps might be filled with assistance from human service organizations?
5. Can the concepts truly improve our ability to measure or to understand love?

The examples that follow illustrate how network analysis can be used to respond to these questions.

RESEARCH ILLUSTRATIONS OF NETWORK ANALYSIS

Although networks are built from specific linkages between individuals, the network is nonetheless an abstraction, for it may include only certain categories of individuals and certain types of links. It may, for example, concern all individuals within a given housing unit, or all those with whom a client interacted in obtaining information about a health problem. Furthermore, some ties that are weak and subject to infrequent use may nevertheless be important because they serve to mobilize people for particular purposes under specific conditions. Such ties are thereby functionally supportive to the individuals comprising the network.

Networks can be arbitrarily defined by addressing one or more specific areas of content or relationships. These areas could include primary and/or secondary kin, or intimate and/or more distant friends. Other content areas might include economic, political, religious, sexual, fraternal, elite club membership, mutual aid, and service relationships.

The Latent Network of Community Power Study. One study of a local center of power made specific use of the concept that networks can be constructed from highly specific types of linkages, to be mobilized for specific purposes. Perrucci and Pilisuk (1970) gathered data on all linkages consisting of common membership, in a decision capacity, in all business, political, fraternal, religious, and human service organizations in a town with a population under fifty thousand. The researchers were able to identify a group of individuals who were all interconnected among several organizations. By matching those individuals with an equally eminent group of individuals who were not similarly interconnected, the authors were able to provide a critical test in the controversy between pluralistic and power elite spheres of social power. Having identified the interconnected web as a latent power network, it was then ascertained that the individuals so identified were all part of each other's social network as well, and that the group maintained a marked homogeneity in values when compared with the matched sample. The same interlocked leaders were found to be the most effective persons during a major community controversy and were the most powerful by reputation as well.

The relevant point of this study is that the hypothesis about the existence of a power elite could only be tested after a *network* was defined and identified. Analyses of the community structure based solely upon the decision-participation model or upon the reputations or positions of individuals were insufficient for determining the power patterns. Network analysis helped define the appropriate unit, or network, of study and was thereby able to critically test the pluralistic versus the elitist theories of community power. Both theories implied the existence of networks by defining transaction routes or exchanges of power and influence. Until the use of network analysis, however, research in support of the two positions had been undertaken largely as a study of individuals; of their decision-participation by the pluralists, their high positions, or their reputations for power by the elitists.

The ability to define a network for loosely structured entities is of importance to the study of those social support networks that overlap with, but are not part of, kinship ties, friendship circles, neighborhoods, or formal memberships in organizations. An examination of supportive social ties can be used to test analogous questions regarding the underlying structures in the way a community offers social support.

Community Structure and Social Ties. Although network analysis makes no assumptions regarding the structure of social units, this aspect does not limit the value of network analysis in the study of social structure. In fact, because of its separation from surface groupings or territorial units, network analysis has become a tool to uncover underlying structures in existing linkages. To better understand the changes often said to have overcome the close knit community, it is possible to make certain hypotheses regarding the underlying network structure of a community and then to test these structural hypotheses against the networks actually found. Wellman (1979) posed three distinct, hypothetical answers to the "community question": How have primary ties been affected by large-scale divisions of labor in the social system?

The *Community Lost* hypothesis posits the present existence of impersonal, transitory, and segmental ties, and of multiple networks that are sparsely knit, loosely bound, and rarely adequate for dealing with contingencies. The *Community Saved* hypothesis asserts the persistence of solidary ties in neighborhoods, kinship systems, and at work. The *Community Liberated* hypothesis lies somewhat between the others. It contends that (1) urbanites are involved in multiple social networks with weak ties; (2) high mobility weakens ties and hampers the formation of new ones; (3) easy transportation and communication systems reduce costs of maintaining dispersed primary ties; (4) opportunities for urban interaction increase the possibilities for access to loosely bounded, multiple social networks; and (5) spatial dispersion and heterogeneity induce those less well tied to densely knit, close communities, to make more links.

According to the Liberated arguments, older forms of dense ties that combined kinship, work, and residence have been replaced with looser networks that are nonetheless prevalent and available as important sources of sociability and support. This aid and friendship is less frequently a matter of obligation than in times past and more often a reflection of the quality of particular dyadic ties, the ease of continued contact, and the ability to mobilize resources beyond the dyad.

Wellman put the three hypotheses (Lost, Saved, and Liberated) to the test in East York, Toronto, where he found general support for the Liberated argument, with most individuals having one or more intimate ties. Although only a small portion of these ties were available for help in daily matters or in emergencies, most persons could get assistance from someone. The relative importance of parent-offspring ties and physical proximity of work ties suggested some elements of the Saved Community hypothesis, although personal networks were clearly dispersed.

Wellman sought out intimate ties by asking the following: "I'd like to ask you a few questions about the people outside your home that you feel closest to; these could be friends, neighbors or relatives." The relation of the respondent to each named person was described in the terms of network analysis, and the ties of the various associates to one another were plotted. This methodology may have encouraged the naming of more intimates than the defenders of the Community Lost hypothesis would countenance. Still, the study is a remarkable example of the capacity of research, guided by network analysis, to study the relationship between the structural nature of community ties and the availability of social support.

Comparable Categories of Social Support. A third illustration helps show the value of formalizing the specific concepts of network theory when studying supportive ties. Tolsdorf (1976) contrasted the networks of recently hospitalized, adult male schizophrenics with those of a matched group of medical surgical patients. This method of plotting relationships used ego as the locus and drew lines to a primary star of network members. Because a variety of content areas (or types of linkage) are possible between the individual and any other individual, the number of content areas to the number of individuals in the star could be expressed as a ratio. The networks of the psychotic group showed fewer multiplex relationships and lower relationship densities. Tolsdorf's model examined three specific functions for the linkages between individuals: *support* (defined as assistance in meeting goals or dealing with demands), *advice* (defined as provision of information), and *feedback* (defined as evaluation of the individual's success in meeting expectations). An actual map of the links showing their directionality was facilitated by the mathematical concepts of directed graph theory (Harary, Norman, and Cartwright 1965). The nature of asymmetries between the individual and others in his/her network was formally described as "indegree" or "outdegree," describing, respectively, the number of functions one receives and the number one provides.

Tolsdorf's analysis provided a useful tool for determining the level of support an individual experiences. He found systematic differences between the medical surgical and psychiatric groups in the size and complexity of their networks. The study showed the possibilities of network analysis, both in refining the categories for describing helping ties among individuals, and for quantification and cross-group comparison of the variables described.

Resource Analysis and Policy Development. Stueve and Fischer (1978) used network analysis to describe support networks of older women. Their study was directed toward developing comprehensive public policy programs in gerontology. They defined the purpose of their study to be the determination of the social networks of the subject population, rather than the examination of the use of existing public services and programs. Social networks, they asserted, constitute a resource for older persons that must be considered in developing public policy, and, consequently, they must be studied and described. Analyzing the networks also provided information relevant to other questions of critical importance to policy development, such as how networks differ as service resources, how people differ in their needs and wants, what gender differences occur in network structure and function, and what changes in networks take place with increasing age (Stueve and Fischer 1978).

Stueve and Fischer conceived of supportive networks according to the constructs of exchange theory. They assumed individuals are rational decision makers who determine which social relations they will and will not engage in; that they make subjective assessments regarding the rewards and costs of relationships; that interpersonal relations are indeed exchanges; and that choices are made within particular social constraints. Individual social networks were analyzed in terms of kinship and friendship ties and in categories of supportive exchange: instrumental (doing things *for*), social (doing things *with*), and personal (emotional sharing). By developing a pattern of existent exchanges, a corresponding pattern developed of resource exchanges that were not made. The latter provided a means for specific evaluation of deficiencies in the system, information of immense value to human services planning.

The Stueve and Fischer study was conducted in several different communities in order to develop a general profile of the support networks of older women. Their methodology could be adapted, however, to study the supportive exchanges occurring in a particular association, such as a senior center, a nursing home, or a support group for bereavement. By using network analysis methodology, the relationships among individuals can be analyzed and described as parts of a system relating to the larger society, thereby linking the social structural and individual levels of analysis to social issues.

CARING: WHAT IS MEASURED AND WHAT REMAINS

The illustrations of network analysis give a healthy boost to the tools of social scientists. The discussion of networks surely adds to our means for studying caring relationships. But network analysis does not appear to capture the whole issue. When we speak of a friendly phone call, the frequency with which it occurs makes a difference. If a particular supportive exchange is an intimate embrace, the source of initiation matters greatly. Moreover, one friend's visit to share your experience of grief may not truly be the same as sharing that experience with perhaps some other person. Nor is an intimate exchange regarding a personal problem to be equated with a loan to get past a financially rough period, even if the source of the exchanges is the same. Furthermore, what is apparently the same exchange with a little different inflection of voice is not really the same. So while network analysis obliges us to be better tuned to the broader context of network patterns and to the different types of links between people, we still have a way to go in directly measuring social support and its adequacy to individuals.

Since some researchers have jumped into this additional task already, it would be wise to review their accomplishments. This review will help formulate our answer to the question: "Can you measure social support?" You might recall that this chapter began with the observation that, as important as social support, caring, and love may be to our health and to our state of mind, they can only be studied, in a scientific sense, to the extent that they can be measured. The purpose for looking at network analysis was to ask whether this new and fashionable set of terms could help measure our caring for one another.

First, it should be pointed out that, though network analysis has proven to be a handy tool, it definitely has not resolved the matter of how love or caring are to be measured. All attempts to get an objective measurement (let us say, a network map) from the information people provide are limited by the accuracy of what people tell us. One study found that people tended to be highly inaccurate in reporting their social networks (Killworth and Bernard 1976). In fact, one group of people added an average of 50 percent more names when nearly identical questions were asked again in the same interview, and more than 25 percent of those named the first time were missing in the second list (Barrera 1980). This problem of reliability is common in the measurement of social and psychological concepts (Dixon 1983). We can, of course, change the wording to tighten up the measures and thereby improve the likelihood of more reliable replies. The cost of this rigidity (to be guarded against), would be the lost opportunity for people to talk about important but unusual relationships or about nuances of interaction not readily recalled or easily described.

The problem in measuring caring relationships is not only a matter of obtaining reliable responses. Another issue is the decision about what to measure. Besides asking who is in the network, we could take a quite different approach and measure the actual help or care that occurs; or, to take a third alternative, we could try to measure the individual's experience of that care. Each of the three approaches to measurement places emphasis upon a different aspect of caring that the researcher thinks is important. For example, when we speak of social marginality or social isolation, the point is made that being embedded in a set of ongoing relationships with others is highly important. This assumption is the basis of an entire sociological tradition dating back to Emile Durkheim's theory of anomie (1951). These ongoing relationships may be demanding obligations as well as personally rewarding encounters; but the point is that the extent of our embeddedness in these relationships is itself something to notice. In fact, many of the public health studies cited in chapter 2 to establish the link between social support and health made use of indicators of social embeddedness: Do you live with other people? Attend church or synagogue? Belong to a group? More embedded individuals tend to have less illness.

Types of Caring Exchanges. When we switch our approach and attempt to measure the actual help or caring that takes place, we elevate the importance of differences among the many possible exchanges between two people. Note Wellman's observation that many interactions are decidedly nonsupportive. Recall also Minuchin's study cited in chapter 1 showing that parental interaction in a therapy situation resulted in elevated anxiety for the sick child.

Some people have tried to select for measurement those forms of interaction that are precisely supportive or helpful. The literature on psychological counseling provides helpful guides to the identification of specific behaviors used in a supportive relationship. Empathetic listening, nonjudgmental reflection, and warmth are examples of such behaviors (Carkhoff and Truax 1967). The types of informal helping behaviors extended to sole-support mothers by family, friends, and neighbors were identified in a study by Gottlieb (1978). The types were *emotionally sustaining behaviors,* ranging from unfocused talking to the provision of an extended period of care; and *problem-solving behaviors,* ranging from focused talking to the provision of a directive for action. Gottlieb's schema included two less direct forms, also of importance in a supportive network: *indirect personal influence* and *environmental action.* Similar categories were developed by Walker, MacBride, and Vachon (1977) to describe assistance available to the recently bereaved individual.

Once types of assistance are identified, it is possible to ask people about a goodly number of situations (illustrating each type) in which they do or do not receive support. We can then improve our original typology by determining which types of support actually tend to cluster. This procedure is exactly what the statistical method of factor analysis is designed to do. Using factor analysis, Barrera (1980) discovered four distinguishable factors (or clusters). By looking over the individual items within each factor, it was possible to name the factor in accordance with the items most central to it. Four factors of social support emerged:

Directive Guidance—including the provision of advice
Nondirective Counseling—including expressions of intimacy, availability, and esteem
Positive Social Interaction—including joking, diversion, and discussing interests
Tangible Assistance—including the provision of shelter or money

Detailed examination of supportive behavior may be getting more precise. Moreover, the overt manifestations of caring can easily be observed and would seem, therefore, to be more objective measures of our caring. Yet this approach, too, has problems. Actions that provide support, for example, your offer to provide me with transportation, can be quite objectively observed. Whether or not the offer is actually supportive, however, is another matter, and a more subjective one. Your timing or your style of offer may be off, or I may be suspicious that the offer is but an effort to make me feel indebted. Also, how are we to weigh or to combine the many different supportive actions? Can a loan of $50 be added to a personal compliment, to advice about your health, or to a hug in order to sum up a total measure of caring? Is a gift of $50 an expression of twice the caring as a gift of $25? Is physical assistance more important than companionship or emotional sharing? Or does the importance of each behavior vary according to the needs of the individual? After the loss of a loved one, there is need for a special kind of attention or affection that may be inappropriate at other times. Such questions suggest that direct observation of supportive behaviors may provide a measurement that loses the holistic or gestalt quality of this thing called love.

FEELING CARED FOR
Assessing social support from the unique experience of the individual who receives it is a more subjective endeavor. This approach also has a long historical tradition. The writings of the symbolic interactionists (Cooley 1902; Mead 1934) claim that social interaction provides the basis for identity, the way we define ourselves and evaluate our worth. The importance of maintaining a positive self-image was quite central to our explanation,

in chapter 2, of how social support can increase our levels of immunological protection. In formulating a self-image, it is the sense we make from the support we receive that is important (Brim 1974). What must be measured in this view is not the breadth of our network, nor even the specific, supportive actions provided by it; rather, we must assess how we feel about this network. Such measurement is highly subjective and poses some problems.

Efforts to measure the perceived quality of support may be worth the effort, however. One study looked at the help available to victims in road accidents. He found that the availability of help was unrelated to the victims' perceptions of help extended. However, the perceived receipt of respect and empathy was highly related (Porritt 1979).

The difference between the approach dealing with specifically defined supportive individuals or actions, on the one hand, and taking a broader perceptual orientation, on the other, comes out clearly in a discussion of negative or undermining social supports. Small, denser networks are sometimes ineffective in supporting an individual's new and different directions. In fact, support from a close-at-hand group could be a source of extreme pressure and have quite adverse effects. Earlier, the personal network map (illustrated in Figure 4) included a section in which to list people with whom interaction tends to be negative. One study specifically asked subjects to list who they most likely encounter in angry or upsetting ways (Barrera, Sandler, and Ramsay 1981). Also, the "hassles" scale (Lazarus 1976) contains quite a few opportunities for people to note their specific, recent, troublesome encounters. The broader and more subjective view was also used in Tolsdorf's previously described study (1976) of the social networks of psychiatric patients and of surgical patients in hospital settings. In addition to differences in the specifics of their networks, the groups differed in another, more subjective way. The surgical patients typically held a "positive network orientation," described as a set of beliefs or expectations that it is safe, advisable, and in some cases necessary to confide in the social network, to draw upon it for advice, support, or feedback in a stressful situation. The alternative, a "negative network orientation," was more typical of the psychiatric patients. This orientation was defined as a set of expectations or beliefs that it is inadvisable, possibly useless, and even potentially dangerous to draw upon network resources. This underlying, subjective feeling about whether or not we are loved or cared for seems to overshadow many of the gains made in getting more precise measurements of other aspects of social support.

We have apparently come full circle. We began by promising to examine network analysis as a tool for measuring caring relationships and for transforming such ties into a more central part of our scientific understanding of social support. We have come to a single study by Tolsdorf that carefully uses network analysis, and, nevertheless, leads us to a conclusion that our own subjective evaluation of our supportive networks may be the key factor to understanding social support.

The detailed examination of caring relationships through the framework of network analysis has been worthwhile. It has enabled us to plot the intricate web of human interconnections and differentiate the variety of exchanges linking people to one another. Originally, however, we sought to test the effectiveness of network analysis in measuring love. For better or for worse, something at the heart of caring still seems to elude precise measurement. We have moved closer to accurate measurement of many things, all of which are related to love. But for love itself we are back to the original, often unreliable method of asking people and listening carefully to what they tell us.

Urie Bronfenbrenner (1977) describes the problem of measurement in his social ecology studies as being "between a rock and a soft place." The rock was rigor, the soft place, relevance. Love is perhaps more relevant to our understanding of the human condition than any other idea. If social scientists cannot yet measure it precisely in every way, they should, at least, be encouraged by the fact that they have started the task, adding both to our understanding and to our appreciation of something majestic yet not within our grasp. In fact, we should be delighted that our opportunities to practice loving do not have to await the ability of scholars and professionals to measure it perfectly.

6
INTERVENTION
ENHANCING SOCIAL SUPPORT

Many of our companions on this planet are ill housed, ill clothed, and ill fed. Most of us need look no further than the poor side of our own communities to find the scars of hunger and malnutrition, of illness or inadequately attended disability, and of pervasive loneliness. Closer even than the bag ladies and the lonesome drinkers are the myriad of friends and neighbors who seem unable to find either each other or themselves. Completely hidden are the teaming prisons, the lonesome rooming houses, the board and care facilities housing an array of former mental patients, and the custodial nursing homes for the discarded elderly. For the public service planners who design programs, and for the human service professionals who deal with the casualties, the situation calls almost automatically for the reply: "Analyze and diagnose each separate problem, design various program options to correct what is wrong, evaluate the consequences of these designs, and place the programs into action."

This chapters has been adapted from a paper by M. Pilisuk, S. Chandler, and C. D'Onofrio, Reweaving the social fabric: Antecedents of social support facilitation, *International Quarterly of Community Health Education*, (1982) 3(1), 45–66. Copyright 1982, Baywood Publishing Company, Incorporated.

This chapter is on professional intervention. Much of what is written here will sound like the diagnoses and prescriptions that follow most assessments of social issues, for that is, unfortunately, the language we as professionals know how to speak and comprehend. It is unfortunate, however, because what we have been discovering about human interdependence suggests the need for something that goes beyond the development of techniques for the concerned professional. The situation is, perhaps, akin to the discovery that some spiritual force affects our health and we must urge health professionals to become more spiritual in order to tap its power. What we have learned, and continue to learn, about networks of caring has already had an impact upon various tools of the professional trades. The purpose of reviewing these applications of the concept of social ties is to show that some, but not all, of the implications are matters of feeling and perspective, not of technique. That said, we will begin nonetheless, with techniques—in fact, with techniques to nourish social support that have long been part of the professional arsenal. Later, we will return to the point of view that gives meaning to the art of helping strangers.

PROFESSIONAL ROLES SUITED TO
AIDING SOCIAL SUPPORT NETWORKS

Professional intervention on behalf of more satisfying human relations has been more art than science; yet, each of the various methods that has emerged within the human service professions has had a distinct rationale and a set of finely differentiated characteristics. Assisting a family in crisis is different from creating a group for recuperating patients. In turn, these tasks are distinct from helping a large organization cope with personnel problems and, different again, from building a sense of community purpose in a deteriorating neighborhood. Each task has its own procedures that have been described in the professional literature. The job of developing supportive interpersonal networks has usually been considered subsidiary to other goals of treatment or assistance. With the newfound relevance of social support to health, however, the task of promoting such support is likely to become more central. For this reason, the various predecessors of this activity should be reviewed to suggest just what form this professional intervention might take. We have selected seven intervention models (see Table 2) on the basis of their apparent relevance to developing networks. Some are designed to assist a family in crisis, others to help an organization or an entire community, and one is designed to help the helpers. All of them, however, involve building supportive ties.

The important question is as follows: If we look closely at each of these different forms of professional helping, will we find a common kernel of wisdom? In other words, will we learn something basic about how to go about nurturing supportive relationships among people? To begin searching for the answer to this question each of the different professional roles will be described. Then we will contrast the seven types by answering some basic questions. How is the client defined? What are the change agent characteristics? What is the goal of the intervention? What is the mode of initiating contact? How long is the typical duration of the intervention, and what specific skills, tasks and interventive behaviors are involved? The answers to these questions will help in describing what human services have already found out about providing nurturant support by developing social support networks.

Table 2 summarizes the comparison of several models of professional helping. With it, we begin a brief review of seven methods, most of which have had volumes written about them. It is necessary, however, to examine them if we hope to find a common element in all forms of professional helping. The seven models chosen represent a variety of disciplinary approaches. For our purposes, it matters little whether the method emerged from the traditions in psychology, psychiatry, public health, social work, or nursing. There are traditions in the matter of helping strangers that are perhaps deeper than the traditional boundaries separating the professions.

Family Systems Therapy. Family therapy developed as a distinct approach when psychotherapists saw a need to work with whole families rather than just with the individuals exhibiting behavior or personality problems. For instance, take the problems of seven-year-old Jed. His hyperactivity and propensity for stealing got him into continual trouble, a matter of great concern to his exasperated parents. Jed's mother was overprotective, his father deeply jealous (though he could not admit it) of the warm attention Jed received. When things were normal, the father's ulcer flared up and he missed work. He was always angry at Jed for something. When Jed actually got into trouble, the father's ulcer subsided and both parents turned their attention to the bad kid. When the problem or behavior was seen as the result of family patterns of communication and activity, it made sense to work with the family as a unit—to help it function more effectively for the benefit of all members as well as for the identified patient.

Families, we have argued, are often the most immediate and unquestioning source of social support. When they are not always able to fulfill these supportive functions the reasons may lie in forces of the economy, in major illness, or in mobility—forces often beyond the control of an individual family. Yet, the family sometimes does not use well even the pool of potential caring that it does command. Sometimes, as in the case of seven-year-old Jed, internal conflicts sap the strength of the family and bring pain

TABLE 2. *Forms of Social Support Facilitation*

	INTERVENTION MODEL			
	FAMILY SYSTEMS THERAPY	FAMILY NETWORK THERAPY	NEIGHBORHOOD ORGANIZATION	COMMUNITY NETWORK THERAPY
DEFINITION OF CLIENT	Nuclear family	Extended family and significant others	Residents in a defined geographic tract	Family, significant others, and human service organizations
CHARACTERISTICS OF INTERVENTION AGENT	One or two professionally trained psychotherapists	Teams of three or more professionals or trainees with family therapy training	A professionally or self-trained community organizer.	An agency-based health or mental health professional
AGENT'S GOAL OF INTERVENTION	Reduce destructive conflict, enhance creative problem solving, and family satisfaction	Establish personal network to assist family with a critical problem	Increase involvement in neighborhood self-help and social action	Enhance family sufficiency, provide direct services and coordinate services, and advocate for family needs
MODE OF INITIATING CONTACT	School, agency, or self-referral for emotional problem	School, agency, or self-referral for emotional problems	Core group seeks organizer to enhance efforts, or agency offers planner to groups	Referral of family by school
TERM (DURATION)	Usually between 3 to 50 weekly sessions	One to four day-long sessions	As long as community maintains interest	Often through school year, or until family uses community resources effectively
SPECIFIC SKILLS AND TASKS INVOLVED	Individual and family diagnosis, therapeutic interpretations of the family system	Organize meetings, build sense of common purpose, facilitate meetings	Establish core group, define community, assess needs, assets and impediments, assess community power structure, be resource to group	Assess family problems and community resources, coordinate and advocate service.
KEY TYPES OF INTERVENTIVE BEHAVIOR	Listen to all members, increase safety for interaction, encourage individual and family growth, interpret patterns	Identify active leaders, clarify problem, acknowledge and praise constructive caring	Hold meetings, arrange meetings or confrontations between residents and power groups, reward participation, and maintain spirit of group	Establish contract with school system, meet with family in home, work with individual family members and friends, advocate with community agencies

Reprinted with permission from Pilisuk, M., Chandler, S., and D'Onofrio, C. (1982). Reweaving the social fabric: Antecedents of social support facilitation. *International Quarterly of Community Health Education,* 3(1), 45–66. Copyright 1982, Baywood Publishing Company, Incorporated.

INTERVENTION MODEL		
SYSTEM CONSULTATION	**SUPPORTIVE CONSULTATION WITH NATURAL HELPER**	**PATIENT GROUP EDUCATION**
DEFINITION OF CLIENT		
Service organization, agencies, units within agencies	Natural helpers (non-professionals)	Patients (often similar patients) or family
CHARACTERISTICS OF INTERVENTION AGENT		
One or more specialists from a number and range of disciplines	An agency-based health or mental health professional	One or more health-care providers and/or concerned patients or former patients
AGENT'S GOAL OF INTERVENTION		
Help organization deal with interpersonal impediments to effective or satisfying work	Enhance the capacities of natural, non-institutional providers of service	Help client understand and adjust to illness, and participate in optimal self-care to speed recovery, assist individual and group feeling of power
MODE OF INITIATING CONTACT		
Agency administration seeks aid from individual or firm, sometimes mandated by legislation	Agency consultant seeks out helper and offers assistance	Provider-referrals, self-referrals, group outreach
TERM (DURATION)		
Contract specifies time from one session to indefinite length	Continued regular meetings, termination not sought	Indefinite duration
SPECIFIC SKILLS AND TASKS INVOLVED		
Set clear contract, assess contract, diagnose system impact of problems, mediate conflicts	Find healthy and capable natural helpers, diagnose service needs, establish mutual consultation agreement	Encourage expression of doubts and feelings, facilitate group interaction, assist in developing alliances, and provide information
KEY TYPES OF INTERVENTIVE BEHAVIOR		
Hear all sides, establish safe environment for affective expression, and set up direct communication channels	Listen, support, offer agency back-up or aid when needed, be available for consultation with special problems	Experiential teaching, developing program, arranging and setting up meetings

to one or another of its members. At this point, typically with one person in distress, the family therapist enters.

Because the family does not necessarily see the individual's behavior as a symptom of a family problem, it is often the counselor's task to relocate the problem in the family system. With the entire nuclear family present, the therapist can directly observe aspects of the disturbed pattern, such as a parent repeatedly interrupting the attempts of a shy child to speak. In other words, the outside intervenor (in this case, a professional counselor or psychotherapist) strives to see the system in motion before interrupting the patterns.

What each therapist does with the family varies according to individual orientation. There are widely differing styles and theories of family therapy; there are also some marked similarities. Ferber, Mendelsohn, and Napier (1972) distinguish between two general types—the conductors and the reactors. While observing the family, the conductors structure the situation in order to manipulate the interactions. The manipulation may be quite direct. Family therapists like Virginia Satir (1967) literally teach family members new and different ways of communicating at the moment they become aware of problems arising from the present pattern. Some family therapists teach negotiating skills to encourage responsibility and power for each person. The less direct conductors will create unfamiliar situations for the family in order to break patterns. The therapist may intentionally break unspoken family rules or taboos (Ackerman 1966). Other therapists will have family members actually enact a situation that breaks their normal pattern (Minuchin and Montalvo 1967).

Reactors respond to the behavior the family presents to them. In actual practice, most family therapists find themselves both assertive and reactive to some extent; however, the reactors are predominantly responsive. In general, reactors are more concerned with understanding family interaction. They take note of internal psychological processes and are particularly alert to how the family operates. Karl Whitaker, perhaps the most famous of this group, "invades" the family by becoming caught up in one of their patterns. Then he backs out, leaving them to react to what he has done. Another pair of therapists (Boszormenyi-Nagy and Framo 1965) work to uncover internal, individual distortions that are being perpetrated on current family relationships.

All contemporary family therapy approaches have as their ultimate goal, a change in the way family members interact. One approach may focus upon providing insight, another may try to direct the action; but much of the basic task—creating a more caring network—is the same.

In most instances, the family is referred or has sought help because of a disturbing behavior by one of its members. The therapist (or two therapists working conjointly) must decide whether the identified problem is primarily a symptom of a family disorder. The major task then becomes to change the focus from one person to the whole unit. Whatever the choice of tactics, the therapist works for recognition of what is going wrong and for change of those problem behaviors. The therapist is a director, a teacher, a role model, an actor, but not an advisor. Family therapists purposely avoid that role in order to assist the family in becoming more self-sufficient.

Prevention of future breakdowns is also a goal when the family is involved. If the therapy goes well, according to the theory of family therapy, the identified patient will be able to give up the problem behavior without another child or adult having to assume symptoms in order to maintain family homeostasis. In the last analysis, family therapy reminds us that suffering and the relief from suffering are not just individual matters of concern.

Family therapy clearly requires intervenors with a high degree of knowledge, of skill, and of sensitivity to the established patterns of interaction that define the family as a network. Their practice also illustrates the importance, when trying to enhance social support, of resisting giving direct advice. Direct advice is probably one of the least useful methods for improving the capacity of the family, or any network for becoming more effective in its tasks of caring.

Family Network Therapy. The concept of family network therapy grew as a variation in family therapy. The network involves the immediate family and a large number of other people significant to it. When the resources of the family are not enough to meet basic needs, the network may be able to provide the necessary support.

Ross Speck and Carolyn Attneave (1973) have outlined the basic process a group of people goes through in family network therapy. Most often, a family in crisis initiates contact with the therapists, who then hold a preliminary meeting with the family. If it is agreed that a network intervention is the best approach, then family members have some work to do. They must contact relatives, friends, neighbors, schoolmates, and work associates (15–100 people) and invite them to participate by coming to a meeting at the family home. During a major crisis that could result in someone being institutionalized, it is hard for family members to imagine that an old acquaintance or distant relative would have an interest. But it is exactly when the problem is a crisis that people can be brought together. Intervention is time-limited—usually only four meetings are held, although the entire process is sometimes planned for one long session. A group of professionals and trainees comprise the intervention team.

The network has come together because of a specific problem or person. The intervenors' goal is to "retribalize" or reunite the entire network into a band of human support for all members of the network as well as for the identified patient. In a society where we have given so much responsibility for caring to formal institutions (Hawkes 1978; Howell 1975), family network therapists are trying to educate a community of people to help itself. This objective is based on the dual beliefs that a nuclear family cannot carry the entire burden and that people are willing to help each other. The basic ideas of network therapy do not focus upon individual pathology. Instead, the intervenors use a model that explicitly looks for strengths.

What actually takes place is a dramatic tour de force. With the help of a team of therapists, people hold hands and sway rhythmically or silently look into one another's eyes. They physically break into or out of certain closed cliques, watch silently while others argue, and often express the deepest emotions. Once feelings are expressed, the group comes up with an amazing variety of resources. The group provides not only emotional reassurance but concrete problem solving, leading to jobs, housing, or respite care to relieve someone who has been shouldering too large a burden for too long.

A brief description cannot do justice to a set of experiences carefully designed to build cohesion in a loose network facing a calamity. In fact, the description makes the activity sound a bit like the practices of certain flashy trends in therapy. But observers note that these activities form part of an integrated process, and that an effective network can be created in this way.

According to the description provided by Speck and Attneave (1973), the process of family network therapy has six phases that intervenors facilitate.

1. Retribalization is described as the feeling of caring and belonging in a group. It begins with the process of reacquaintance, is developed through a series of group exercises, and is reinforced by the excitement that follows successful resolution of a problem. During this time, intervenors explain the presenting situation to the assembled "tribe" and make clear that the network is there to work on the problem. Their own roles are clearly stated—to assist or to provide resources but not to be leaders. This step leads to the second phase.
2. Polarization is a typical phase wherein the group divides into opposing factions around the issues and the persons involved in the problem.
3. The mobilization phase is one of action, in which group members decide what must be done and who will do it. Most frequently the solutions found do not prove entirely successful, and there is a subsequent drop in morale.

4. The depression phase describes a temporary let-down from the more energetic stages that came before.
5. Breakthrough is a stage in which new and more realistic plans are made, and group members have an opportunity to verify the group's progress.
6. Exhaustion and elation occur as the group members experience success. That phase leads back to retribalization and a recycling of the process, which may continue long after the departure of the facilitators.

During this process, network members are learning new skills—communication with clarity and organizational problem solving. They are developing natural leaders and gaining a sense of their ability to help themselves (as well as the identified patient). Ultimately it is the sense of community and mutual supportiveness that sustains the network through crisis. This would be true whether the crisis is external, as in a home destroyed by fire, or internally imposed (by fear of people to speak openly).

One might argue that this entire process could be done without the therapist. In fact, that is the goal of therapists—to see the network function on its own. Intervenors in family network therapy try to present models of open exchange through their own behavior. In so doing, they create the freedom in the group that will allow change. They tighten, stimulate, and coalesce the sense of belonging. Via exercises and suggestions, they set up situations in which members can be creative. They strive to build trust in the entire network by being open, flexible, and caring, but not allowing themselves to become authorities. One lesson from family network therapy is that a healing bond or tribe still exists. It needs some help to get mobilized, but the results are worth the effort. Like family systems therapy, the task requires the help of highly skilled facilitators. Unlike family systems therapy, the definition of who is being helped is not assumed. Instead, a primary task of the method is to help bring into being a group capable of sharing an intense sense of common purpose.

Neighborhood Organization. Community organizing is frequently associated with activities designed to help the poor to protect their rights through organized protest, pressure, and confrontation. These concepts, frequently associated in the 1960s with the work of Saul Alinsky and with the Student Non-Violent Coordinating Committee in the Southern States, provide excellent examples of developing mutual support on behalf of a concern that would not otherwise be voiced. In the field of health, organizing has often supported the right of people to participate in their own health care as well as to obtain adequate medical services. Health care organizing has a long-standing tradition that cuts across national boundaries.

One study of community organization and self-help in twelve Japanese settings (including rural, semiurban, urban-industrial, and traditional city) concluded that community organizing was the core of all health activities in the community. It was related to the provision of health education by professionals for lay persons, by community leaders for lay persons, and by lay people for themselves. It also related to the development of "health awareness," as in nutrition, and to the greater task of participation in program planning for preventive activities (Myasaka and Kavata 1979).

The field of community organization has developed several models for intervention, some using outside professional persons who assist local groupings in a variety of tasks. This outsider attempts to involve groups in organized activity on their own behalf. The organizer wants to enhance the participation of individuals in decisions that affect their well-being.

One classic description of community organization presents three models: *locality development* (in which the group has not yet become aware of the extent to which the problems they each experience are part of á common community pattern), *social planning* (in which professionals, experts, and government agencies are aware of the problem and are the initiators), and *social action* (in which conflicting interests are known and the task is to mobilize the less advantaged sector for change) (Rothman 1970). Each type has somewhat different goals and makes somewhat different assumptions about the task to be addressed. These differences have implications for the various practitioner roles. Actual occurrences of community organization, however, often include several of the models, so although neighborhood (or locality) development is the primary focus here, the roles we are describing for the practitioner will have more diverse elements.

The first job of the outside practitioner is to obtain an invitation, since, as organizer, the practitioner must strive to leave responsibility for all major choices with the community. Where there is no organized group to do the asking, the practitioner's first task is to engage people in conversation in order to hear what needs or problems are salient for people in the neighborhood. Frequently, unbeknown to one another, neighbors have common concerns. The organizer's next task is to bring people together where they can discover that the problem is not theirs alone and that their efforts toward a solution can be strengthened by working together.

The organizer serves as a catalyst or coordinator, acknowledging the concerns, affirming the value of individuals getting together to work on them, and encouraging natural leadership. The organizer helps the group discover its area of concensus and the array of activities that will provide a course of action. The organizer's communication skill is used to enhance participation and involvement. The practitioner must also be sensitive to community resources and to the obstacles involved in any particular problem. The group may enlist the organizer's guidance on a long list of tasks.

How can we reach more people with similar concerns? How are we to locate and to approach relevant decision makers? Where will we discover potential allies for a broader coalition? How does one organize a lobbying visit? How do you make committee decisions known to the larger group? And, perhaps most common, how do we raise money?

In developing tactics to advance the group's goals, the organizer can serve as a fact finder. When does the council meet? Who owns the land? How does the crime rate differ from other areas? What have other groups with similar problems done? What do we do next? In this role, the organizer must be careful not to use factual information to dictate the group's direction. This precaution is necessary for two reasons. First, it avoids making the group dependent on the organizer, and, second, it assumes that the group knows its own culture and its own needs better than an outside practitioner.

The organizer can assist the local group in negotiating or in confronting tactics to secure immediate objectives, but the ultimate goal is to make people feel more powerful and able to come together to make their needs heard. Sometimes this will involve leaving the community with an ongoing, neighborhood self-help organization to serve as a continuing channel for participation (Howell 1975; Kotler 1969).

Neighborhood organizing efforts are commonplace. Two illustrations hold particular relevance to the promotion of both health and interpersonal support. In San Francisco's Tenderloin district, a preventive health program was established for isolated, older occupants of single-room occupancy hotels. The setting was in a high crime area with extreme social isolation for older people and with the consequent problems of alcoholism and failure to obtain necessary health checkups. The project was set up in the hotel lobby. It began with health screening and blood pressure checks, but its latent agenda was to help residents meet each other and discuss common problems, to socialize, to assist each other, and to develop a sense of group solidarity. The project served a switchboard function, gradually bringing together formerly isolated individuals to assist each other in shopping or to find a card partner. Gradually, they began to organize meetings to address collectively the hotel landlord about issues of rent and living conditions (Minkler 1981). Eventually, the local groups expanded to include eight hotels. Their projects resulted in "safe houses" and better police protection in high crime areas. They led to meetings with the mayor and the press to address problems, and produced a continuing organization that dispelled the previous isolation from personal contact.

A second example, in a small rural community, was begun with a preventive mental health focus. Here, the practitioners' goal was to enhance community empowerment and the community's capacity for natural helping. The organizer made use of a powerful umbrella group, a list of natural helpers in the community, and, of most importance, a special type of community forum. Each forum drew forth constituencies from the community concerned with a particular issue. The forum used a modification of the nominal decision-making technique,[1] designed to assist the group in specifying needs, priorities, and action plans. Among the outcomes were a Chicano community celebration, the use of volunteer counselors, a youth program, and the creation of a friendly visitor program for mentally disturbed residents of board and care homes. The community established a system for barter exchange, making every individual who came to the office for help the potential helper for someone else needing a different type of assistance (Pilisuk et al. 1982).

In both instances, in San Francisco and in the rural community, the projects' contributions to health came via fostering networks of supportive ties. Neighborhood organizing shows us that it is still possible to build mutual help on a community basis. This type of organization extends the scope of supportive interventions that were targeted to families. It adds a dimension to the task of enhancing supportive ties. The distinctive activity is sometimes called "networking"—linking the people in a community and providing a setting in which they can deal with problems.

Community Network Therapy. The family therapies we have mentioned assume that the natural network has the goods to deliver if only it can be freed of its destructive linkages or if a larger, "natural" network could get involved. That assumption is not always true. Community network therapy tries to enlarge the natural mix by using a couple of trained advocates and, through them, by putting certain community services into the picture.

Community network therapy is an approach that combines working directly with troubled children using family systems therapy, school consultation, patient advocacy, nurturance of supportive networks, and education on broader problems of the culture and society. The method, as described by Gatti and Coleman (1976), frequently begins with a referral from a public school for assistance with a child's behavior problem. A team of two mental health professionals meet regularly with the school's adjustment counselors, nurses, principal, and assistant superintendent in charge of students with special needs. Where family evaluation or therapy appears war-

---

[1] The technique was originated by Delbeque, Van de Ven, and Gustafson (1975). It requires active participation from everyone present and assures that the group will assign responsibilities for the various suggestions.

ranted, school counselors will suggest that the family consider either the consultant team or another family therapist.

Four basic principles guide the work of the consultants with the family. The first is to address the family in an open, concrete, problem-solving style. This aim requires one preliminary meeting with the parents to help strengthen the parents' authority. They are encouraged to question whether they wish to work with this particular team. The consultants also obtain written permission to communicate with school personnel. The second meeting takes place in the home with the entire family. Subsequent meetings may be with one or all family members, in restaurants, schools, or parks, or as a part of family outings. The purpose is to meet the important people in the lives of family members. Such meetings are followed by more conventional home or office discussions.

Second, the team establishes a continuing contact with as many of the important extrafamilial people and institutions affecting the child as are accessible. The team becomes a part of the child's network. The network includes extended families, neighbors, and friends. Representatives from school, welfare, employment, housing, courts, and charitable or church groups are also brought ito the network. Even the child's companions and other professionals such as doctors and ministers are included when necessary.

Third, the team assumes that people in the child's world can come to see the child's behavior as human and comprehensible, even though problematic. To nourish this understanding, they avoid psychological jargon, are very concrete, and provide formulations worded in everyday language. Labeling is avoided, and the focus is on the system rather than on the individual. These emphases, plus the availability of the team for feedback, reduce problems inherent in sharing information through larger, interlocking systems. Focusing on the system reduces blame and frequently points to resolution of problems without the need to reveal specific, embarrassing details.

Finally, the consultants present a cultural perspective. This perspective can reduce personal guilt or shame and promote an active sense of choice. Hence, problems of social isolation, sexual standards, sex role styles, changing authority structures, and political and economic issues such as unemployment, inflation, and health care are addressed. By keeping a broad perspective, the team takes the blame for larger societal stressors away from the individual. They teach about the use of available resources and act as advocates to intercede on the family's behalf. Social isolation, as we saw in chapter 3, is a common family problem. Here, the team borrows from the family network approach to help the family to invoke the assistance of their existing network or, if they are truly isolated, form a new one.

Members of the team do not look upon themselves as managerial or parental authorities. Rather, they are expert consultants whose special talent lies in their ability to describe and sort out family relationships, to coordinate the use of the various service facilities in the community, and to adjust their own views and roles according to the community network's influence. In contrast to the support therapists previously discussed, the community network therapist is in the distinct position of being an advocate, helping clients find a path to existant, but not easily obtainable, resources. In sum, this method shows that professional advocates can help natural community networks work better.

System Consultation. Individuals and families feel the pain of social duress, but the workplace is often closer to the source. For many who labor, work has no intrinsic rewards. From piecework workers to professionals in bureaucratic settings, work stress is a common theme. It evolves from structures wherein the rules do not provide options for action or are too limited. This stress reflects the setting, whether it be the factory or the brokerage house.

Program-centered consultation is a systems intervention. "Systems" is one of those horribly overused words. Here, system merely means a point of view that focuses upon the interrelations of all human as well as nonhuman parts of an organization and upon how the whole organization is doing. The consultation is initiated by one or a group of consultees to obtain help with problems in programs, policies, training, administering, or in any aspect of a human service. A rather common problem, for example, is staff burnout. Disenchantment, fatigue, and defeatism often overtake concerned professionals in the human services when facing excessive regulation, shrinking budgets, and truly heartrending needs for services (Brager and Holloway 1978). In such settings, supportive assistance can provide an effective antidote to burnout (Maslach and Jackson 1984; Pines 1983).

Ideally, the consultant will first collect extensive information about the organization and the problems it faces. A useful assessment must be thorough and it must reflect the various biases and concerns. Large organizations inevitably develop factions with different skills and different attitudes. Often, the differences are unspoken (Argyris 1964). To avoid alienating members of a system, consultants must show respect for designated authority, and for other administrative staff, as well as for board members and workers at all levels who may be affected by the consultation. Unbiased listening and concern are the means used to create a positive atmosphere and model a process in which openness can exist and willingness to change is possible.

The organizational development (O.D.) specialists have developed a number of techniques or exercises designed to get more honest participation and to speed up the process of working together. After an assessment of needs, goals, and objectives is completed, the consultant may propose a plan of action to fit the needs, taking agency limitations, attitudes, and goals into consideration. By presenting a tentative plan to the consultees for feedback, the consultant increases the likelihood that the final plan of action will belong to and work for the organization. Another means of ensuring commitment to the course of action is for consultants to stimulate agency members to create their own plan of action.

The intervenor focuses upon developing the skills and abilities of consultees and on helping them learn how to cope with problem situations. Organizational development began with this kind of consultative focus, attempting to "sensitize" organization members to each other—to create the openness and honesty felt necessary for an organization to function both humanely and effectively (Bennis 1966; Bennis, Benne, and Chin 1969). Although the value of "sensitivity training" in changing organizational structure (Golembiewski and Blumberg 1979; Zandler 1982) has been questioned, the method continues to be an important part of organizational development.

Consultation may be directly with one individual, but is also a method well applied in group situations. As an ongoing process, consultation can help different members of an organization deal with specific problems when they arise. Particularly in a long-term arrangement, the consultant must be careful to maintain attention to work-related problems or interactions rather than to intrapsychic phenomena unrelated to optimal or satisfactory functioning within the system. By drawing from knowledge of systems theory, organizational behavior, and interpersonal dynamics, the consultant can impart information and assist with problem solving. The consultant's role also includes modeling appropriate communication skills and facilitating group discussions (Epstein and Warren 1974). The often unsung yet vital activity is to give support.

Flexibility and sensitivity are among the professional skills viewed as essential to any consultant role. The basic process for addressing a problem involves an assessment of needs and establishing a workable contract. This process will involve planning a course of action, implementing it, and evaluating the outcome (Spencer and Croley 1977). The emphasis in consultation today is more on the system than on individuals. There is a recognized need to reach more people and to foster growth on a broader scale (Signell and Scott 1971). The task has expanded into providing community education, developing self-help projects, and organizing communities. The mental health consultant can now offer training in skills and new behaviors (e.g., assertiveness), as well as in the interpretation of the change process itself. The potent consultant is both a model and a facilitator of growth and change. He or she tries to work in egalitarian relationships, leaving the consultee able to stand alone. The more enhanced are the consultees' abilities to plan, solve problems and grow independently of outside help, the more effective is the consultant as an agent of change. Systems consultation provides one way of bringing supportive concern for people back into the big organization.

Building supportive and caring relationships within the walls of a huge organization shares some of the communication network building characteristics used with families and with communities. Much of contemporary life is dominated by our associations with large institutions in the world of work, education and health care, welfare, the legal system, and shopping for goods and services. The consequences of these bureaucracies include a segmentation of experience into very specific categories and the restriction of communication according to an equally strict definition of positions and regulations. That is why certain consultants have focused their efforts upon alternative or collective work settings, where the group is already committed to a more supportive environment (Reinharz 1983). Systems consultation is not a panacea or a quick cure for the evils of impersonal, uncaring, and often degrading circumstances in the bureaucracy. In fact, the methods have been used in some corporate settings to make people feel more cared for by the company without actually dealing with their genuine needs for flexible time schedules, better pay, or better health care. Still, the methods do speak to the most pervasive problems and do show that a measure of caring and human concern can be brought into formal organizations, just as it can be promoted for families or for informal community groups.

Consultation for Natural Helping Networks. A lot of helping in a community is never planned. It just grows through the efforts of people who are "natural helpers." They take care of old people or young people, offer advice, encouragement, transportation, food, or health care. One form of professional helping is directed toward assisting these helpers. Alice Collins and Diane Pancoast (1976) describe a type of consultation designed to strengthen the ability of neighbors to be helpful to those in their social network. This type of consultation is consultee centered, the major focus is on enhancing the consultee's abilities to cope with current "clients" and future "clients" with similar problems. The clients in these cases are friends, neighbors, or acquaintances of the natural helper. Natural helping neighbors may be providing child care, assisting lonely people in single-room dwellings, or providing health services, as in the case of *curanderos* in a Mexican-American community. Here consultation differs from the traditional consultee-centered form of consultation, because the role of natural helper does not necessarily correspond to that of a professional or a paraprofessional worker and the consultee is not performing a paid job under an administrative structure.

In such instances, the first and sometimes difficult task is to identify the natural helping neighbors. A primary aim is to become very familiar with the setting. This familiarity permits a preliminary selection of candidates who are positive forces in their neighborhoods. The choice is made of one or two individuals who are natural helpers and who meet the "freedom from drain" criterion, that is, they are sufficiently healthy, able, and self-confident to allow consultation to focus upon their helping roles rather than merely on their own personal needs. The consultant tries to set up a collaborative arrangement. Help goes in both directions. The consultation is a form of mutual problem solving, in which the client's knowledge of the community is a crucial factor. The consultant listens, learns, and establishes a partnership during meetings set up at the discretion of the consultee. Although a goal may be to provide more natural services, the consultant avoids pressing this objective on the client. After all, the natural helper is the one who has begun the operation and is also the one who must continue to run the show.

All forms of professional collaboration with folk healers makes some use of consultation with natural helpers. In fact, when the real value of natural helpers is recognized, they are sometimes brought in to help the professionals. Two spiritual healers, a *curandero* and a minister familiar with voodoo, have even been brought into a psychiatric facility of a major university hospital to help the professionals with particular cases (Goode et al. 1982). Consultation with natural helpers is a way in which professionals can make the most of natural helping.

Bringing consultation to natural helpers probably introduces no special techniques of intervention beyond those already discussed. The method does, however, require a great deal of diagnostic acuity in finding out just who is providing supportive care. Most child care still occurs in informal, unlicensed facilities, as does most care for the elderly. Bartenders and hairdressers, funeral home representatives, and, of course, clergy, represent a literal army of confidants and counselors providing social support to those in need. Providing consultation to such natural helpers is a method of recognizing, respecting, and, where possible, assisting the promoters of caring in the community.

Patient Education. When describing the effects of social support upon health, we observed that support played a major role in helping people stay with a difficult program of medical care. The medical establishment has long known that a physician's advice to engage in certain exercise, to avoid certain foods, or to take certain medications is no assurance that the advice will be followed. Successful treatment, as described in chapter 2, is often dependent upon social support and that principle has been behind the use of supportive groups in patient education.

The nurturance of social support systems through patient education can take many forms. All these forms, however, are focused on helping the patient (and/or those close to the patient) cope with problems arising either from a condition requiring medical care or from consequences of medical treatment. The three types of patient education that address the supportive task include patient and family orientation meetings, patient education groups, and patient self-help groups.

In *family orientation meetings,* information about the patient's illness is given, natural systems of social support are activated, and lines of communication for patients and their families are opened. The professional assists communication by acknowledging the anxieties of family members, by sharing observations about the patient's condition and options for treatment, and by providing easy opportunities for questions to be raised and discussed. Optimally, the professional can provide authoritative medical information while respecting the information families may have received from other sources.

Concern for the needs of patients and family members is demonstrated by adjusting the amount and timing of information to family readiness and by selecting a place for discussion that assures privacy. There is also a need to provide time for family members to digest what has been said and, then, for the professional to respond empathetically. Specific ways in which family members may help the patient are identified, and members are encouraged to assume these roles. Family involvement may be of critical value in stimulating compliance to a medical regimen, and one approach has included the use of home visits by the professional to meet with family and friends of the patient (Toledo, Hughes, and Sims 1979). Compliance is a grave problem, considering that most studies of traditional methods of offering information to the patient show that one-third of the patients fail to comply with instructions, and one review of compliance studies shows rates of 50 percent or greater noncompliance (Davis 1968). The support of family and peers can make the difference.

A related type of educational group prepares patients and their families to assume an active role in health care delivery (Silver, 1974). A classic example is of training couples to participate in the Lamaze method of childbirth. However, patients and their families have also been taught to control bleeding in hemophiliacs, conduct kidney dialysis at home, and carry out a variety of tasks related to management of hypertension, diabetes, and other chronic diseases. Because specific skills in medical care are taught, emphasis is on the physical aspects of the condition. At the same time, participation of the family in the treatment process represents a tangible form of social support often recognized as having its own therapeutic value. Less widely appreciated is the impact of such involvement on the family member, who, rather than being isolated from a loved one in need of help, is assigned a supportive role within the health care setting.

Family orientation meetings are set up either in organized classes or in the patient's home to teach specific techniques integral to the patient's care or treatment. Depending upon the complexity of tasks to be learned, teaching may be limited to an hour or two or it may extend over the course of several weeks. Sensitivity to the feelings of others and ability to foster supportive, psychological relationships are critical skills for helping patients and family members learn how to cooperate in meeting the patient's physical needs, especially when these needs involve changes in former patterns of privacy, authority, and independence.

The professional often has a trying task here. What is the right way to provide information about an incurable, degenerative brain disease or about a child with leukemia? How does one speak to people about a medical procedure that will bring major disfiguration or restriction of activity, or about a needed treatment the family just cannot afford? And how does one communicate when the client is from a refugee family, never before in a hospital, and speaking only the Mong language? The work of helping here is, clearly, not a matter of doing only what comes naturally.

Patient education groups provide another form of education having strong implications for the development of social support. Such groups provide peer support through interaction among patients with a similar problem or with family members of patients with a similar condition. The groups are based on the assumption that people facing similar medical problems can provide a unique form of help for each other by sharing their feelings, difficulties in coping, mutual encouragement, and practical suggestions for adjustment (Schwartz 1977; Veninga and Fredlund 1974). Learning more about the condition and the skills related to its care are also common objectives. The emphasis upon information and/or skills varies according to the purposes for which the group is formed. A typical format might involve a presentation, film, or demonstration, followed by an open discussion session.

Some patient education groups are organized by health professionals, often working as an interdisciplinary team, to help participants comply with a therapeutic regimen or to make a health-promoting change. One notably successful effort trained a group of mostly elderly lay persons as leaders of group sessions for arthritis patients. These nonprofessional elders were able to bring about strong personal involvements, increased participation in exercise, and decreases in pain (Long et al. 1980). Family members can also be involved, as in a program where patients with congestive heart failure were invited to group meetings with the suggestion that each bring a relative (Rosenberg 1971). Entry to such groups is traditionally by physician referral. In recent years, however, religious organizations, community service agencies, and commercial enterprises as well as health care providers have sponsored weight loss, exercise, and smoking cessation groups that anyone could join.

A contrasting pattern of leadership occurs in *self-help health groups.* These groups of patients or family members have as their primary purpose the provision of mutual aid for adapting to problems created by chronic illness, addictive disease, and other physical or mental impairments. Since this concept was first popularized with the formation of Alcoholics Anonymous in 1935, self-help health groups have been organized by patients, former patients, and family members around a host of conditions, most of which medicine has been unable to cure or which are socially stigmatizing. The number of persons involved is large and growing still larger. In part, this growth has occurred because surgical advances in the 1950s, made possible by the development of antibiotics, have enabled us to keep more people with serious problems alive and functioning. Many groups have formed to help patients cope with the socially disabling aftereffects from procedures such as mastectomy, colostomy, and laryngectomy. Since the 1950s, the number of mutual aid health groups has accelerated, according to two social scientists, "to the point where their national ubiquity constitutes an emerging and viable social movement" (Tracy and Gussow 1976:381).

The vast majority of these self-help or mutual aid groups are consumer initiated (Back and Taylor 1976; Levy 1976). They arise typically out of deep frustration from the failure of existing institutions to provide assistance with the overwhelming needs felt by patients or family members. In some cases, these problems relate to a life-threatening crisis. More often, they concern physical and social obstacles that inhibit human interaction and full acceptance by others. The goal of these groups, although often unstated, is to develop or restore the integrity and independence of the whole person.

Accordingly, an essential characteristic of these groups is that they deal with the needs identified by group members. These needs tend to focus upon personal and social problems related to a condition rather than upon the medical aspects per se (Katz and Bender 1976b; Schwartz 1977). Initially, discussion seems to center around the sharing of feelings and concerns participants previously thought were theirs alone. The discovery that others have experienced similar problems helps assure members that their anxieties are normal—a source of relief that helps develop individual morale and a sense of identification among group members. This sharing then leads to an exchange of ideas about effective ways to handle problems. It leads also to peer encouragement and to development of active coping skills.

As part of this process, members may retrieve information about their condition that was unavailable to them during their medical care or that was not heard or understood at the time it was offered. Such information is important in helping group members to accept their situation realistically and evaluate their options. There is another function of this information sharing, however. Medical advice is not always the best advice. The groups assist members in assessing the adequacy and appropriateness of the care they have received. From these insights, members gradually begin to resolve their own problems and to turn their energies outward. The group may then reach out to help others with similar afflictions, and it may also attempt to make health professionals and institutions more responsive to their needs. They may thus develop educational programs and informational materials both for patients and professionals. They might visit new victims of the disease and invite them to join the group, engage in fund raising for research or services, or become active in legislation and lobbying. Some groups also organize alternatives to traditional health services that they regard as ineffective or too expensive. In self-help health groups, professionals are not always welcome. For the most part, however, assistance is sought wherever it is in keeping with the objectives of the group. An outside intervenor, whether a professional or former patient, may be asked to lead meetings, assist in developing an organization, or participate in fund raising or advocacy activities.

The need for consumer-initiated, self-help groups is nowhere more clearly articulated than in Freudenberg's (1981–1982) account of the potentials and limitations of a self-help program for asthmatic children and their parents within a medical institution. The study found, on the one hand, that health groups were greatly effective when discussing prime social causes of problems, in linking people to community services, and in getting better services from the medical institution. Yet the location of the program, within a medical institution, imposed certain important constraints. For example, the meeting time and place (and hence accessibility to the groups) were rigidly planned around the institution's medical care schedule. Mutual help groups strive to circumvent such limitations. Patient education reminds us again of the relevance of social support to health.

Like consultation for natural helpers, patient education includes a set of tasks connecting the formal helping system to the natural providers. The mutual help revolution has extended far beyond health-centered activities and into the variety of voluntary natural helping systems discussed in chapter 4. As with each of the previously mentioned forms of intervention, the focus is upon the existing abilities of the participants to help themselves. Also like each of the other forms, this one requires certain resources, a place to meet, a person with time to contact the others, and some money for operating expenses—more so if professional time is needed.

DEFINING THE ROLE OF SOCIAL SUPPORT FACILITATOR

We noted before that encouraging social support involves more than conducting a set of professional activities. The professional activities described so far demonstrate a lot of effort. What do they tell us about how social support can be nurtured? The various change agent roles concerned with assistance to social support are compared in Table 2. The particular attempt in this chapter is to compare forms of assistance that have been self-consciously formulated by external change agents. We have, therefore, selected no instances in which a natural helper such as a friendly aunt, neighbor, or religious helper provides assistance, although such occurrences certainly do take place. In reviewing the array, several common attributes of these forms of helping are visible. Together, the commonalities help define the collective, professional heritage appropriate for assisting groups of people in their efforts to provide more supportive, caring, effective, and satisfying interpersonal environments. We will call this Social Support Facilitation.

1. Social support facilitators are all trained and experienced. Although training may or may not be professional, it always involves either experiential or didactic preparation in understanding individuals and groups.
2. Social support facilitators are not a permanent part of the unit being assisted. In all cases, the facilitator is engaged, as are all professionals, in the work of helping strangers. The work is to assist the group to meet needs not necessarily those of the social support facilitator. One variation from this general rule occurs in patient education groups where the initiator/facilitator occasionally has the same condition as the persons in the group and organizes the group for his or her own benefit as well as for the benefit of other patients.
3. The group defines the need for service. Despite the particular referral route, a need for assistance is not assumed until the group has set forth such a need. This request for assistance might originate with one individual or with a faction of the client system. In some instances, the social

support facilitator helps the group crystallize the problem to the point where assistance can be sought.

4. The limits of the relationship are made clear. In all cases, the social support facilitator clarifies the nature of the contract, what and how much he or she is willing to do, and what is expected of the client.

5. The social support facilitator is a listener. Attentive, nonjudgmental listening to client(s) includes a reassurance that the client's views have been heard. The social support facilitator(s) always checks the understanding between himself/herself and the client(s).

6. The social support facilitator's interventive behavior models the type of social interaction being encouraged. In most instances, the social support facilitator engages in supportive behavior, shows respect for continuity of relationships despite differences, invites increasing participation, and follows through on an obligation undertaken.

7. The interventive behavior of social support facilitators is directed toward enhancing the group's own values as well as their members' competencies to provide real caring for each other.

8. The social support facilitator works with a growth model or a systems model, but not with a pathology model. In all examples, the social support facilitator assumes that the participants of the unit have competencies to contribute to the social unit. The social support facilitator helps look for problems in the system rather than in the individual, and searches for more effective patterns of behavior that will permit richer and more rewarding experiences for the individuals.

9. The social support facilitator in all instances appears to make use of his or her own skills and of the talents of the group members in group problem solving and interpersonal communication. Skills of the participants are critical in achieving autonomous, healthful functioning, apart from long-term dependence on the facilitator.

10. In all but perhaps the supportive consultation to natural helpers, the social support facilitator expects to change people's behavior. This fact has implications for both the technical and the ethical training of the change agent.

Beyond the above similarities, certain factors in each of the seven intervention models are clearly distinguishable. Although all the social support facilitators examined are external to the unit and all require skills and experience, professional requirements may vary greatly. Some facilitators are clearly and necessarily professional; others can be paraprofessionals or lay persons.

So far, we have been looking only at the means professionals have used in developing supportive ties. Of course, the professional is not typically working with a set of disconnected individuals, but with an existing web of network ties. We have already seen in chapter 3 how the family forms the first line of resources for many people. With an additional inner circle of close friends, family members are typically the most intimate, the most available resources for the broadest range of assistance. There are other voluntary ties of the network, many of which were discussed in chapter 4. These connections include helping neighbors and other "natural helpers" within a community. For some of these natural helpers, their assistance is superimposed upon a particular role (of minister, bartender, or letter carrier), while others will meet with those in need because they have a common problem. Volunteers also constitute a source of help that was, at one point, arranged by an agency. There are, indeed, some overlapping bits of wisdom. In this review of social support methods, we intend to ask just what good is likely to come of this divergency. First, it will be useful to discover who the professionals are trying to help.

THE TARGET FOR HELP

There are a variety of perspectives one can take in assessing this set of natural helping linkages. One strategy focuses upon the individual client's support system. This method has been called *personal network intervention*.[2] Family therapy in general and family network therapy are examples of this effort to encourage the informal supports of the family, friends, and neighbors of an individual.

There are four other areas of focus. Where existing ties are limited, efforts may go into making *volunteer linkages*. This process involves matching lay helpers to the client who has a special need for companionship, for support, or for advocacy. Some of the more successful programs to assist former mental patients' transition to life in the community use this form of network building.

Building *mutual aid networks* involves intervention to link people who share a common problem or interest. The professional focus here has been to help such people find one another in order to share experiences and to reduce the isolation or the stigma associated with a particular condition. In one of our own studies of a group to assist abusive parents, we found that isolation was a major characteristic of the people in the group. However helpful the members could be to each other, some outside help was needed just for the people to become acquainted with one another. Afterwards, the leader could help members help one another confront the stigma associated with rage against one's own children, identify the causes of this anger,

---

[2] The terms are selected from a study in Oregon (Froland, Pancoast et al. 1979).

and eventually find alternative ways for handling it. This group was essentially a self-help assemblage, but some outside force had to get the ball rolling or it never would have begun (Pilisuk and Parks 1980).

Consultation for natural helpers is a prime example of the *natural helper strategy*. This strategy involves identifying these special people, helping people in need find these natural helpers, and helping the helpers in their existing patterns. Sometimes, natural helpers need advice on how to deal with a particularly difficult person. More often, what is needed is help on getting a waiver on a regulation that, in its effort to guard people against quacks or neighborhoods against crowding, somehow restricts a highly successful, natural helping operation.

The final focus, upon *community empowerment*, is not so concerned with the individual, but with a set of people who are discovering their potential to do for themselves, and for each other, what cannot be achieved from the beneficence of others. Community organizing efforts are typically vocal about the objective of empowerment. Power is so badly distributed, it is argued, that the barest resources needed for a minimal sense of dignity must be demanded by collective action. Yet, this chapter addresses only one aspect of the problem of what to do to promote a more caring social order. Even power redistributed to those previously without it offers no guarantee that human connections will be enhanced. To address the broader issue, it is helpful to step back and review our understanding of the resources available to people and what has been done with these resources so far. Only by stepping back from the immediacy of particular problems and the review of specific intervention techniques can we clearly see those requirements of a caring human community that we have failed to address so far.

THE MYTH OF PROGRESS

A sweeping indictment of where organized human efforts have led us so far is given in Theodore Roszak's *Where the Wasteland Ends*.

The Last Days were announced to St. John by a voice like the sound of many waters. But the voice that comes in our day summoning us to play out the dark myth of the reckoning is our meager own, making casual conversation about the varieties of annihilation . . . the thermonuclear Armageddon, the death of the seas, the vanishing atmosphere, the massacre of the innocents, the universal famine to come. . . .

Such horrors should be the stuff of nightmare or the merely metaphorical rancors of old prophecy. They aren't. They are the news of the day, by now even growing stale (for some) with reiteration. They descend upon us, not as the will of capricious gods, but as the fruit of a politics held to be preeminently practical, of down-to-earth policy and tough-minded, dollars-and-cents realism. Governing elites, empowered by the consent of multimillionfold majorities, have piloted us deliberately along our way. We have not stumbled into the arms of Gog and Magog; we have *progressed* there. The peculiar genious of our culture—"*our culture*" meaning the culture of white, western masculinity and its many admiring or envious imitators—only now reaches its full height. Never before so much power, knowledge, daring, opulence, dynamism. Never so many great adventures in the making. And that is the worst of it—that even the genocidal end we prepare for our species shines with a Promethean grandeur (1972:2).

Western ideology educates us to linear and hierarchial thinking about space and time. We get our fix upon just where the problem is and start prescribing ways to handle it. As long as our approach to building social support is restricted to describing techniques, the method has not differed basically from our approach to repairing a malfunction in the plumbing of a house or the design of a company. The ultimate in program design is to find a specific set of rules to deal with a specific task. The process leads to a fragmentation of human services, each offered by a highly trained specialist. The organizational structures needed to offer these services often become inefficient, self-serving bureaucracies. With time, the most innovative solutions to the problems get washed away by a withdrawal of funding or a burnout of leadership.

The various professional models of enhancing social support have been presented here. They are imaginative, certainly useful, and unfortunately limited. Some analysts of modern life believe that Western thought lacks the richness for addressing broader problems. In Western thought, we assume that when we have defined a specific problem, we therefore know what the problem is. All that remains to be found, then, is a specific solution. Yet, problems have a way of being linked. Every ecologist knows how often we destroy while we are building, and, throughout this book, we have examined how we have lost much of our social glue in the winds of our personal development. The magic in the community network approach does not lie in its specific techniques but, rather, in its willingness to step outside of typical, single-problem procedures and meet the family on its own turf, bending its efforts with the ebb and flow of available community resources. This general approach is termed *ecological*, and some of its major advantages have been discussed by psychologists dissatisfied with the restrictions of their discipline (Bronfenbrenner 1977; Sarason 1976).

THE TRANSACTIONAL FIELD
AND THE CONCEPT OF BALANCE

If there was magic in the family network approach, it too came from the involvement and flexibility of its techniques. The approach truly values the interrelatedness of people—the network—the web. It views human problems almost as rips in the tapestry of social life and its purpose is to reweave the torn fabric. Although the practice is full of concrete problem solving, its stength lies mainly in the less tangible art of strengthening the cloth. Its stress upon interpersonal ties still lacks the concentration on finding a balance within the larger ecology, but surely both the family network and community network approaches speak to an image of people as parts and participants of something greater.

The *transactional* view, perhaps encompassing both these concepts, has been proposed by the family therapist John Spiegal. The thrust of this concept is that relationships always move in more than one direction. The "transactions" avoid blame and blaming labels (a rather useful idea in family therapy) and describe who and what comes and goes in the "ecological niche" of each person. No little hideaway, this unique niche is elaborated into a transactional field—containing just about every conceivable influence in our lives and extending from the cosmos to the nucleus of the atom.

> The Universe is concerned with the nonliving world in general, all the way from the cosmos to the atomic nucleus. It includes the house or dwelling in which a family lives; the land on which that house is built; the surrounding terrain, urban or rural; the quality of the air a family breathes; and the food resources it consumes. Processes included in Universe are in transaction with processes in Soma, the anatomical structures and physiological processes within the human organism. The next focus, Psyche, takes in cognition, perception, problem-solving, conflict elaboration and reduction, emotional arousal, habit formation, and communication. Personality results from the integration of processes within Psyche, and from its transactions, on the one side, with Soma and, on the other, with the focus called Group. It is in groups such as the family, that behavior receives situational definitions and role attributions. However, groups do not exist in isolation from each other. They receive their forms and functions in accordance with their place in the larger network of social systems that we label Society. Finally, the family as a social institution, along with the other religious, educational, economic, legal, governmental, recreational, and voluntary institutions that make up Society, is anchored in a set of beliefs and values about the nature of the world and human existence known as Culture. Culture in turn contributes to the survival of a society in its ecological niche, as well as forming the basis of a people's beliefs about the nature of the Universe, thereby completing the circling of the transactional field (Spiegel 1982:35).

Broad concepts such as a "transactional field" are not always welcomed by the practitioner who has a job to get done. We are never able to tell whether they are profound or vacuous, a key to a new understanding or scholastic jargon. We think there is a worthwhile kernel in this idea, but the concept is at once delicate, imprecise, and somewhat alien to our Western ways of thought; yet, successful intervention on behalf of more caring relationships and more caring communities might require just such a perspective.

The transactional field perspective keeps us tuned into our connectedness. Is this awareness important? That question is one of values. Although there is an orientation that values these interconnections, it is culturally remote. In Western society we see two possible relationships to the surrounding world—mastery of the world to make it serve our ends, at one pole, and a fatalistic subservience to a harsh order, at the other. The concept of balance between control and acceptance, of harmony between one's own efforts and the natural order, barely seems to have meaning. Yet, without such a balance, it is difficult to intervene with flexibility and with continued dedication. One of the most effective groups ever in their efforts to build a more peaceful, humane, and caring social order has been the Society of Friends. With amazing effectiveness for their numbers, the Friends have brought a high level of energy to bear upon almost every form of human suffering or degradation. In addition, they have continued this effort without regard to the popularity of the cause. What sustains the effort?

At Friends' meetings, there is no sermon, but people sit in quiet meditation, interspersed occasionally by one or another participant's expression of thoughts and feelings. Meditation slows the frenzied rush to find solutions among spinning wheels. Afterward, each person joins hands with someone nearby and exchanges a warm greeting. It is a Quaker belief that God is within each of us. There is also a tradition in which statements of conscience and acts of helping contribute to personal fulfillment. Deep also within the Quaker ethic are assumptions that have been well voiced by people not of the Quaker faith. Eleanor Roosevelt once noted that "it is better to light a single candle than to sit and curse the dark." Gandhi taught that "the end never justifies the means." Native American teachings have taught us to love the Mother Earth the giver of life. From Judaic teachings comes a lesson that certain moral codes are a given part of humanity. From the teachings of Christianity we have been admonished to love our neighbors, and from the East we have learned that for every force there is a counterforce leading us to an eternal balance. The Society of Friends has found a way to be guided by such basic teachings. In what seem to be simple ways, they have found a piece to the professionals' puzzle—the part that recognizes the "transactional field" and reviews the commitment of each individual through affirmation of basic beliefs and through interconnectedness with others.

The Society of Friends has not found the only way to nurture the caring so needed in society. They have, however, found one way to retain a broad view of social problems and to retain their dedication during times of budget cuts, reorganization, repression, and apathy. Surely then, their approach is a lesson on balancing one's own efforts with the flow of world forces, and it can teach professionals about what is needed to nurture social support over a sustained period of time. This spiritual and ethical dimension adds to the professional methods of intervention. The nurturing of social support is a matter deserving the finest professional methods for helping people. It is a result, also, of the values embedded in a humanitarian heritage of love and commitment to the human family.

7
CARING AND HEALING FROM A CROSS-CULTURAL PERSPECTIVE

Throughout our writing so far, we have been asking what is happening to caring relationships in the contemporary United States and in industrial Euro-American society. The struggles and changes we have been noticing in families, in friendships, and in communities have consequences for our health and for our survival. The stakes are large enough to warrant a look at how the particular Western brand of relating interpersonally contrasts with that of other cultures, which view health, well-being, and survival in ways more closely related to their established patterns of supportive interpersonal ties.

Of course, contemporary Western society includes a tremendous amount of internal cultural and ethnic diversity. With the exception of Native Americans, we have chosen not to focus upon these divergent subcultures. This decision was made because many of them reflect strong accommodations to the Western mainstream, for cultural traditions result from the gradual evolution of the human modalities for dealing with a particular environmental reality. They also reflect accommodations to a minority status made necessary by restrictions set by a more powerful majority. Our understanding of the social networks found among minority cultures is enhanced by taking a cultural perspective. For example, consider the effects of early immigration statutes restricting Asians from the United States, but only after a substantial number of Asian men had already been permitted, in fact, recruited to settle here. The resulting sex imbalance had both immediate and enduring effects. Some Japanese men were able to select brides through pictures, then imported their picture brides into the United States. This pattern certainly enhanced a cultural tradition regarding women's domestic subservience. The absence of women in traditional caretaking roles was also met, in Chinese-American communities, with the development of powerful community organizations for many caretaking functions. These internal networks in Chinese-American communities have tended to persist (Lyman 1970).

A somewhat different cultural imposition affected the networks of Black Americans. Mainstream efforts to depict the ideal family with a woman fully occupied as homemaker kept many white women out of the work force. The lowest rungs of nonorganized labor, either as domestics or as service workers, were available to Black women, often when Black men could find no work at all (Ovington 1969). Hence, the ethnic pattern of three-generational, female-dominated families, including real and fictive kin, that Carol Stack (1974) found in contemporary low-income Black communities has a historical root lying somewhat outside any inherent cultural tradition. In extreme cases, the oppression or suppression of a cultural group and the omnipresence of poverty push toward eradication of many traditional cultural patterns, leaving only the common patterns concerned with basic existence (Lewis 1966a; Valentine 1970). Such accommodation often discloses more richness and ingenuity in forms of caring than one would imagine; but, for purposes of contrast, we have selected examples a bit further removed from the Anglo-American mainstream.

The illustrations that follow are but a few from the myriad of cultural forms. The example of salaried, organization men in a Tokyo suburb is selected to show a change from traditional, rural society to a modern, industrial one with fewer costs of isolation or alienation than have occurred in the West. The case of the Jewish shtetl in Eastern Europe, like the Shaker and Mennonite communities of the United States, exemplifies cultures whose patterns of internal caring have managed to withstand pressures of assimilation, and to retain protective communities often within hostile environments. Highly cooperative and cohesive communities also existed among certain Native American tribes, and we shall look briefly at the West Coast Miwok and the midwestern Salteaux.

These illustrations of communities more caring than our own are followed by a discussion about the role of elders. In modern Western society, the worth of an elder is typically no greater than the wealth he or she has been able to accumulate. Beyond that, the grandparent era has become identified with society's problem of providing special institutions for their housing, health care, or amusement. But people are not merely problems. Care for people constitutes something more than management of their needs. It also means recognizing their contribution to our values. A cross-cultural example of the elder's role helps make this point clear.

The chapter goes on to examine health care as one type of supportive concern. Its methods, even its purposes, differ greatly. The illustrations suggest approaches for meeting the health needs of the individual that are far more congruent to the person's beliefs and interpersonal role than methods of health care in the West.

Finally, we review the chilling evidence that contemporary Western society has learned little from the successes of these alternative ways of organizing supportive ties among peoples. Even worse, we appear to be hell-bent on eradicating such examples from the face of the earth. Such callousness will result in a loss to all of us.

In presenting these contrasts, it is imperative to point out that the particular cultural aspects we have selected can only be fully appreciated in the context of their own surroundings. Transplanting one or another aspect of supportive caring that is different from modern Western examples does not mean the practice could be made to work here. Nor should the success of one set of practices in a culture blind us to difficulties of that culture in other areas of life. Still, if our goal is to learn about caring, an item our own culture frequently lacks, there is potential advantage in reviewing our own values by examining those of different cultures.

CHANGE WITHOUT ALIENATION IN JAPAN

Much of the uprooting of traditional family and community ties in Europe and North America has been associated historically with the transition from a rural society to an industrial and urban society. The transition, occurring over one hundred years, was a jolt to the traditional patterns of social ties. In Japan, however, a predominantly rural nation changed to an urban, industrial one in less than three decades. The traditional, paternalistic arrangements between land owners and tenants was largely replaced by land reform. A rigid class system gave way to an open one, and the extended family dominated by the male line was, in a significant measure, replaced by the nuclear family. Meanwhile, large firms came to dominate the economic picture. These changes have produced a number of pressures acknowledged by the Japanese, but some of the differences with the West in accommodating the change are remarkable. The divorce rate has risen only slightly in Japan. Likewise, the crime rate has remained relatively low. During this period of migration to the cities, certain features of Japanese society have apparently served as buffers. Some of this buffering is due to ties with the family, and part of it relates to a perspective about the passage of time.

In the Japanese family, the oldest son was the heir, and other sons were expected to migrate and make their way through long, patient apprenticeships in the city. The family home was always present in emergencies, but the younger sons had little choice but to adapt to a new locale with little interference from family. The authority of the home setting was reinforced because the family, or the local village elders, was instrumental in arranging a place for the young people in the city. The new employer was the one who provided paternally for the second or third son, even to the extent of arranging or assisting in his marriage. Women traditionally went with their husbands. The new employer provided a new group of colleagues for loyalty and comradery. In Japan, the history of mobility has been one of ordered transitions from one group to another rather than of individuals on their own.

Modern Japan builds upon its tradition of family responsibility. Mamochi is a middle-class Tokyo suburb that was the site of a study of a large, expanding group of salaried workers in large organizations. The residents of Mamochi describe their neighborhoods as *shizuka* (quiet and peaceful). Their Japanese-style homes are less luxurious and less cluttered than those of their Western counterparts. Living in Mamochi is greatly ordered by the affiliation of men to their place of work. This affiliation is permanent, typically the man's first employment. The pay is modest at first, but incentives for seniority, loyalty to the firm, and good performance over the long-term include a set of graded rewards and the complete assurance of security. Many women find this future attractive, and the salaried corporation worker is a highly desired spouse. This security is particularly important since welfare in any form is considered quite demeaning. The Japanese corporation places little value on experience, since changing from one company to another is a sign of weak loyalty. The critical point in the life of a corporate salary man is therefore upon his selection to the firm.

Selection in Japanese society may sometimes be aided by personal recommendations, but the procedure always includes selection from a prestigious university. The deciding point, then, occurs during entrance examinations to these universities. The tests are referred to in Japanese as *shiken jigoka*, "examination hell." They place adolescents and teenagers under tremendous tension, an unfortunate circumstance that is reflected in high rates of suicide within this group. Even secondary schools require competitive examinations for admittance. Some *escarseta* (accelerated) schools make initial selection with kindergarten and assure a clear line of advancement through the university at that time. Success to the student means eventual selection into a company that offers a sense of belonging and a sense of security—qualities once associated with a large extended family and a successful family farm. Once students have been accepted into the university, remarkably few failures or dropouts are reported. Competition there, as within the firm, is greatly reduced.

A striking feature of competitive pressures for achievement in Western societies is that they create a sense of rivalry among people—between siblings, schoolmates, across generations, and with fellow workers. In Japan, this rivalry is definitely muted. Grades are unimportant, and the success of one family member is shared by all. Friends preserve a sense of loyalty; rivalry is reserved for strangers. In keeping with Japanese religious and philosophical thought, success is not a sudden, dramatic event, but evolves over a long period of time through discipline and patience.

When people make the transition, whether to a large firm or to some smaller, usually more paternal enterprise, the tie with the initial family or clan is carefully preserved and serves as a backup security system. There is, however, a great deal of security in this ferocious sense of loyalty to the company and the feeling that one's advancement and successes are incontrovertibly tied to the well-being of one's group. The individual is eager to see the group change, accommodate, and succeed and is cautious about departing from its wishes. This sense of group loyalty has provided a remarkable buffer against the anomie of individuals, so common during rapid social change (Vogel 1968).

Americans tend to confuse the Japanese sense of loyalty and group identification with an absence of individuality and lack of definition of self. Those more familiar with Japanese culture find that the self concept is alive and well in Japan but that it has a different meaning. For the American, identity is obtained by creating a trail of individual attainments. For the Japanese, identity is within, to be found by discovering one's connection with other people. Hence, a role may have some highly individualistic components, but role dedication and loyalty are the normal forms of Japanese self-expression. The Japanese word "*uchi*" means house. It also means family or family circle. There is still more richness in the meaning, however, for it is used to mean a company or a group in which the spirit of family connection exists. The concept is highly important to our understanding of supportive ties. The more we look outside of the values of Euro-American culture, the more we see our own culture as the odd one, the one that places little basic value on our connections with others and focuses more concern upon ourselves. The American response to Japanese successes has been to look upon the Japanese firm as a set of techniques that, if competitively successful, can be taken over by American firms. If we copy Japanese techniques without the values, however, the experiment seems likely both to fail in this country and to endanger the concept's lasting value in Japan.

Finally, it would be wise to note that the organizational affiliation that has cushioned the Industrial Revolution for many Japanese men has not provided as secure a cushion for Japanese women. The women are still quite disadvantaged in the quest for a good organizational position for themselves, and, by Western standards, are often oppressed in their marital and community roles.

THE JEWISH FAMILY AND COMMUNITY CARING

Survival takes many forms. The shtetl, the small, Jewish community of Eastern Europe, traces its origins to the biblical creation and the exodus from Egypt. The walk from Mt. Sinai to the shtetl spanned more than three thousand years for a people almost always without dominion over a native land. Throughout the wanderings of this band, there were perhaps two elements that sustained life and identity. The first was the Torah, a covenant with God so detailed in its prescriptions that the highest achievement was to learn all its teachings, an attainment far outweighing any other measure of worldly success. The second was a particular sense of "we" that was embodied in the shtetl. Typically, the shtetl was isolated from the environs of its host country. The mode of life within it existed from the time the Crusades drove the local infidels eastward until the pograms and Nazi exterminations destroyed it.

Every aspect of life in the shtetl was enhanced by religious overtones. The aspect of most concern to us here has to do with the responsibilities of people to one another. The worlds of joy and obligation were combined in the concept of a "mitzva," or any happening both good and just. Though the "mitzvas" were God's just rewards, they were earned, particularly by following the commandments prescribing relationships among human beings. God forgives sins against God, but He does not forgive sins against people who do not forgive one another. There were ritual opportunities to atone and seek forgiveness from one's neighbors, but it was safer and smarter to earn one's blessings through daily living.

The task of making children into good Jews was the great goal of parenthood. To this end, the shtetl mother was constantly toiling, worrying, and sacrificing. Parents in particular—but also all elders—were recipients of a special feeling of *derekh erets,* (respect). The shalom (peace) of the home was not one of tranquility, since argument was frequent and not particularly discouraged. Rather, it came from reciprocation of parental love, not only in direct repayments but in the *nakhes* (joys) the family found in each other's joys and successes.

The extended family was also expected to give without being asked—whether it be money for a dowry, a place to live, or a meal—although the relative might be only remotely connected. Such generosity was a mechanism for social justice within the family circle as well as being insurance, for who knew when the giver might also be in need.

The responsibilities of shtetl residents extended well beyond ties of kinship. The community was an extension of the family, and those from the same shtetl had a bond that persisted across the continents. Within the community, charity was an important part of the good deeds one collected in the eyes of God. Every celebration, from birth to death, was accompanied by a donation to the needy—placed in a tin box in every home. Even a poor person who lived on charity was obliged to give charity from that which was given.

The style of giving was itself part of the "mitzva." The best gifts were given in ways delicately designed so that the self-esteem of the recipient would be carefully protected against feelings of weakness or subordination.

> We had a grocery store. . . . There were some poor Jews who used to come. We served them just like the others but they did not have to pay. However, nobody was to see this and they were helped just like the other customers. Mother used to say that to be generous you had to have three things: one, the means to give; two, a kind heart; and three (most important), good sense (Zborowski and Herzog 1972:200).

Parents taught charity by allowing their children to make gifts or donations to others, but responsible caring was not perpetuated by force of habit nor even an instilled sense of altruism. Under the covenant with God, people were interdependent. Not only did the acts of one person affect the fate of all, but each had need of the others. Those less privileged, therefore, depended upon those who had more for instruction or for material aid. Those more privileged, however, could only validate their spiritual identities by sharing their valuables with those who lacked. Interdependence was recognized not only in charitable activities but in every aspect of human relations—the personal as well as the communal.

The shtetl was part, albeit an aberrant part, of Western society; yet, in this aberration, the homeland of the fiddler on the roof, a lesson about the human condition was preserved for centuries. The example did not inform the surrounding Western civilization, however; rather, the carriers of this tradition were, in large numbers, exterminated, leaving the more competitive, self-aggrandizing forms of Western culture one less reminder of ways in which human relationships can be embedded in more caring communities.

AMERICAN INDIAN COMMUNITIES AT PEACE
In the past, most Native Americans lived in clans, groups linked directly by a common lineage and recognized as an entity of loyalty. The

Miwoks, who settled the shores and coastal valleys of northern California, were organized into such scattered clans. They caught shellfish and ground acorns into flour, using only primitive tools. They shared their temperate environs with the grey fox, the grizzly, and the field mouse, and like them were residents, sharing the hospitality of the earth they used so sparingly. The Miwok clans—Esalon, Costanoor, and Salinas—were different linguistic groups, none of which had a word for, or a concept of, warfare. They lived as neighbors, enjoying the bounty of the earth, peaceful and undisturbed for ten thousand years. These people had mastered a way of living with nature and with each other, a way that sustained them for a longer time than other human orders. While successive generations quietly replaced one another among the Miwok, other entire civilizations ascended and declined.

> Civilizations came into being in Sumer, Babylon, and all other ancient places of the earth only to recede into dust and forgotten decay. Troy, Mycenae, Athens, and Rome rose, flourished and collapsed. Still the people along the shores of California lived out the measured, undisturbed course of their days (Crouch 1973).

When the Spaniards arrived, they corralled the Indians into large missions behind the strength of the sword and the cross. The zealous effort to save their souls assured the obliteration of the Indian way of life, and within one hundred years it was gone.

Little remains in accounts of Miwok life to explain the peaceful stability that characterized their existence. The bounty and mildness of the California coast were most certainly a factor, yet several Algonkian tribes of the northern woodlands of the United States and Canada maintained a similar interpersonal peace amid harsher environments. One observer of the Montagnais-Naskapi, an Algonkian offshoot in the Labrador peninsula, noted, "Strife is scarcely present, violence strenuously avoided; competition even courteously disdained" (Speck 1933:559–594). The same outward harmony appears characteristic of another branch of Algonkians, the Salteaux. These Ojibwa-speaking people live in the general area of Lake Superior and eke out an existence by hunting and fishing. Observers of the Salteaux notice a great deal of cooperation, laughter, harmony, patience, and self-control. They have never been at war, either with whites or with other Indian tribes. Among the related Papago, war is the linguistic equivalent of "insanity" (Hagen 1971). With the Salteaux, there are no records of murder, suicide is unknown, and theft is rare. There are few open expressions of anger, and it is extremely rare for a quarrel to lead to actual physical assault.

Father LeJeune, a Jesuit missionary, once observed a disparity between the outward harmony among the Salteaux and an inner sense of malice. Anthropologist Irving Hallowell (1954) noted similar indications of ambivalence, citing the invocation of sorcery in their interpersonal lives. The pacific pattern, however, is the more obvious one.

Several reasons for this harmony, cooperation, and tranquility have been tendered. The first is that hunting, fishing, and trapping provide a modest existence with very little opportunity for storage of surplus. The sense of interdependence reflects a true condition of interdependence. With virtually no differences in affluence and no chance to save for a rainy day, the best strategy is to cooperate in the hunt and to share food. An equally compelling source of the harmonious, interpersonal life lies in the kinship system. Among the Salteaux, everyone with whom one has contact falls within the category of a relative. Furthermore, by extension of a few primary terms, no linguistic differentiation is made between those with blood ties and those whom we would regard as in-laws. Hence, open quarrels are tantamount to hostility among blood relatives. Such hostility does, of course, occur, but among the Salteaux solidarity is far more important. Cooperation and inhibition against openly expressed aggression is not only a socially approved ideal, but also but a pattern of living that seldom breaks down. To ward off hostile forces, the Salteaux maintain a sense of inner power, granted through the blessings of supernatural powers. They believe that true power can allow itself to be tested. With confidence in one's powers, aggressive exploits are unnecessary, and the best defense is to avoid offense. Such behavior will lead to *pimadaziwin*, or life in the fullest. This value is far distant from the ideas of the white trappers, whose ancestors are more likely to be victims of type A behavior and have probably never been able to share *pimadaziwin*.

RESPECT FOR THE ELDERLY

In Western society, status reflects individual success in the marketplace. Those who can achieve are socially recognized, and the contributions of others, barely noticed. We have become a society in which major categories of people—the old, the disabled, the young, the unemployed—are viewed as problems rather than as people. A different perspective about the contribution of others can be found in societies out of this mainstream. The elderly in particular often have specially valued roles.

We once had the opportunity to hear of a thirty-five-year-old Native American educational psychologist's travel through reservations in the Southwest to discuss with tribal elders some of the serious problems associated with Indian boarding schools. His message was straightforward.

> Your children go off to these schools. Their native languages and culture are often not respected and the schools are inferior to the schools of white people.

They are left with little pride in themselves and little opportunity. You and the leaders of other tribes will have to come together to make known your concerns for a better educational system to the Bureau of Indian Affairs.

His message was usually not met with immediate affirmation. A typical reply would be, "We have heard what you say. But you are a young man and not yet wise. Think more about this, and we shall also." The educator would leave quietly and go on to the next tribe. He persisted in this activity for many years. "Why," he was asked, "do you continue with so little apparent agreement or response?" He replied, "I am an outsider. I have my views but they know their ways and must be respected. I would not want my own children to grow up in a culture where the wisdom of their elders was not respected." One cannot help but be struck by the depth of that conviction.

In Emmy Werner's book *Kith, Kin and Hired Hands* (1984), references are made to the role of grandparents in several minority groups. In the Native American communities (particularly Ojibwa and Hupa tribes), the grandmother is the cornerstone of the family and often is primarily responsible for the socialization of her grandchildren. Support was also provided by grandparents for unwed mothers. In nine out of ten cases, children born of unwed mothers were reared by the grandparents. In Native American communities in the Southwest United States, "92 percent of the elderly generations fulfilled the traditional family role on a daily basis for their children, grandchildren, and great grandchildren" (Werner 1984).

Margaret Mead (1932) once remarked that, surprisingly, Indian women could be such poor mothers but such wonderful grandmothers. The pattern, however, made cultural sense. The younger woman had difficult work to do, work that required mobility. She skinned animals, gathered medicinal and edible plants, set up, brought down, and transported teepees, and carried water in skins or pots. A mother, typically still in her teens, found her youthful strength to be needed for tasks that would be seriously encumbered by the presence of toddlers. The grandmother, however, knowing the ways of the world and the tribe, could gather up a group of grandchildren and provide daily succor.

The Hopi of the Southwest have no nouns in their native language: everything in life is part of a process, intimately related. All nouns, therefore, are linguistically verbs. To the Western mind, this thinking can best be understood by reflecting on a wave on the ocean. For Western linguists, "wave" is a noun, but "waving" might also seem appropriate because we can watch the wave take form, change form, and disappear into the larger whole. Hopi philosophy recognizes the temporal aspect of all living, whether or not their changing form is immediately recognizable. A person, in the Hopi view, is always in the process of becoming, as is a tribal community. Elders, therefore, are an important part of the human process, which is inseparable from the spiritual process and from things of nature.

In many Native American communities, the role of grandparent accompanies the status of sage and tribal elder. This role is crucial within the community context and carries with it a sense of judicious authority. Whereas younger individuals carry on the cultural rituals, elders have the specific responsibility of standing in judgment, and in a sense, of being the conscience of the younger generations. A Cherokee woman from Oklahoma told of her impressions of being an elder, which included being a "grandparent" to many of her youngsters, most of whom were not related by blood. She explained that the grandmother is the glue that binds the generations together. She is the nurturer as well as the stern judge.

> I like my role as an elder; it's a respected, responsible, heavy role—too sacred to give up. I have been here sensing, feeling, tasting, looking, and gathering masses of knowledge.
>   I believe in feeding people. It is one of my responsibilities as a woman and as an elder. You share what you've got no matter how much you have (Hutchison 1984).

The woman's reference to "feeding" has not only a literal connotation, but also refers to taking care of community members without regard to blood kinship. This idea is quite different from the way most Americans are socialized, particularly in responsibility and ownership.

The crucial issue here is context. The Indian culture does not place importance upon either material possessions or upon individual ownership. The land and its fruits are not to be hoarded, but are to be preserved. There is no sense of ownership, instead, stewardship. If one is a guardian of land, food, and other material goods, it becomes one's responsibility to see that they are shared.

Feeding in its literal sense symbolizes the process of sharing and giving. During the same interview, the Cherokee woman said,

> In my tribe, if you respect someone, you cook when they come. You feed them because it is vital to life. And so I cook. I love to cook, and I love to go to the sacred fire and see the little old women who do the cooking. Always, it's wonderful food, and one takes a tiny morsel of food from each pot and puts it on the ground for the great spirit (Hutchison 1984).

The role of grandparent is so important in some cultures that a surrogate grandparent might be taken into a family that is without a resident elder. In the Spanish-American communities in northern New Mexico and southern Colorado, many of the old ways have been preserved. The literature coming from this population speaks eloquently of the elder's role; a particular family is described in Rudolfo Anaya's autobiography, *Bless Me, Ultima,* (1972). Ultima, a matriarch of the small community described in Anaya's account, was a midwife/healer. As is common in many Spanish-speaking communities in the Southwest, the *curandera* linked the people of the community. A *curandera* is, in the most classic sense, an elder of the community who fills a supportive role wherever needed. In *Bless Me, Ultima,* Ultima moved in with the author's family and became a surrogate grandparent.

> Ultima slipped easily into the routine of our daily life. The first day she put on her apron and helped my mother with breakfast. It was as if she had always been there. My mother was very happy because now she had someone to talk to and she didn't have to wait until Sunday when her women friends from the town came up the dusty path to sit in the sala and visit.
>
> My father was pleased. Now he had one more person to tell his dreams to.
>
> And I was happy with Ultima. We walked together in the llano and along the river banks to gather herbs and roots for her medicines. She taught me the names of plants and flowers, of trees and bushes, of birds and animals; but most important I learned from her that there was beauty in the time of day and in the time of night, and that there was peace in the river and in the hills. My soul grew under her careful guidance (1972:1314).

Successful aging requires that elders play a reciprocal role, offering something of importance to others and receiving the care they need. In small Mexican villages, the responsibility for that care is carefully woven into the family structure. There, the traditional pattern of paternal dominance gives the father some land or other possessions, to bestow in exchange for care from his family. For the aging mother, protection comes through the cultural image of *marianismo.* This concept of the woman's role was studied in two central Mexican farming communities. In Tepetlaoxtoc Villa de Hidalgo, the people are mestizo and clearly Hispanic in language and culture. In San Geronimo Amanalco, the villagers are identified as Indian and speak Nahuatl, the language of the Aztecs. In both places, *marianismo* is a dominant factor in the relationships surrounding the adult woman. In this concept, the woman, or more accurately the mother, is thought of as undergoing a great deal of sacrifice and self-abnegation in giving birth to children and in nursing them. Birthing is considered a major forbearance, and breastfeeding, which lasts from ten to twenty months, is considered a moral obligation, not pleasurable for the mother. In fact, friends and family help the mother by supporting her special requirements of diet, abstinence, and sweat baths, and by helping her avoid emotional states such as *susto* (fright)—all actions related to the production of healthy breast milk. Built into the culture is a deep sense of indebtedness by the children, who wish to repay the obligation to their mother who has given so much and who will always be counted upon to give for her children. As an elder, she will not be neglected. Her unquestioning nurturant role will assure the concern of her children (Graham and Millard 1983).

HEALING AS A CULTURAL
FORM OF SUPPORTIVE ARRANGEMENT

Anthropologist Margaret McKenzie once told us that in her work in a Melanesian community, she was impressed by the astuteness of the natives, whose translation of the Department of Health was the Department of Illness. The people were not opposed to health. In fact, a major portion of their cultural practices were devoted to enhancing it, promoting it, and preserving it. They recognized, perhaps correctly, that the Department of Health dealt only with sickness. For health they relied upon their own tribal religious leaders, who combined a stored wealth of tribal tradition on healing with an intimate knowledge of the individual, the family of the individual, and the particular behavior considered antithetical to healthful living. Their practices resembled those of Hopi Indian shamans halfway around the world whose use of dreams was part of their preventive health methods, a concept much different from Western ideas. Often, Hopi shamans used dreams to find a compatible life role for an individual. This practice greatly contrasts with the Western medical tradition where, after years of unsuccessful somatic remedies, the individual might visit a psychoanalyst who uses the dream to interpret the frustrations that have evolved from playing a role incompatible with the person's own needs and desires (Duarand 1984).

Medical care in Western society has not always been so exclusively geared to the treatment of highly specific illnesses. In the past, folk practitioners of many stripes peddled their remedies, and there was once a highly organized form of holistic medical practice—homeopathy—that stressed the acquisition of proper nutrients and the reduction of toxins so that the body's own defenses might best redress any imbalance of pathogenic agents. To practice homeopathic medicine required more time in school than did even the contrasting allopathic medicine of contemporary medical schools, and it required large amounts of the practitioner's and patient's time (Vithoulkas 1979). Preventive health care lost out in the rush to find quick cures and, perhaps, higher medical incomes. The American Medical Association favored a model focused more upon symptoms and the treatment of specific diseases than upon the underlying causes of ill health. This position received a great boost when large amounts of financial assistance to symptom-focused medical education were provided by the Rockefeller Foundation (Brown 1979). The result has been the near monopoly of symptom-oriented medicine, which dominates the contemporary scene.

Lost with homeopathy are cultural traditions that viewed both health and treatment as more than the cure of specific, distinct illnesses. There has been a tendency among ethnographers to study folk healers and healing rituals as exotic practices, interesting for their symbolic or religious significance but not for their contribution to a more general understanding of health and disease. The legacy of such work has been to conceal important parts of a holistic perspective from the general study of health. In chapter 2, we discussed the importance of perceived symbols in understanding the mechanism by which social support fortifies one's resistance. Here we look at some cultural symbols and practices that illustrate more interpersonal origins of illness and of treatment. The medical beliefs of preliterate societies are frequently well-developed systems. Among the Ndembu, a small African tribe, specific symbols are linked to psychophysiological reactions, on the one hand, and to specific tensions in social relationships on the other. The view is enbedded in a complete cultural system of health care practices (Turner, 1967). The cross-cultural perspective reveals not only differences in health practices, but also a view of health more closely linked to natural patterns of interpersonal caring.

THE FAMILY, THE TANG-KI, AND THE M.D. IN TAIWAN

In Taiwan today, there exists an amazing mixture of medical and pharmaceutical treatments, some in the Western tradition, some with elements of traditional Chinese medicine. The same individual might visit both a Western-style and a Chinese-style doctor. To supplement the Western medicine, the individual could purchase a medicinal "one hundred herb tea," said to lower the internal hot energy (*huo ch'u*), or purchase an amulet for *Pao sheng la ti,* the god of the healers. Chinese healers provide an almanac containing information on treating or preventing illness that follows traditional Chinese beliefs about fate, family, and ancestors. A fortune teller in the temple gives advice in health matters. On certain occasions, a Taoist priest conducts ceremonies that we in the West would consider medical or psychiatric—although a part of the procedure involves driving away ghosts and evil spirits or placating the responsible gods. Nearby, a shaman can be consulted. In the ornate pharmacies, people can be found perusing an array of deer antlers, rhinocerous horns, dried lizards, pickled snakes, and aromatic herbs—although the herbalist's store will have a far richer variety of grasses, roots, and flowers. Close by in the market, people buy high nutrition food supplements, vitamins, and Western patent medicines. The costs and effectiveness of treatments are sometimes discussed with family members or neighbors—usually older women commonly knowledgeable about illness and healing (Kleinman 1980).

Those with firmly entrenched Western views wonder at the apparent inconsistencies and dismiss all but the physician call as visits to the realm of superstition. But for the Taiwanese, the Western-style doctor is not one who understands his or her illness, its long-term causes, the best methods for its prevention, or its impact upon one's life and family obligations. The Western-style physician is looked upon as one who asks few questions of his patient, gives a shot as a quick fix, and prescribes a drug. The more traditional shaman or *tang-ki* refers to the client as *k'e-jen* (literally guest), has no fee (but accepts donations), and obtains a great deal of family information. The *tang-ki* gives extensive personal support to the individual and the family and prescribes a treatment procedure. The ritual symbolism and the occasional induction of trancelike states are part of the *tang-ki* repertoire, as is the prescription of traditional Chinese medicines. Observers of *tang-ki* note that these healers are warm, empathic, and supportive, while still authoritarian in their admonitions of what must be done. Most important, the healing activities occur in an environment of group support given by the assistants of the *tang-ki,* by other clients (guests), and particularly by the family.

Beyond the elements of magic and faith, strong psychological forces in their own right, the *tang-ki* healing process speaks to the Taiwanese cultural conception of healthful living. Traditional Chinese differentiate a large repertoire of physical or physiological maladies, believe in a large range of important, cross-generational obligations to the family, and the extended family, and differentiate a small number of individual emotional expressions. Direct expression of negative concerns is considered potentially disrupting for long-term kin obligations. Surface harmonious behavior accompanies the individual's denial of negative feelings. Frequently, suppressed feelings find somatic expression. The function of the shaman is to help the client reassess concerns about the family and about responsibilities to one's kin. The causes of somatic disturbance are then addressed, and symbolic expressions of feeling are permitted (Kleinman 1980).

The shaman's skill lies in finding forms of expression that respect the custom of removing such feelings from everyday life. A continuity of caring about people in one's network, living and dead, is established, and with this act comes an affirmation of the rightness of continuing to live in health.

NAVAJO HEALING

Among the Navajo, the priest and the doctor are one and the same person. Religion, healing, and art are intrinsically woven into an amazing unity. The religious ceremonies, with but few exceptions, are ceremonies of healing intended to restore health and harmony with the environment.

The Navajo world of illness and ill fate is anchored in a fear of possession by evil spirits. The fear is balanced by a strong reliance upon reason and knowledge as regulators of ethical behavior. Healing practices are pragmatic, based upon what is good for the individual and the community and what has worked in the past. At the core of healing is a belief that there exists a natural and universal order, and that imbalances, disharmonies, and disease are best met by its restoration. There is no concept of sin, but there are concepts of being in error or out of order in one's relations to others or to more cosmic forces. The ceremonies of healing are ritual modes for restoring the order. They are said to have been laid down in the beginning along with other laws that govern the universe.

Earlier we described the way in which symbolic representation of those to whom we are connected becomes part of a psychic system capable of protecting one's self against overwhelming stress and breakdown in health. We next attempted to use a scientific mode of thought to help in understanding how social support might confer immunological protection. The importance of these symbols of people, however, cannot be fully appreciated without taking a deeper look into the place of cultural symbols.

The path from infancy to death inevitably involves a measure of suffering. Some obstacles in this path increase the measure of distress producing painful symptoms. Specialized healers in any society learn that the suffering most difficult to endure is pain devoid of meaning. Close to the heart, then, of all methods of cure is a symbolic structure that gives meaning to our discomfort—meaning to the dull routine of daily life, to sudden strikes of illness or accident, to the gross misfortunes of intemperate seasons, or to the malice and ignorance of people. The symbols are not simply words in a language (what Susanne Langer calls *discursive* symbols). Instead, they are *presentational* symbols—larger sequences of meaning only understandable within a broader structure. The most comprehensive of these, such as musical compositions, or myths, songs, healing rituals, or religious ceremonies, are what Langer called *life symbols*. These life symbols present a view of the origins of civilization, of the purposes of life, and of the causes for all that happens. Life symbols are the molds for our thought and feelings in each culture. The prevailing myths lead to a set of rituals, which tend to be observed with the force of religion (Langer 1942).

The Western faith in science is just such a life myth, and from it follows the healing practices centered upon the physician and the pharmacist. These particular practices are viewed as effective quite apart from one's beliefs. The symbols do more, however, than provide a vocabulary for explanation. Their most compelling power would extend to folk healing as well as to scientific forms. According to Carl Jung, the added potency lies in the ability to transform psychic energies from basic urges into aesthetic potentials, from fragmented acts, and thoughts, and feelings into a path of life that has both direction and a power for growth and enrichment (Jung 1964).

It is this psychic energy that the ritual healings of the Navajo seek to tap with appeals to the life symbols. There are a variety of ways in which healing energies are mustered. The Appache seek visions to help reconnect aberrant sufferings to the spirits of the healing myths. For the Navajo, the process that leads to a cure combines elaborate, prearranged symbolic rituals with a decidedly social setting. Our contention is that social participation is an essential part of the cure.

The diagnostic and treatment functions are sometimes led by separate individuals. The former is done by highly sensitive, intuitive individuals, usually women; the latter is conducted by a medicine man or woman and assistants who have studied the many chants, the folk myths of healing, and the ritual forms of sand painting. Whether the problem is pneumonia, a broken arm, or a feeling of weakness, the procedures always require elaborate preparation involving cleansing and the appropriate herbs. The healer orchestrates a ceremony that frequently goes on for four or five nights. The common nine-night chant and healing would be impossible without the active help of the family in planning the meals. Before the entire procedure is ended, there will have been several sweat baths. A large sand painting symbolizing four directions which stand for the major polarities of life, will be created on the ground. The chants are recited flawlessly, and masked dancers, sometimes in frightening forms, represent various spirits. In the Navajo religion, there is always an attempt to integrate all things within a framework of cosmic harmony. There is also always a residue, sometimes seen as an omission or an imperfection in the sand paintings, that cannot be included. This part is called *tundi*. It is a part associated with sorcery and witchcraft. The songs and ceremonies of the medicine man will either help banish the evil spirits or to isolate and disarm them. Since they are a part of the life symbols of Navajo culture responsible for certain ills, their removal at the hands of other potent symbols of life is tantamount to cure.

The myths of the Navajo are detailed, and their characters may experience punishment and renewal such as losing one's skin or being ingested, dismembered, banished, reborn, or reanimated sexually. As the healing goes on, patients identify with the Coyote Woman, the Beggar Boy, Eagle Girl, Child Born of Water, or Monster Slayer and experience the characters' transformations in the myth as their own. The shaman, the assistants, and the family help enact the drama under conditions evoking basic emotional involvement.

The chant ritual "Blessing Way," in which the entire family takes part, fills the patient with joy and peace, with a sense of renewal. The Changing Woman spirit renews herself with every cycle of the seasons. The ritual contact with her in the chant produces a state of internal and external harmony, helping to achieve the cultural goal of "walking the path of beauty in old age."

Navajo medicine men have long been more tolerant of Western medicine than the reverse. If a person is going off to the hospital for an operation, the ritual is used to provide an adequate preparation, mobilizing the forces of healing before the event. There are recent examples of modern physicians, who, recognizing the special power of the shaman and the ritual, have invited their help with a difficult case, but such instances are uncommon.

Increasingly, modern technological society has encroached upon the Navajo. Donald Sandner, a Jungian psychiatrist, describes the remaining Navajo medicine men and women as a small group who have spent their lives immersed in religion. They weigh their words carefully but display a deep and searching mentality. They maintain a delicate balance between giving and withholding.

> They have lived lives of hardship and poverty, yet many of them have attained the goal that is the crowning jewel of a life spent in service. They have become the embodiment of the wise old men and women who are thoroughly at home in their own culture, and yet universal in the depth of their vision. Such wise old men and women are rare in our own society in spite of the comparative ease and comfort we enjoy. Perhaps that is just what has made us blind to the path that has always been there—the path to inner wisdom. Perhaps a life of hardship and ascetic living makes the path plainer and more acceptable. Whatever the reason, these old singers of the desert have preserved the vision of the path which can still form the basis for the wisdom of the future (Sandner 1979:9).

To the medical specialist in Western society, disease is the affliction of a particular organ of the body. Its cure most frequently lies in mechanical or chemical removal of the infecting source. For most hosts of disease, the experience is one of illness, pain, discomfort—an interference with the pursuit of one's life and the fulfillment of one's roles in relation to others. The means to deal with this state necessarily require tapping the strengths of inner subjective experience. Those who deny this method because it is inherently subjective deny a major part of human nature. Lewis Mumford writes,

> without that underlying subjective flux, as experienced in floating imagery, dreams, bodily impulses, formative ideas, projections and symbols, the world that is open to human experience can be neither described nor rationally understood. . . . When our age learns that lesson, it will have made the first move toward redeeming for human use the mechanical and electrified wasteland. . . . (Mumford 1967:75).

In Western society, the poet and the artist contact this symbolic cultural reality for those few who are curious. This symbolic reality, reflecting the meeting of our sense of inner physiological, happenings with external social happenings is used only on the fringes of Western medical practice by certain psychotherapists. By contrast, the Navajo religion has been described as

> a profound meditation upon nature and its curative powers. Through the centuries their visions have crystalized into living symbolic units like the prayers and the sand paintings, which are easily reproducable and may be transmitted from one generation to the next (Sandner 1979:273).

It is a dogma connecting all things and every detail, large or small, of nature and of experience. It links each bone of the body to a universal destiny. It omits nothing, no matter how small or hidden, and extends even to inconceivable space. Not only are the elements all present, but they are part of an interlocked unity in which the individual has a significant function. Healing ceremonies help redirect this function. In the Navajo view, the final dissolution of the individual means becoming one with an ultimate harmony. The teaching of the young by the elders makes such life symbols as natural to understand as any other simple truths of experience. "On that foundation, the Navajo have constructed an edifice of symbolism that can take its place among the great healing systems of the world" (Sandner 1979:273).

There is a sense in which Navajo, Hopi, and other Native American healing practices have served their communities well. Whereas other cultures have rushed into the melting pot, welcoming their own assimilation, Native Americans have persisted in maintaining their culture following their physical conquest and their removal from the land of their ancestors.

Their culture has survived in spite of unfulfilled treaty obligations to provide adequately for the health and education for those remaining on tribal reservations. But the extent of the accommodation to Western culture is reflected in the 1980 census on Indian elderly. The Navajo are but one—the largest—of 333 tribes, altogether containing 109,000 persons over age sixty. Though more than 50 percent of all Indians are now urban residents, the elders are disproportionately found on the reservation (Curley 1982). During the 1960s and 1970s, when middle America was discovering the nursing home and the senior center, Indian communities persisted in the belief that they could take care of their own. Such was the way it had always been; as one got older, there was an increase in status.

A majority of this over-sixty group (96 percent) are not employed, and most are unable to meet their costs for heating or basic repairs on their decaying homes. Many homes still lack indoor plumbing, and 75 percent of these elderly receive no Medicare or Medicaid benefits despite their low income. An unusually high proportion of Indian males die between the ages forty-five and sixty. One national study showed that Indians at age forty-five exhibit the functional characteristics of non-Indians at age sixty-five (National Indian Council on Aging 1981a).

The values of kinship and harmony with the universe are still believed, but they are not fulfilled for many people. When their children went off to school, the elders thought they would return to embrace the old ways. Most did not. The traditional gift of the elder was to pass on knowledge and wisdom to children and to grandchildren. The sharing of ways of healing and of living provided the elder with a unique and valued place. Now the barriers of distance and language preclude the family status that would ordinarily go with such a gift. There is a sense of isolation and of failure among some Indian elders, who know things that may be of great value to all of us. Their wisdom is of family and tribal cohesion, of living with the ecology as partner rather than as exploiter, of healing as a holistic practice, and of respect for the wise. As much as these lessons may be needed, Western society goes on barely noticing the loss. The ideas are as strong as ever, but no one is listening.

The cultural practices we have looked at are not excerpts from perfect societies. Women in changing Japan have major role conflicts, and adolescent pressure there is enormous. Mothers in Mexican villages and in Eastern Europe endure the anguish as well as the rewards of giving at one's own expense. The healing cosmologies in Taiwan and among the Navajo are less protective than many basic innoculations. Our culture's strength is its capacity to develop highly specific techniques. We are being tested now to see whether our efforts to learn from other cultures and to develop a more caring society can counter the effects of other changes that have led to a loss of concern for the human community.

Sometimes, when looking beyond our own horizons, we are able to see a vision of community that still has much to teach. In her autobiography *Blackberry Winter,* Margaret Mead reminds us, "There is hope, I believe, in seeing the human adventure as a whole and in the shared trust that knowledge about mankind, sought in reverence for life, can bring life" (Mead 1972:296).

8
THE POLITICAL
ECONOMY
OF CARING
RELATIONSHIPS

THE WAYS OF LOVE

The hope and the joy that some followers of Taoist thought are able to find comes from the basic premise that the Tao or "the way" just is. It does not have to be studied, built, saved for, or invented. In fact, with too much sophistication in our search for the way, or too much detailed knowledge, the way is lost, and we may find ourselves opposing the tide rather than contributing to this remarkable universe and its gifts of life and of consciousness. The ways of life are surely not utopian, for hardship, anguish, and death are as much a part of our history as are the joys of living. If the Freudian concept of the death wish were to be understood in broader biological terms, it would state that this script, written directly into our protoplasm, contains not only the seeds for our vitality, our building, our nurturing, and reproducing of life, but the seeds of our destruction as well.

In this book we have tried to achieve a measure of distance, both from the ravages of destructive tendencies in our civilization and from the specific rush to find solutions. By stepping back, we have been able to ask what has become of the force for life, for nurturance, for social building that is also part of the way. This subject is not one for which one finds a single, definitive answer. We have approached the task in much the same way as the six blind men described the elephant. In separate chapters, we have looked upon the relation of human nurturance to our health and to our culture, to blood ties and to ties of choice, to the scientific quest to measure our affections for others, and to the practice of translating the impulse of caring into intentional, professional practice. We have found a thousand places where loving attachments remain a powerful protector of health and well-being, but also a thousand places where the ties that heal are being unraveled. We have also found places where threads merge strongly and are rewoven into the social fabric. In fact, everything we have learned confirms the words of Malvina Reynolds' folk song: "Love is something—if you give it away, you keep on getting more." But is individual effort adequate to reweave the weakest connections in the most threadbare parts of the social fabric?

RESOURCES FOR CARING

Clark University sociologist Robert Ross has been a vigorous advocate of community self-help for many years. The political limitations of mutual help can be seen from the perspective of one who has worked with local groups to help obtain decent living conditions and a fair share of the opportunities for food, for housing, for employment, and for unpolluted and safe neighborhoods.

Caring exchanges occur at the most microscopic of social levels. A willingness to listen, a kind word, or a helping hand affirms others and ourselves as part of the human community. Surely a foster grandparent arrangement can enrich the lives of two people at both ends of the life span, while a community project can help an abused or sick child or adult, or assist a hungry and homeless one in feeling less alone, more hopeful. The illustrations we are citing all occur locally. When we examine whole communities, entire cities, states, or nations to see if we have spread the fruits of the earth to those in need, however, the outlook is less optimistic. Ross quotes the wisdom of his grandmother in explaining the paucity of resources: "You can't squeeze blood from a stone" (Ross 1982).

The stone in this case is the reality that resources reflect larger economic arrangements. It was not only Karl Marx and Friedrich Engels who noted that social arrangements are often derivatives of economic ones. Anthropologists have shown that the primitive societies that practice female infanticide have been those in which food was scarce and physically difficult to acquire (Sahlins 1967). Ways of gathering and distributing food have also been related to sex roles in the family and to the patterns of ruling and of caring for the elderly (Sahlins 1972). The larger, institutional arrangements of the economy often affect the smallest and most intimate personal exchanges.

During the late nineteenth century, in Western society, we witnessed the growth of the nationally oriented, quasi-monopolistic firm as a partial replacement for the private business that was dependent upon a specific locality. The large mill or factory did not have to locate in the center of a city, but could command workers into its more isolated, suburban site and could sell its produce in every town the railroads could reach. The policies of these corporate giants set limits on the capacities of families and neighborhoods to develop self-help or mutual help. Amidst degrading working conditions, women and children were first assigned to work in the factories and then banished from them to their homes, where it was not possible to earn a living (Oakley 1974). Public charity became a demeaning symbol of what life could be for those who could not play the game in accordance with the then current manner of allocating the resources needed to live (Edwards 1979; Piven and Cloward 1971).

In the 1980s, the scale of economic activities has expanded even further. Large firms are now global, and moderate-sized firms are increasingly so. Investment in United States facilities or communities is not their only locus of activity. In fact, certain Third World countries are emerging as the more lucrative sites to produce shirts, blouses, headsets, automobiles, and computer components for sale not only to individuals but to other corporate giants and to governments. For the local community as well as for the city or state, the losses from industry relocation have had a sobering effect upon local populations. The competition is open. Those areas with more forgiving tax structures, more corporate inducements, and weaker unions hold the edge. In the bitter competition between communities, we deny those human needs that express the measure of our mutual caring—for children and their schools, for the disabled, for family health services—as they struggle for a place in the local agenda. We find the priorities becoming not housing rehabilitation but industrial parks, not child care centers but convention centers.

Unlike neighbors, who may become a strong part of one's personal network of support, the international corporation has no community loyalty. Investors have the upper hand where unemployment is high. Wages stagnate, more people fall into poverty, and more will accept any work at any wage. When investors choose to move on, they leave deteriorating neighborhoods with inadequate resource bases for providing the needed services for job training and for feeding and housing the families whose lives have been uprooted by the loss (Bluestone, Harrison, and Baker 1981). What happens, then, to the nurturant care so necessary to cushion our defeats, to protect our health? Some find the health-giving or life-preserving efforts of a natural helper. Others become part of a mutual help group with all its promise and strength. What happens when the group raises its voice to ask the local board of supervisors for help in providing truly adequate services? Well—you can't squeeze blood from a stone.

In developed Western societies, the 1960s were a decade of rising expectations for poor and working people. Labor and civil rights movements were able to command a greater portion of industrial benefits than before or since. The unprecedented rise in social expenditures such as pension schemes, health benefits, disability programs, and educational programs for minorities amounted to a shift in social consumption. On a social scale, these programs reflected the same values of nurturant attention to one another that supportive ties address at the interpersonal level. In fact, this social consumption provides the supportive ecology and the hope in which deeper interpersonal ties can flourish (Pilisuk and Minkler 1985).

The 1970s, however, found multinational firms facing a period of economic stagnation, and a movement toward governmental austerity followed that substantially reduced social programs. In addition to reductions in health and medical care, education, social security, and community programs, we have witnessed a privatization of such services. For example, health care is increasingly contracted to private facilities—even tax-supported health care. Matters of occupational or environmental health have been relegated a lower priority, and expanding corporate profits to promote reinvestment has been given high priority. Health, education, and other services are increasingly justified not for their contributions to social consumption—creating a better quality of life—but rather as contributions to the process of industrial expansion.

BLAMING THE POOR AND POWERLESS

Accompanying a reduction in the hope for a greater level of consumption among working people (or among the unemployed, the disabled, or single parents) is an ideological message saying that government services are the enemy, that their costs have placed an unbearable burden upon the taxpayer and, particularly, upon the investor, who is to be solicited at every level. This message is a far cry from the ideology of the generation before. Then equality was considered an ideal, and the outrages of poverty were viewed with scorn. The fruits of the mainstream were considered of value to everyone, and those whose health, culture, or education departed from the main were considered just targets for a host of remedies. This analysis may have been wrong. The poverty of the time may have been less a result of the lack of skills, knowledge, health care, or "head-starts," than of the fact that large amounts of affluence had accumulated and were not circulating to the poor. Then, as now, the reason some people were poor and powerless was that others were rich and powerful (Gitlin and Hollander 1970). Nonetheless, the war on poverty, though not removing destitution, did attack the consequent miseries of many people. It gave people programs; it broke their despair (Pilisuk and Pilisuk 1973).

The newer ideology looks upon these same programs as the very stuff that hurt the industrial investor: promising too much, costing too much. Too many benefits, it is argued, can kill the goose that lays the golden egg; those who are not investors should learn to expect less from their government, from their work, from their lives. The new philosophy extends to ideas about those who fall victim to the new industrial appetite and to public belt tightening. The emphasis is turned upon the self and upon individual and familial responsibility for our health, for our well-being. One is poor for reasons of inherent failure to achieve, ill because of failure to take precautions (Crawford 1977; Ryan 1976). This ideology blames the victim for the circumstances that have descended upon him or her (Estes 1982; Minkler 1983). According to this theme, we are free from collective responsibility for those who die of starvation, who are killed with weapons supplied by our dollars, or who succumb after breathing toxic air. England's Prime Minister Margaret Thatcher notes, "We have to get away from collectivism. Democracy is people taking care of themselves." Or is it?

RESOURCES AND POWER

There is surely greed in this world, but to so honor it is perhaps to lose the natural balance between self and others, between self and the universe. The individualistic value is culturally masculine and macho. It favors individual virtuosity and performance, but, more than that, it favors winning: winning in work, winning in relationships, winning even above the requirements of survival. This sense of competitive striving has been the flywheel of Western industrial development. David McClelland's imaginative study of the motivation for competitive achievement in earlier societies shows the clear relationship of such motives to indicators of economic expansion.

When motivation for achievement appeared in elementary schoolbooks, it was followed twenty-five years later by massive developments of hydroelectric power. The rise and fall of motivated pursuit of excellence has been followed by the rise and fall of patents for inventions. Themes of achievement in ballads and sonnets preceded the transport of coal into London to fuel the first machines of the Industrial Revolution. Even the fifth century B.C., the Golden Age of Greece was preceded by a rising achievement orientation, as expressed in the writings of the time (McClelland 1961). Mostly men led the charge to the more exacting enterprise, the larger edifice, the grander empire, showing the relation of competitive striving to masculine identity. If success could not always be found in the pursuit of excellence, it could sometimes be obtained in the pursuit of power, in the intense quest for status through the manipulation and control of others. A characteristic of successful managers in David McClelland's studies was a drive for power; whereas the less successful were distinguished by a greater concern for being liked (McClelland 1975; McClelland and Burnham 1976).

The power and influence of women have surely been limited. Individuals socialized to express their needs for power in less directly aggressive ways or to see specific tasks not as narrow rites of manhood but as parts of interpersonal activity, are often passed over. As man-made history proceeds from one isolated event to the next, new problems are created as old ones are attacked in stepwise fashion (Van Wagner and Swanson 1979). Often, a voice deep within tells us, men and women alike, that this method is not the way. Traditional female modes that we have chosen not to cherish hold answers that can lead us away from the excesses of power and domination.

Our theory is that there is a connection between the history of psychological development and the history of economic development. When children, particularly male children, are raised to be independent strivers for long-term achievements, they force upon themselves and many others the conditions needed for development. Such efforts have brought great technological advances, as well as more heart ailments and ulcers. The stress of this pursuit has encouraged some to replace the striving for individual excellence with institutionalization of what they have already achieved. The establishment of dynasties of power have followed—institutions that maintain the fruits of individuals' efforts, for their own ends, by manipulating people, the law, and police powers (Rudin 1965).

Motivation for power can be passed on in our modes of socializing our children. These power orientations necessarily create some who rule and many who are subservient. The values permit false advertising and embezzlement and condone robbery, homicide, and war. Historically, societies built on such exclusive domains of power have spawned segments of the population that refused to worship the success they had no power or desire to obtain. Early Christians evoked a faith alien to the powers of Rome, and the "flower children" of the 1960s turned against a society that could conduct a war in Vietnam (Roszak 1969). In both cases, we can identify a move to revive the buried concerns about affiliating with others.

Affiliation, or the emphasis upon supportive ties, is not a panacea for all social woes. The price of a social order leaning exclusively upon such values tends to be both a measure of conformity and a fear of contesting individual grievances, as was the case in the southern United States before the civil rights movement. Survival at that time was often predicated upon being of mutual assistance; however, it was also important to keep people in their places. The assertive demands of the civil rights movement were needed to correct a great imbalance. Now, however, the society as a whole is witnessing a different imbalance—an extraordinary centralization of power.

At this moment in history, we see the encapsulation of power in the form of multinational business firms and their links to energy, communication, the environment, institutions of health and education, and war. The enterprises insurmountably commandeer the resources needed to promote human growth at the local level. In the women's movement, in the human potential movement, and in the civil rights movement, we hear voices saying, "We, too, need resources to nourish ourselves and our contribution to the common good." To this request comes the reply: "Governmental austerity."

The move toward government austerity has not uniformly attacked all those who live on government handouts. California's Congressmember Ronald Dellums once remarked he had to be elected to Congress before he finally understood the difference between welfare and subsidy. "Subsidy," he noted, "is a larger check that goes to a smaller number of people."

Government spending for the tools of war has grown markedly. The money, a resource no longer available to the community in need, is abundantly spent in accumulating and deploying weapons of mass destruction. This action makes sense to no one but strategic gamesters. From the latter perspective, there is no reality other than the competitive one, and it must be acknowledged even in nuclear preparedness, where the stakes have grown so high that neither winning nor losing has meaning. Military competition extends as well to smaller arenas of conflict, to poorer nations in which the struggle for food, for health, and for literacy are dominant.

The competitive military game takes on special meanings in poorer nations, where there is little capital for development and where agriculture is for export and not for home consumption. Here, military expenditure protects local pockets of wealth and branches of transnational corporations. The game of special military forces has become one of winning, or coercing, the population away from efforts to redistribute their country's limited wealth. In many countries where such military operations ply their special craft, the families no longer own land on which to nurture their corn, their beans, their rice, their children or elders. Their infants die in great numbers while they work sporadically at indecent wages to produce a cash crop that is exported (Navarro 1982). If the special military forces succeed, some of these people may one day have steady jobs, working long hours for low pay, assembling computer chips in crowded factories. The factory moves from Massachusetts to South Korea or Brazil, and so go the resources needed to nurture American local communities.[1]

---

[1] See *Controlling Interest* (1978) for an excellent documentary film showing the connections between corporate policy, international poverty, and domestic unemployment.

A TRAUMATIC LOSS

What happens to a community suddenly deprived of ways of life and livelihood? The answer helps us understand the imbalance in the larger society in the matter of caring. Several studies of people in New England mill towns and in midwestern factory towns have documented the suffering that occurs following closure of a major industry. All point to a loss both in self-esteem and in the sense of community. Perhaps the most sensitive account of a sudden and more complete loss of community is preserved in Kai Erikson's account of Buffalo Creek, West Virginia.

On February 26, 1972, a makeshift mining company dam burst and 132 million gallons of muddy water and debris crashed through and demolished a narrow valley, home to a group of people since the days of their mountaineering ancestors. Before the disaster, this community had fierce pride in the domestic skills that allowed a most modest survival. Men made their own repairs, distrusted strangers, and accepted no favors that smelled of charity. Women married in their teens, raised a dozen children, cooked, spun, served, fed and slaughtered livestock, fetched water from the creek, milled corn, built fences, midwifed their neighbors, and nursed their ill. Life contained both the tradition and the resignation characteristic of long-standing poor communities everywhere. Kinship ties, however, were very strong, and the patterns of neighborhood caring provided a safety net to deal with emergencies. Perhaps it was this bond that brought people back to the area after excursions to find work in Ohio or Illinois failed to take root.

After the flood, the survivors of the once tightly knit community were crowded into thirteen trailor camps, where makeshift housing was the concern, not neighborhood and community. The individual traumas of death and loss proved to be more than a matter of transient adjustment. When individuals are beset by trauma, they withdraw into themselves. They feel numbed, frightened, vulnerable, and alone. The collective trauma has even deeper consequences—the realization that a supportive community no longer exists. The sense of "we" is gone, and the healing of individual trauma is retarded when the remaining social life has lost its cohesion. One Buffalo Creek man noted, "It used to be that I cared for all people, but anymore I just keep myself alive. That's the only thing I study about" (Erikson 1976:217). Another survivor said, "Each person in the family is a loner now, a person alone. Each of us is fighting his own battles. We just don't seem to care for each other anymore" (Erikson 1976:222).

The traumatic consequences of the flood in Buffalo Creek are not unlike reactions visible among many people whose trauma has been less sudden. The reaction is visible among the victims of war and among evacuees from urban neighborhoods demolished to accommodate a new condominium, shopping mall, or office building. It has been reported in the model camps into which the Indians of Guatamala have been moved, and on American Indian reservations one hundred years after they were transferred from the ways of life that gave meaning to their existence. The same numbness of spirit is seen in migrant worker camps or on skid rows and in the growing number of nursing homes. Now, the dull despair, a vague apprehension overpowers such lives where once the strength of long-term ties to others were the strands of a safety net, nourishing the roots of community, validating the purposes of each member.

Newer fears of dangerous contaminants in our most trusted foods, our waters, or our atmosphere have now come upon a people searching for communities of meaning that can interpret our dangerous realities or can provide collective support for facing them. To many, the danger of a nuclear war remains too raw a source of underlying apprehension to be permitted a conscious voice. For some, the search for new ties is too tenuous to permit attention to anything but a sharing of the most pleasurable escapes with the closest people. Here, we find a lure to retreat into the privacy of our protected family or into the intimacy of a warm support group. But Richard Sennett has noted that the horrors of nineteenth-century capitalism were followed by the privatization of the family as an effort to make the family warm and snug against the outside. The attempt, he observed, "constantly failed because the alien world organized personal relations within the house as much as impersonal relations without" (cited in Erikson 1976).

IN SEARCH OF A CURE

There is a great deal of encouragement now for self-help, mutual help, and aid from the private sector. Those who become part of the movement to reweave the interpersonal fabric of caring are part of a move to kindle a sense of local community and social responsibility in this fast-paced, modern society. Yet, in a larger sense, local love is not enough. The priorities of modern industry, by cutting the funds available for local services, produce more casualities, more illness, more broken homes, more people in need than all our mutual help groups can assist. Massive involvements in warfare in poor countries creates more homeless, more refugees, more hungry, more bereaved people than support groups can help. Our world has grown small, and the cries of the excluded pierce our circles of small concern.

If there is to be a coming together, it will depend upon our recognizing how much we need one another in the continuous fight for a more caring social order. This idea was well expressed by the Reverend Caldwell, interviewed in William Beardslee's study of the civil rights leaders of the

1960s who sustained their efforts long after the fanfare and the publicity had died down. Caldwell and his family continue to address the economic servitude of poor farm workers. He and his family live at the subsistence level, pooling their farm livelihood with a group of people. In his words,

> I didn't lose hope, although it was, and is a very troubled hope, and I kept a group. I think the group is the biggest thing we've got going for us, and I always told everybody else that. You can't make it in this kind of thing by yourself. You have to have something to reassure you. Not only that, you have to have something to keep you straight so you don't give in to the rewards of this society. The group is working amid all the failures as the source of comfort and support for us. I am encouraged by the hope that some day we can join our piece of land with other pieces of land owned by other people. Then we will finally have the strength and togetherness that cannot be broken. I have not given up the idea of changing this damnable monster that we have (Beardslee 1982).

Frank Reissman, editor of *Social Policy* and director of the National Self-Help Clearinghouse at City University of New York, has examined the paradox faced by a conservative political administration that favors self-help but reduces support for programs to assist local citizen initiative. The administration notes, with some displeasure, that self-help groups do not always follow the apolitical model of Alcoholics Anonymous, which avoids attention to the sale or advertising of alcoholic beverages or to alleviating social conditions that increase drinking. Their focus is restricted to the victims. Aid to the victims of alcoholism, of addiction, or of abuse, is an important first step to help people, but it is not sufficient to handle the causes of the problem. By contrast, the Association of Retarded Citizens, begun in the 1950s as a national support group of parents, has become an important interstate organization, successfully advocating legislation to provide free schooling for handicapped children in the least restrictive environments. Women's health groups, like the Sisterhood of Black Single Mothers, and such groups as the Gray Panthers and Centers for Independent Living, have become proponents of needed social action. Citizen Action, Reissman notes, has grown from local groups concerned about traffic or crime to a twenty-state organization of more than one million members. Its 1,500 full-time staff workers have been advocates for social security, safe toxic waste disposal, and lowered gas prices. In similar fashion, local women's groups of the 1970s evolved in the 1980s into a national woman's movement (Reissman 1984).

Hopefully, our efforts will grow and become mutually supportive in their advocacy. Hopefully, they will not lose sight of the small group origins of interpersonal caring that nourish people and fulfill them, even as they work to help others. Hopefully, the coalition will mirror in its political spectrum the vast spiritual and ecological bonds that underlie the interdependence of our species.

If there is a cure to be found for our aloneness, it will not only be in our coming together as individuals, but in our connecting into circles, tied to other circles of all people and of all cultures. In this connecting, the boundaries of individual circumstances, of city, and of nation will merge with the boundaries of nature, and we can become allied once again in a reverence for all our living earth. These connections appear to be part of the Tao of survival. They are not only paths of political commitment, but also a state of mind and of heart.

The transitions from "you or me" to "you and me," from "me" to "all of us," are profound. They will not, however, enable us to draw blood from a stone. The obstacles of aggressive competition, of troubled economies, and of radically differing ideologies will remain. It is our connections, perhaps only our connections, that will help us transcend such differences and focus upon an independent and loving world.

REFERENCES

Abelson, R. (1958). Modes of resolution of belief dilemmas. *Journal of Conflict Resolution, 3*, 343–352.

Aberle, D., and Stewart, O. C. (1957). *Navaho and Ute Peyotism: A chronological and distributional study.* Boulder: University of Colorado Press.

Abrams, H. S., Moore, G. L., and Westervelt, F. B. (1971). Suicidal behavior in chronic hemodialysis patients. *American Journal of Psychiatry, 127*(9), 1199–1204.

Abramson, L., Seligman, M., and Teasdale, J. (1978). Learned helplessness in humans: Critique and reformulation. *Journal of Abnormal Psychology, 87*, 49–74.

Ackerman, N. (1966). *Treating the troubled family in New York.* New York: Basic Books.

Ader, R., ed. (1980). *Psychoneuroimmunology.* New York: Academic Press.

Ainsworth, M. (1969). Object relations, dependency and attachment: A theoretical review of the infant-mother relationship. *Child Development, 40*, 969–1025.

Ainsworth, M. (1979). Infant-mother attachment. *American Psychologist, 34*(10), 932–937.

Ainsworth, M. (1982). Attachment: Retrospect and prospect. In C. Parkes and J. Stevenson-Hinde (eds.), *The place of attachment in human behavior,* 330. New York: Basic Books.

Albee, G. W., and Joffe, J. M. (1977). *Primary prevention of psychopathology: The issues.* Hanover: University Press of New England.

Allport, G. W. (1962). Psychological models for guidance. *Harvard Educational Review, 32*(4), 373–381.

Amoss, P., and Harrell, S., eds. (1981). *Other ways of growing old.* Stanford: Stanford University Press.

Anaya, R. (1972). *Bless me, Ultima.* Berkeley: Quinto Sol Publications.

Andrews, F., and Withey, S. (1976). *Social indicators of well-being: Americans' perception of life quality.* New York: Plenum.

Andrews, G., and Tennant, C. (1978a). Being upset and becoming ill: An appraisal of the relationship between life events and physical illness. *Medical Journal of Australia, 1,* 324–327.

Andrews, G., and Tennant, C. (1978b). Life event stress, social support, coping style and the risk of psychological impairment. *Journal of Nervous and Mental Disease, 166*(7), 605–612.

Antonovsky, A. (1967). Social class, life expectancy and overall mortality. *Milbank Memorial Fund, 45,* 31–73.

Antonovsky, A. (1973). The utility of the breakdown concept. *Social Science and Medicine, 7,* 605–612.

Antonovsky, A., ed. (1979). *Health, stress and coping: New perspectives in mental and physical well-being.* San Francisco: Jossey-Bass.

Antonucci, T. (1982). Attachment: A life-span concept. *Human Development, 19,* 135–142.

Argyle, M. (1969). *Social interaction.* New York: Atherton Press.

Argyris, C. (1964). *Intergrating the individual and the organization.* New York: Wiley.

Asher, S. R., and Gottman, J. M., eds. (1981). *The development of children's friendship.* Cambridge: Cambridge University Press.

Atkinson, J. (1971). *Developing an extended family program.* (Available from the Unitarian Church, 1535 Santa Barbara, San Francisco, Calif.).

Attneave, C. (1981). Interdependence unbound by time and space. Commencement Address, May 9, Saint Vincent College, Penn.

Axelrod, M. (1956). Urban structure and social participation. *American Sociological Review, 21,* 13–18.

Back, K. W. (1951). Influence through social communication. *Journal of Abnormal and Social Psychology, 45,* 9–23.

Back, K. W., and Taylor, R. C. (1976). Self-help groups: Tool or symbol? *Journal of Applied Behavioral Sciences, 12*(3), 295–309.

Bacter, J. (1975). Corticosteroids as immunosuppressive drugs. In E. A. Friedman (ed.), *First International Symposium on Corticosteroids,* Vol. 7, 1–55. New York: Grune and Stratton.

Baekeland, F., and Lundwall, L. (1975). Dropping out of treatment: A critical review. *Psychological Bulletin, 82,* 739–732.

Barnes, J. A. (1954). Class and committees in a Norwegian island parish. *Human Relations, 7*(1), 39–58.

Barnes, J. A. (1969). Networks and political processes. In J. Clyde Mitchell (ed.), *Social networks in urban situations: Analyses of personal relationships in Central African towns,* 51–76. Manchester: Manchester University Press.

Barnes, J. A. (1972). *Social networks.* Reading, Mass.: Addison-Wesley.

Barrera, M. (1980). A method for the assessment of social support networks in community survey research. *Connections, 3,* 8–13.

Barrera, M., Sandler, I. N., and Ramsay, T. B. (1981). Preliminary development of a scale of social support: Studies on college students. *American Journal of Community Psychology, 9,* 435–447.

Bartrop, R. W., Luckhurst, E., Lazarus, L., Kiloh, L. G., and Penny, R. (1977). Depressed lymphocyte function after bereavement. *The Lancet, 31,* 834–836.

Baruch, G., Barnett, R., and Rivers C. (1984). *Lifeprints: New patterns of love and work.* New York: McGraw-Hill.

Bauman, D. J., Cialdini, R., and Kenrick, D. (1981). Altruism vs. hedonism: Helping and self-gratification as equivalent responses. *Journal of Personality and Social Psychology, 40,* 1039–1046.

Baxler, E., and Hopper, K. (1982). The new mendicancy: Homeless in New York City. *American Journal of Orthopsychiatry, 52*(3), 393–408.

Beardslee, W. R. (1982). *The way out must lead in: Life histories of the civil rights movement.* Westport, Conn.: Hill.

Bell, R. R. (1981). *Worlds of friendship.* Beverly Hills, Calif.: Sage Publications.

Bell, W., and Boat, M. D. (1957). Urban neighborhoods and informal social relations. *American Journal of Sociology, 62,* 391–398.

Belle, D. E. (1982a). The impact of poverty: Social networks and supports. *Marriage and Family Review, 5*(4), 89–105.

Belle, D. E. (1982b). *Lives in stress: Women in depression.* Beverly Hills, Calif.: Sage.

Bengtson, V. L., Burton, L., & Manglin, D. (1981). Family support systems and attribution of responsibility: Contrasts among elderly Blacks, Mexican-Americans, and whites. Annual meeting of the Gerontological Society and the Canadian Association of Gerontology, Toronto, Canada, November 1.

Bengtson, V., and Dowd, J. J. (1980–1981) Sociological functionalism, exchange theory and life-cycle analysis: A call for more explicit theoretical bridges. *International Journal of Aging and Human Development, 12,* 55–73.

Bennis, W. G. (1966). *Changing organization: Essays on the development and evolution of human organizations.* New York: McGraw-Hill.

Bennis, W. G., Benne, K. D., and Chin, R. (1969). *The planning of change.* New York: Holt, Rinehart and Winston.

Berger, P., and Kellner, H. (1964). Marriage and the construction of reality. *Diogenes, 46,* 1–24.

Berkman, L. (1977). *Social networks: The health effects of social disconnection.* Unpublished doctoral dissertation. School of Public Health, University of California, Berkeley.

Berkman, L., and Syme, L. (1978). Social networks, host resistance and mortality: A nine year follow-up study of Alameda County residents. *American Journal of Epidemiology, 109*(2), 186–204.

Berkner, L. K. (1972). The stem family and the developmental cycle of the peasant household: An 18th century Austrian example. *American Historical Review, 77,* 398–418.

Besedovsky, H., and Sorkin, F. (1977). Network of immune-neuroendrocrine interactions. *Clinical and Experimental Immunology, 27,* 112.

Bettleheim, B. (1965). The problem of generations. In E. Erickson (ed.), *The challenge of youth,* 26–38. New York: Doubleday.

Bettleheim, B. (1967). *The empty fortress: Infantile autism and the birth of the self.* New York: Free Press.

Bianchi, E. C. (1982). *Aging as a spiritual journey.* New York: Crossroads Press.

Bigelow, B. J. (1977). Children's friendship expectations: A cognitive-developmental study. *Child Development, 48,* 246–253.

Billings, A. G., and Moos, R. H. (1981). The role of coping responses and social resources in attenuating the stress of life events. *Journal of Behavioral Medicine, 4*(2), 139–157.

Black, S., Humphrey, J. H., and Niven, J. S. (1963). Inhibition of mantoux reaction by direct suggestion under hypnosis. *British Medical Journal,* (June), 1649–1653.

Blau, P. (1967). The second individuation process of adolescence. In A. Freud (ed.), *The psychoanalytic study of the child,* Vol. 22, 218–236. New York: International University Press.

Blau, Z. (1981). *Aging in a changing society,* 2d ed. New York: Franklin Watts.

Bloom, B., Asher, S., and White, S. (1978). Marital disruption as a stressor: A review and analysis. *Psychological Bulletin, 85*(6), 867–894.

Blos, P. (1962). *On adolescence: An analytic interpretation.* New York: Free Press.

Bluestone, B., and Harrison, B. (1982). *The deindustrialization of America.* New York: Basic Books.

Bluestone, B., Harrison, B., and Baker, L. (1981). *Corporate flight: The causes and consequences of economic dislocation.* Washington, D.C.: Progressive Alliance.

Boardman, V. (1975). School absences, illness and family competence. In B. Caplan, and J. Cassel (eds.), *Family and health: An epidemiologic approach,* 63–89. Chapel Hill, N.C.: University of North Carolina, Institute for Research in Social Sciences.

Bonacich, P. (1967). Associational contiguity: A critique. *American Sociological Review, 32,* 813–815.

Borkman, T. S. (1976). Hemodialysis compliance: The relationship of staff estimates of patients' intelligence and understanding to compliance. *Social Science and Medicine, 10*(7–8), 385–392.

Boszormenyi-Nagy, I., and Framo, J., eds. (1965). *Intensive family therapy.* New York: Harper and Row.

Bott, E. (1957). *Family and social networks.* London: Tavistock Publications.

Boussevain, J., and Mitchell, J. C., eds. (1973). *Network analysis: Studies in human interaction.* The Hague: Morton.

Bowen, M. (1966). The use of family therapy in clinical practice. *Comparative Psychiatry, 5*(7), 365–374.

Bowlby, J. (1973). *Separation.* New York: Basic Books.

Bowlby, J. (1982). Attachment and loss: Retrospect and prospect. *American Journal of Orthopsychiatry, 52*(4), 664–678.

Brager, G., and Holloway, S. (1978). *Changing human services organizations.* New York: Free Press.

Brecher, E. M. (1972). *Licit and illicit drugs.* Boston: Little, Brown.

Brennan, T., and Auslander, N. (1979). *Adolescent loneliness: An exploratory study of social and psychological predisposition and theory.* Boulder, Colo.: Behavioral Research Institute.

Brett, J. M. (1980). The effects of job transfer on employees and their families. In C. L. Cooper and R. Payne (eds.), *Current concerns of occupational stress*, 99–136. New York: John Wiley and Sons.

Brim, J. A. (1974). Social network characteristics of avowed happiness. *Journal of Nervous and Mental Diseases, 58*, 432–439.

Broeck, E. T. (1974). The extended family center. *Children Today, 3*, 2–6.

Bronfenbrenner, U. (1970). *Two worlds of childhood: US and USSR*. New York: Russell Sage.

Bronfenbrenner, U. (1974). The origins of alienation. *Scientific American, 231*, 53–61.

Bronfenbrenner, U. (1977). Toward an experimental ecology of human development. *American Psychologist, 32*, 513–531.

Bronfenbrenner, U. (1979). Contexts of child rearing: Problems and prospects. *American Psychologist, 34*(10), 844–851.

Brown, E. R. (1979). *Rockefeller medicine men: Medicine and capitalism in America*. Berkeley: University of California Press.

Brown, G. W., Bhrolchaim, M. N., and Harris, T. (1975). Social class and psychiatric disturbance among women in an urban population. *Sociology, 9*, 225–254.

Brown, G. W., Davidson, S., and Harris, T. (1977). Psychiatric disorder in London and North Ulster. *Social Science and Medicine, 11*, 367–377.

Brown, G. W., and Harris, T. (1978). *Social origins of depression: A study of psychiatric disorder*. New York: Free Press.

Brown, G. W., Harris, T., and Copeland, J. R. (1977). Depression and loss. *British Journal of Psychiatry, 30*, 1–18.

Bryant, B. K. (In press). The neighborhood walk: Developmental perspectives on sources of support in middle childhood. *Monographs of the Society for Research in Child Development, 50*(3, Serial 210).

Bunch, J. (1972). Recent bereavement in relation to suicide. *Journal of Psychosomatic Research, 16*, 361–366.

Burgher, P. L. (1981). *Social network characteristics, social support and compliance to chronic hemodialysis regimen*. Unpublished doctoral dissertation. University of Windsor, Ont.

Burke, R. J., and Weir, T. (1978). Maternal employment status: Social support effects on adolescents' well-being. *Psychological Reports, 42*, 1159–1170.

Butler, R. N. (1975). *Why survive? Being old in America*. New York: Harper and Row.

Butler, R. N. (1982). The life review: An interpretation of reminiscence in the aged. *Psychiatry, 26*, 65–76.

Cameron, N. A. (1963). *Personality development and psychopathology: A dynamic approach*. Boston: Houghton Mifflin.

Candy, S. (1978). A comparative analysis of friendship functions in men and women through the adult years. Paper presented at the Family and Sex Role Seminar, Ann Arbor, Mich.

Cantor, M. H. (1979). Neighbors and friends: An overlooked resource in the informal support system. *Research on Aging, 1*, 434–463.

Caplan, G. (1962). Types of mental health consultation. Paper delivered at the annual meeting of the American Orthopsychiatric Association, 22 March, Los Angeles.

Caplan, G. (1974). *Support systems and community mental health: Lectures on concept development.* New York: Behavioral Publications.

Carkhoff, R., and Truax, C. (1967). *Toward effective counseling and psychotherapy: Training and practice.* Chicago: Aldine Publishing Co.

Cassel, J. (1976). The contribution of the social environment to host resistance. *American Journal of Epidemiology, 104,* 107–123.

Cassel, J., and Tyroler, H. A. (1961). Epidemiological studies of culture change: Health status and recency of industrialization. *Archives of Environmental Health, 3,* 25–33.

Chan, K. B. (1977). Individual differences in reactions to stress and their personality and situational detriments: Some implications for community mental health. *Social Science and Medicine, 11,* 80–103.

Chen, E., and Cobb, S. (1960). Family structure in relation to health and disease. *Journal of Chronic Disease, 12,* 544–567.

Chess, S., and Thomas, A. (1982). Infant bonding and reality. *American Journal of Orthopsychiatry, 52*(2), 213–222.

Chiriboga, D. (1977). Life event weighing system: A comparative analysis. *Journal of Psychosomatic Medicine, 21,* 415–422.

Chiriboga, D. and Lowenthal, M. F. (1975). Response to stress. In M. F. Lowenthal, and D. Chiriboga (eds.), *Four stages of life,* 146–162. San Francisco: Jossey-Bass.

Clark, K. B. (1980). Empathy: A neglected topic in psychological research. *American Psychologist, 35,* 188.

Cobb, S. (1976). Social support as a moderator of life stress. *Psychosomatic Medicine, 38*(5), 300–313.

Cobb, S., and Erbe, C. (1978). Social support for the cancer patient. *Forum on Medicine,* (November), 24–29.

Cobb, S., Kasl, S. V., French, J., and Norstebo, G. (1969). The intrafamilial transmission of rhematoid arthritis: Why do wives with rheumatoid arthritis have husbands with peptic ulcer? *Journal of Chronic Disease, 22,* 279–293.

Cochran, M. M., and Brassard, J. A. (1979). Child development and personal social networks. *Child Development, 50*(3), 601–616.

Coe, C. L., Mendoza, S. P., Smotherman, W. P., and Levine, S. (1978). Mother-infant attachment in the squirrel monkey: Adrenal response to separation. *Behavioral Biology, 22,* 256–263.

Coelho, G., Hamburg, D., and Adams, J., eds. (1974). *Coping and adaptation.* New York: Basic Books.

Cohen, C. I., and Sokolovsky, J. (1980). Social engagement vs. isolation: The case of the aged in SRO hotels. *The Gerontologist, 20,* 36–44.

Cohen, F., and Lazarus, R. (1973). Active coping processes, coping dispositions, and recovery from surgery. *Journal of Psychosomatic Medicine, 35,* 375–389.

Cohen, S., and McKay, G. (1982). Social support stress and the buffering hypothesis. In A. Baum, S. E. Taylor, and J. E. Singer (eds.), *Handbook of psychology and health,* 253–267. Hillsdale, N.J.: L. Erlbaum Associates.

Cohen, S., and Wills, T. A. (1984). *Stress, social support and the buffering hypothesis.* Carnegie-Mellon Institute, Pittsburgh. Unpublished manuscript.

Collins, A., and Pancoast, D. (1976). *Natural helping systems*. Washington, DC: National Association of Social Workers.

Colvin, B. K., Greenwood, B. B., and Hansen, S. (1981). A look at today's families. *Tips and Topics in Home Economics, 21*(3), 4–9.

Conger, J. J. (1981). Freedom and commitment: Families, youth, and social change. *American Psychologist, 36*(12), 1475–1484.

Conner, K. A., Power, E. A., and Bultena, G. L. (1979). Social interaction and life satisfaction: An empirical assessment of late-life patterns. *Journal of Gerontology, 34*, 116–121.

Controlling interest: The world of the multinational corporation. (1978). San Francisco: California Newsreel. Film.

Cooley, C. H. (1902). *Human nature and the social order*. New York: Scribner and Sons.

Cooper, D. G. (1970). *The death of the family*. New York: Vintage.

Coser, R. L. (1975). The complexity of roles as a seedbed of individual autonomy. In L. A. Coser (ed.), *The idea of social structure: Papers in honor of Robert K. Merton*, 237–263. New York: Harcourt Brace and Jovanovich.

Cowan, C. P., and Cowan, P. A. (1985). Becoming a father, individual and marital aspects of father involvement. In P. Berman, and F. Pederson (eds.), *Fathers' transition to parenthood*, 180–195. Hillsdale, N.J.: Lawrence Erlbaum Associates.

Crawford, R. (1977). You are dangerous to your health: The ideology and process of victim-blaming. *International Journal of Health Services, 7*(40), 663–679.

Crockenberg, S. (1981). Infant irritability, mother responsiveness and social support influences on the security of infant-mother attachment. *Child Development, 52*, 857–865.

Crouch, S. (1973). *Steinbeck country*. Palo Alto, CA: American West Publishers.

Csikszentmihalyi, M., and Larson, R. (1984). *Being adolescent: Conflict and growth in the teenage years*. New York: Basic Books.

Curley, L. (1982). Indian elders: A failure of aging policy. *Generations, 28*–52.

Cutrona, C. E. (1982). Transition to college: Loneliness and the process of social adjustment. In L. A. Peplau, and D. Perlman (eds.), *Loneliness: A sourcebook of current theory, research and therapy*, 29–130. New York: John Wiley and Sons.

David, D., Greico, M., and Cushman, P. (1970). Adrenal gluco-corticoids after twenty years: A review of their clinically relevant consequences. *Journal of Chronic Disease, 22*, 647.

Davis, J. D. (1976). Self-disclosure in an acquaintance exercise: Responsibility for level of intimacy. *Journal of Personality and Social Psychology, 33*, 787–792.

Davis, M. S. (1968). Variations in patients' compliance with doctor's advice: An empirical analysis of patterns of communication. *American Journal of Public Health, 58*, 274–276.

Dean, A., and Lin, N. (1977). The stress buffering role of social support. *Journal of Nervous and Mental Disease, 165*, 403–417.

Dean, A., Lin, N., and Ensel, W. M. (1981). The epidemiological signficance of social support systems in depression. In R. G. Simmons (ed.), *Research in community mental health*, Vol. 2, 77–110. Greenwich, Conn.: UAI Press.

Delbeque, A. L., Van de Ven, A. H., and Gustafson, D. H. (1975). *Group techniques for program planning: A guide to nominal group and Delphi processes.* Glenview, Ill.: Scott Foresman.

Demos, J. (1970). *A little commonwealth.* New York: Oxford University Press.

DeNour, A. K., and Czaczkes, J. W. (1972). Personality factors in chronic hemodialysis patients causing non-compliance with medical regimen. *Psychosomatic Medicine, 34*(4), 333–334.

Depner, C., Wethington, E., and Korshavn, S. (1982). How social support works: Issues in testing theory. Paper presented at the American Psychological Association Meetings, August, Washington, D.C.

Diamant, L., and Windholz, G. (1981). Loneliness in college students: Some theoretical, empirical and therapeutic considerations. *Journal of College Student Personnel,* (November), 515–522.

Dickens, W. J., and Perlman, D. (1981). Friendship over the life-cycle. In S. Duck and R. Gilmour (eds.), *Personal relationships: Developing personal relationships,* 91–122. New York: Academic Press.

Dixon, M. R. (1983). Measuring the social context of the family. University of California, Davis. Unpublished manuscript.

Dohrenwend, B. S., and Dohrenwend, B. P. (1974). *Stressful life events: Their nature and effects.* New York: Wiley.

Domhoff, G. W. (1967). *Who rules America?* Englewood Cliffs, NJ: Prentice-Hall.

Duarand, E. (1984). *Archtypal consultation: A service delivery model for Native Americans.* Geneva: Peter Lang.

DuBois, C. (1974). The gratuitous act: An introduction to the comparative study of friendship patterns. In E. Leyton (ed.), *The compact: Selected dimensions of friendship,* 15–32. Newfoundland, Canada: University of Newfoundland Press.

Duncan, G. J. (1984). *Years of poverty, years of plenty.* Ann Arbor: University of Michigan Press.

Durkheim, E. (1951). *Suicide: A study in sociology.* New York: Free Press.

Duwe, A. K., Fitch, M., and Ostwald, R. (1981). Effects of dietary cholesterol on antibody dependent phygocytosis and cell-mediated lysis in guinea pigs. *Journal of Nutrition, 111,* 1672–1680.

Edwards, R. (1979). *Contested terrain. The transformation of the workplace in the 20th century.* New York: Basic Books.

Egar, R., and Sarkissan, W. (In press). Reviewing the Australian suburban dream: A critique to neighborhood change with the family support scheme. In M. Satir, M. T. Mednick, D. Izraeli, and J. Bernard (eds.), *Women's worlds: From the new scholarship.* New York: Praeger.

Eisenberg, L. (1973). Poverty, professionalism, and politics. In M. Pilisuk, and P. Pilisuk (eds.), *How we lost the war on poverty,* 313–322. New Brunswick: Dutton.

Engel, G. (1977). Emotional stress and sudden death. *Psychology Today, 11,* 114–115.

England, M. J. (1980). Children's services in Massachusetts ". . . and the first shall be last." *American Journal of Orthopsychiatry, 50*(2), 205–210.

Epstein, J. H. (1974). *Divorced in America.* New York: Penguin.

Epstein, J. H., and Warren, R. H. (1974). The role of behavioral science in organizations. In G. Henderson (ed.), *Human relations: From theory to practice,* 211–220. Norman: University of Oklahoma Press.

Erikson, E. H. (1964). Human strength and the cycle of generations. In E. Erikson (ed.), *Insight and responsibility*, 109–134. New York: Norton.

Erikson, E. H. (1968). *Identity: Youth and crisis*. New York: Norton.

Erikson, E. H. (1974). *Dimensions of a new identity*. New York: Norton.

Erikson, E. H. (1978). *Adulthood*. New York: Norton.

Erikson, E. H. (1980a). *Identity and life cycle*. New York: Norton.

Erikson, E. H. (1980b). Themes of adulthood in the Freud-Jung correspondence. In N. J. Smelser and E. H. Erikson (eds.), *Themes of work and love in adulthood*, 43–47. Cambridge, Mass.: Harvard University Press.

Erikson, E. H. (1982). *The life cycle completed: A review*. New York: Norton.

Erikson, K. T. (1976). *Everything in its path: Destruction of community in the Buffalo Creek flood*. New York: Simon and Schuster.

Escalona, S. K. (1982). Growing up with the threat of nuclear war: Some indirect effects on personality development. *American Journal of Orthopsychiatry, 52*(4), 600–607.

Estes, C. L. (1982). Austerity and aging in the US, 1980 and beyond. *International Journal of Health Services, 12*(4), 573–584.

Estes, C. L. (1983). Have courage: Aging in an era of new federalism. *Western Gerontological Society Connection*, (May-June), 5–10.

Evans, R. I., and Erikson, E. H. (1981). *Dialogue with Erikson*. New York: Praeger.

Fairbairn, W. (1952). Theoretical and experimental aspects of psychoanalysis. *British Journal of Medical Psychology, 25*, 122–127.

Fairchild, H. H., and Tucker, M. B. (1982). Black residential mobility: Trends and characteristics. *Journal of Social Issues, 38*(3), 51–74.

Fairchilds, C. (1978). Female sexual attitudes and the rise of illegitimacy: A case study. *Journal of Interdisciplinary History, 7*, 627–667.

Fallcreek, S. (1980). Health promotions for older persons. Paper presented at the 10th Annual Meeting of the American Public Health Association, 20 October, Detroit.

Farber, B. A., ed. (1983). *Stress and burnout in the human service professions*. New York: Pergaman.

Fengler, A. P., and Goodrich, N. (1979). Wives of elderly disabled men: The hidden patients. *The Gerontologist, 19*(2), 175–183.

Ferber, A., Mendelsohn, M., and Napier, A. (1972). *The book of family therapy*. New York: Science House.

Festinger, L. (1957). *A theory of cognitive dissonance*. Evanston, IL: Row Peterson.

Festinger, L., Schachter, S., and Back, K. (1950). *Social pressures in informal groups*. New York: Harper.

Fischer, C. S. (1982). *To dwell among friends: Personal networks in town and city*. Chicago: University of Chicago Press.

Fischer, C. S., Jackson, R. M., Steuve, C. A., Gerson, K., Jones, L. M., and Baldassare, M. (1977). *Networks and places*. New York: Free Press.

Flacks, R. (1971). *Youth and social change*. Chicago: Markham.

Folkman, S., and Lazarus, R. S. (1980). Coping in an adequately functioning middle-aged population. *Journal of Health and Social Behavior, 21*, 219–239.

Forrest, B. T. (1984). Life span, culture and psychosocial factors. *Academic Psychology Bulletin, 6*, 127–139.

Frank, J. (1979). Mental health in a fragmented society. *American Journal of Ortho-psychiatry, 49*(3), 397–408.

Freud, S. (1930). *Civilization and its discontents.* New York: Cape and Smith.

Freudenberg, N. A. (1981–1982). Self help within a medical institution: Its potential and limits. *Quarterly Journal of Community Health Education, 2*(3), 215–223.

Fried, M. (1982). Endemic stress: The psychology of resignation and the politics of scarcity. *American Journal of Orthopsychiatry, 52*(1), 4–19.

Friedenberg, E. Z. (1971). *The anti-American generation.* Chicago: Aldine.

Fries, J. F., and Crapo, L. M. (1981). *Vitality and aging.* San Francisco: W. H. Freeman.

Froland, C., Brodsky, G., Olson, M., and Stewart, L. (1979). Social support and social adjustment: Implications for mental health professionals. *Community Mental Health Journal, 15*(2), 82–93.

Froland, C., Pancoast, D. L., Chapman, N. J., and Kimboko, P. J. (1979). Professional partnerships with informal helpers: Emerging forms. Paper presented at the American Psychological Association Annual Meeting, September, New York.

Fromm, E. (1947). *Man for himself.* New York: Holt, Rinehart and Winston.

Frye, M. (1983). *The politics of reality: Essays in feminist theory.* New York: Crossing Press.

Garbarino, J. (1976). A preliminary study of some ecological correlates of child abuse: The impact of socioeconomic stress on mothers. *Child Development, 47,* 178–185.

Gartner, A., and Riessman, F. (1977). *Self-help in the human services.* San Francisco: Jossey-Bass.

Gartner, A., and Riessman, F. (1984). *The self-help revolution.* New York: Human Sciences Press.

Gatti, F., and Coleman, C. (1976). Community network therapy: An approach to aiding families with troubled children. *American Journal of Orthopsychiatry, 46*(4), 608–617.

Gilligan, C. (1981). Moral development in the college years. In A. Chickering (ed.), *The modern American college,* 139–157. San Francisco: Jossey-Bass.

Gilligan, C. (1982). *In a different voice.* Cambridge, Mass.: Harvard University Press.

Gitlin, T., and Hollander, N. (1970). *Uptown: Poor whites in Chicago.* New York: Harper and Row.

Goffman, E. (1963). *Stigma.* Harmondsworth: Penguin.

Goldman, W. J. (1980). The psychology and economics of scarcity in human services. *American Journal of Orthopsychiatry, 50*(2), 198–199.

Golembiewski, R. T., and Blumberg, A. (1970). *Sensitivity training and the laboratory approach.* Itasca, Ill.: Peacock Publishing.

Goode, W. J. (1964). *The family.* Englewood Cliffs, N.J.: Prentice-Hall.

Goode, W. J., Herrera, H., Delvecchio, A., Goode, M., and Cooper, J. (1982). Reflexivity and countertransference in a psychiatric cultural consultation clinic. *Culture, Medicine and Psychiatry, 6,* 281–303.

Gordus, J. (1981). *Plant closings and economic dislocation.* Cleveland: Upjohn Institute.

Gore, S. (1978). The effects of social support in moderating the health consequences of unemployment. *Journal of Health and Social Behavior, 19,* 157–165.

Goswick, R. A., and Jones, W. H. (1981). Loneliness, self-concept, and adjustment. *Journal of Psychology, 107,* 237–240.

Gottlieb, B. (1978). The development and application of a classification scheme of informal helping behaviors. *Canadian Journal of Behavioral Science, 10,* 105–115.

Gottlieb, B. (1981). *Social networks and social support.* Beverly Hills, Calif.: Sage.

Gottlieb, B. (1983). Opportunity for collaboration with informal support systems. In S. Cooper and W. E. Hodges (eds.), *The mental health consultation field,* 181–204. New York: Human Science Press.

Gottleib, B., and Todd, D. M. (1979). Characterizing and promoting social support in natural settings. In R. F. Munoz (ed.), *Social and psychological research in community settings,* 183–231. San Francisco: Jossey-Bass.

Gottschalk, P., and Danzieger, S. (1984). Macroeconomic conditions, income transfer and the trends in poverty. In D. L. Bawden (ed.), *The social contract revisited,* 185–219. Washington, D.C.: Urban Institute Press.

Graham, M. A., and Millard, A. V. (1983). Breast feeding and family economics in rural Mexico. Paper presented at the annual meeting of the American Anthropological Association, 16–20 November, Chicago.

Granovetter, M. S. (1973). The strength of weak ties. *American Journal of Sociology, 78,* 1360–1372.

Green, B. (1978). The politics of psychoactive drug use in old age. *The Gerontologist, 18*(6), 525–530.

Greenburg, J. (1980). Beneficial altruism. *Journal of Economic Theory, 22,* 12–22.

Gross, W. (1973). Stressor effects of initial bacterial exposure of chickens as determined by subsequent challenge exposure. *American Journal of Veterinary Research, 35*(9), 1225–1228.

Gutmann, D. (1981). Observations on culture and mental health in later life. In J. E. Birren and R. B. Sloane (eds.), *Handbook of mental health and aging,* 429–447. Englewood Cliffs, N.J.: Prentice-Hall.

Guttentag, M., and Secord, P. (1983). *Too many women.* Beverly Hills, Calif.: Sage.

Haan, N., ed. (1977). *Coping and defending.* New York: Academic Press.

Haber, C. (1983). *Beyond sixty-five.* Cambridge: Cambridge University Press.

Habif, V., and Lahey, B. (1980). Assessment of the life stress-depression relationship: The use of social support as a moderator variable. *Journal of Behavioral Assessment, 2,* 167–173.

Hafer, M. A., Wolff, T. C., Freedman, S. B. and Mason, J. W. (1972). A psychoendocrine study of bereavement, Part 2: Observation on the process of mourning in relation to adrenocordical function. *Psychosomatic Medicine, 34,* 492–504.

Hagen, W. T. (1971). *American Indians.* Chicago: University of Chicago Press.

Haley, J., and Hoffman, L. (1968). *Techniques of family therapy.* New York: Basic Books.

Hallowell, A. I. (1954) Aggression in Salteaux society. In C. Kluckholm, H. A. Murray, and D. M. Schneider (eds.), *Personality in nature, society and culture,* 260–275. New York: Knopf.

Hamill, P. (1973). *The gift.* New York: Random House.

Hammer, M. (1963). Influence of small social networks as factors on mental hospital admissions. *Human Organization, 22,* 243–251.

Hammer, M. (1972). A therapy for loneliness. *Voices, 8,* 24–29.

Hammer, M. (1981). Social supports, social networks, and schizophrenia. *Schizophrenia Bulletin, 7,* 45–57.

Harary, F., Norman, R., and Cartwright, D. (1965). *Structural models: An introduction to the theory of directed graphs.* New York: John Wiley and Sons.

Harburg, E., Erfurt, J. C., and Chape, C. (1973). Socio-ecological stressor areas and black-white blood pressure. *Journal of Chronic Disease, 26,* 595–611.

Harlow, H., and Harlow, M. (1962). Social deprivation in monkeys. *Scientific American, 207*(5), 136.

Harris, J. (1964). *The nature of cultural things.* New York: Random House.

Harris, M. (1968). *The rise of anthropological theory: A history of theories of culture.* New York: Thomas Cromwell.

Hartsock, N. C. M. (1983). *Money, sex and power: Toward a feminist historical materialism.* New York: Congerman.

Hawkes, G. R. (1978). Who will rear our children? *The Family Coordinator,* (April), 159–166.

Hayden, D. (1984). *Redesigning the American dream: The future of housing, work and family.* New York: Norton.

Haynes, R. B. (1979). Determinants of compliance: The disease and the mechanics of treatment. In R. B. Haynes, D. W. Taylor, and D. L. Sackett (eds.), *Compliance in health care,* 49–62. Baltimore: Johns Hopkins University Press.

Haynes, R. B., and Sackett, D. L. (1974). Compliance with therapeutic regimens. Annotated bibliography. Department of Clinical Epidemiology and Biostatistics, McMaster University Medical Centre, Hamilton, Ont.

Heider, F. (1946). Attitudes and cognitive organization. *Journal of Psychology, 21,* 107–112.

Heller, K. (1978). The effects of social support: Prevention and treatment implications. In A. P. Goldstein and F. H. Kanfer (eds.), *Maximizing treatment gains: Transfer enhancement in psychotherapy,* 353–382. New York: Academic Press.

Henderson, S. (1977). The social network, support and neurosis: The function of attachment in adult life. *British Journal of Psychiatry, 131,* 185–191.

Henderson, S., Byrne, D., Duncan-Jones, P., Adcock, S., Scott, R., and Steele, G. (1978). Social bonds in the epidemiology of neurosis: A preliminary communication. *British Journal of Psychiatry, 132,* 463–466.

Hennessy, J. W., King, M. G., McClure, T. A., and Levine, S. (1977). Uncertainty, as defined by the contingency between environmental events and the adrenocortical response of the rate to electric shock. *Journal of Comparative Physiological Psychology, 91,* 1447–1468.

Henry, J. (1980). Loneliness and vulnerability. In J. Harton, J. R. Audy, and Y. A. Cohen (eds.), *Anatomy of loneliness,* 95–110. New York: International Universities Press.

Henry, J., and Cassel, J. (1976). Psychosocial factors in essential hypertension: Recent epidemiological and animal experimental evidence. *American Journal of Epidemiology, 104*(1), 1–8.

Hetherington, E. M., Cox, M., and Cox, R. (1977). The aftermath of divorce. In J. H. Stephens, Jr. and M. Mathews (eds.), *Mother-child father-child relations*, 149–176. Washington, D.C.: National Association for the Education of Young Children.

Hinkle, L. (1974). The effect of exposure to culture change, social change and changes in interpersonal relationships on health. In B. P. Dohrenwend and B. S. Dohrenwend (eds.), *Stressful life events: Their nature and effects*, 9–44. New York: John Wiley Interscience.

Hirsch, B. J. (1979). Psychological dimensions of social networks: A multi-method analysis. *American Journal of Community Psychology, 7*, 263–277.

Hirsch, B. J. (1980). Natural support systems and coping with major life changes. *American Journal of Community Psychology, 8*, 159–172.

Hofer, M. A., Wolff, C. T., Freeman, S. B., and Mason, J. W. (1972). A psychoendocrine study of bereavement, Part 2. Observation on the process of mourning in relation to adrenocortical function. *Psychosomatic Medicine, 38*, 344–357.

Hoffman, L. W. (1974). Effects on the child. In L. W. Hoffman and F. Nye (eds.), *Working mothers*, 32–62. San Francisco: Josey-Bass.

Holmes, D. (1983). *Other cultures, elder years.* Minneapolis, MN: Burgess.

Holmes, T. (1956). Multidisciplinary studies of tuberculosis. In P. Sparer (ed.), *Personality, stress, and tuberculosis*, 65–152. New York: International Universities Press.

Holmes, T., and Masuda, M. (1974). Life change and illness susceptibility. In B. S. Dohrenwend and B. P. Dohrenwend (eds.), *Stressful life events: Their nature and effects*, 45–72. New York: John Wiley Interscience.

Holmes, T., and Rahe, R. (1967). The social adjustment rating scale. *Journal of Psychosomatic Research, 11*, 213–218.

Holstein, C. (1976). Development of moral judgment: A longitudinal study of males and females. *Child Development, 47*, 51–61.

Homans, G. C. (1961). *Social behavior: Its elementary forms.* New York: Harcourt, Brace, and World.

Homans, G. C. (1962). *Sentiments and activities: Essays in social science.* New York: Free Press.

Horney, K. (1937). *The neurotic personality of our time.* New York: W. W. Norton.

Horowitz, M., Schaefer, C., Hiroto, D., Wilner, N., and Levin, B. (1977). Life events questionnaires for measuring presumptive stress. *Psychosomatic Medicine, 39*(6), 413–431.

Howell, M. (1975). *Helping ourselves.* Boston: Beacon Press.

Hutchison, S. (1984). Personal communication. University of California, Davis, CA.

Huxley, A. L. (1946). *Brave new world.* New York: Harper and Row.

Jaffe, D. T. (1979). The holistic family. *New Realities, 2*(1), 3–6.

James, W. (1950). *Principles of psychology.* New York: Dover. (Originally published in 1890.)

Janis, I. (1958). *Psychological stress.* New York: Academic Press.

Janis, I., and Rodin, J. (1979). Attribution control and decision-making: Social psychology and health care. In G. Stone, F. Cohen, and W. Adler (eds.), *Health psychology*, 487–522. San Francisco: Jossey-Bass.

Jeffrey, K. (1972). The family as utopian retreat from the city: The nineteenth-century contribution. In S. TeSelle (ed.), *The family, communes, and utopian societies*, 21–41. New York: Harper and Row.

Jephcott, P., Seear, N., and Smith, J. H. (1962). *Married women working*. London: Allen and Unwin.

Jones, W. H. (1981). Loneliness and social contact. *Journal of Social Psychology, 113,* 295–296.

Jones, W. H. (1982). Loneliness and social behavior. In L. A. Peplau and D. Perlman (eds), *Loneliness: A sourcebook of current theory, research and therapy*, 238–254. New York: John Wiley and Sons.

Jones, W. H., Freeman, J. E., and Goswick, R. A. (1981). The persistence of loneliness: Self and other determinants. *Journal of Personality, 49,* 27–48.

Jones, W. H., Hobbs, S. A., and Hockenbury, D. (1982). Loneliness and social skills deficits. *Journal of Personality and Social Psychology, 42,* 682–689.

Jordanova, L. J. (1981). The history of the family. In B. Antonis, V. Binney, P. Brown, J. Caplan, K. Granwood, and L. Jordanova (eds.), *Women in society: Interdisciplinary studies*, 41–54. London: Virago Press.

Jung, C. G. (1956) *Symbols of transformation*, Vol. 5. (Bollinger Series 20). New York: Pantheon.

Jung, C. G. (1964). *Man and his symbols*. New York: Doubleday.

Jung, C. G. (1966). *Modern man in search of a soul*. New York: Brace, Harcourt and World.

Kagan, J. (1979). Family experience and the child's development. *American Psychologist, 34*(10), 886–891.

Kahn, R. (1978). Aging and social support. Talk presented at the 1978 Annual Meeting of the American Association for the Advancement of Science. Washington, D.C., February 13.

Kahn, R., and Antonucci, T. (1980). Convoys over the life course: Attachment, roles and social support. In P. Baltes and O. Brim (eds.), *Life-span development and behavior*, 253–286. New York: Academic Press.

Kalish, R., and Knudtson, F. W. (1976). Attachment vs. disengagement: A life span conceptualization. *Human Development, 19,* 171–181.

Katz, H. A., and Bender, E. L. (1976a). Self-help groups in Western society: History and prospects. *Journal of Applied Behavioral Sciences, 12*(3), 265–282.

Katz, H. A., and Bender, E. L. (1976b). *The strength in us: Self-help groups in the modern world*. New York: Franklin-Watts.

Katz, J. L., Weiner, H., Gallagher, T. F., and Hellma, L. (1970). Stress, distress and ego defenses. *Archives of General Psychiatry, 23,* 131–142.

Keesing, R. M. (1975). *Kin groups and social structure*. New York: Holt, Rinehart and Winston.

Kelley, H. H. (1979). *Personal relationships: Their structure and processes*. New York: Erlbaum Assoc.

Keniston, K. (1965). *The uncommitted: Alienated youth in American society*. New York: Harcourt Brace and World.

Keniston, K. (1977). *All our children: The American family under pressure*. New York: Harcourt Brace and World.

Keyes, R. (1973). *We the lonely people.* New York: Harper and Row.

Kiecolt-Glaser, J. K., Garner, W., Speicher, C. E., Penn, G. M., Holliday, J., and Glaser, R. (1984). Psychosocial modifiers of immunocompetence in medical students. *Psychosomatic Medicine, 46*(1), 7–14.

Kiecolt-Glaser, J. K., Ricker, D., George, J., Messick, G., Speicher, C. E., Garner, W., and Glaser, R. (1984). Urinary cortisol levels, cellular immunocompetency, and loneliness in psychiatric inpatients. *Psychosomatic Medicine, 46*(1), 15–23.

Kiecolt-Glaser, J. K., Speicher, C. E., Holliday, J. E., and Glaser, R. (1984). Stress and the transformation of lymphocytes by Epstein-Barr virus. *Journal of Behavioral Medicine, 7*(1), 1–12.

Kieth, J. (1982). *Old people as people.* Boston: Little, Brown and Co.

Killworth, P. D., and Bernard, H. R. (1976). Informant accuracy in social network analysis. *Human Organization, 35*(3), 269–286.

Kimmel, M. (1974). *Adulthood and aging.* New York: John Wiley and Sons.

Kitson, G. C., Moir, R., and Mason, P. F. (1982). Family social supports in crises: The special case of divorce. *American Journal of Orthopsychiatry, 52*(1), 101–105.

Kivett, V. R. (1985). Consanguinity and kin level: Their relative importance to the helping network of older adults. *Journal of Gerontology, 40*(2), 228–234.

Klaus, M., and Kennel, A. (1977). *Maternal infant bonding.* St. Louis: Mosby.

Kleinberg, N. L. (1981). Fair allocations and equal incomes. *Journal of Economic Theory, 23*(2), 189–200.

Kleinberg, O. (1979). *Student values and politics: A cross-cultural comparison.* New York: Free Press.

Kleinman, A. (1980). *Patients and healers in the context of culture.* Berkeley: University of California Press.

Klemke, E. D., ed. (1981). *The meaning of life.* New York: Oxford University Press.

Klumburg, S. J. (1980). The systematic study of urban women. In M. Cantor, and B. Laury (eds.), *Class, sex and the woman worker,* 20–42. Westport, Conn.: Greenwood.

Kohlberg, L. (1969). Stage and sequence: The cognitive-developmental approach to socialization. In D. A. Goslin (ed.), *Handbook of socialization theory and research,* 347–480. Chicago: Rand McNally.

Kohlberg, L., and Kramer, R. (1969). Continuities and discontinuities in child and adult moral development. *Human Development, 12,* 93–120.

Kosa, J., Antonovsky, A., and Zola, L. (1969). *Poverty and health: A sociological analysis.* Cambridge, Mass.: Harvard University Press.

Kotler, M. (1969). *Neighborhood government: The local foundations of political life.* New York: Bobbs-Merrill Co.

Kraus, A., and Lilienfeld, A. (1959). Some epidemiological aspects of the high mortality rate in the young widowed group. *Journal of Chronic Disease, 10,* 207–217.

Kulys, R., and Tobin, S. S. (1980). Older people and their "responsible others." *Social Work, 25*(2), 138–145.

Kuster-Ginsberg, C. (1970). Family by choice: A "Gross Familie." Talk delivered to Offentlilches forum mit der Evangelischen Studentengemeinde, November, Dusseldorf, Germany.

Laing, R. D. (1967). *The politics of experience.* New York: Ballantine.

Lamb, M. E. (In press). The changing roles of fathers. In M. E. Lamb (ed.)., *The father's role: Applied perspectives.* New York: John Wiley and Sons.

Lambert, B. G., Rothschild, B. F., Allard, R., and Green, L. B. (1972). *Adolescence: Transition from childhood to maturity.* Monterey, Calif.: Brooks, Cole.

Langer, E. J., and Rodin, J. (1976). The effects of choice and enhanced personal responsibility for the aged: A field experiment in an institutional setting. *Journal of Personal Social Psychology, 34,* 191–198.

Langer, S. (1942). *Philosophy in a new key: A study in the symbolism of reason, rite and art.* Cambridge, Mass.: Harvard University Press.

Langway, L., Lord, M., Reese, M., Ellis, P., Maitland, T., Gelman, E., and Whitman, L. (1980). The superwoman squeeze. *Newsweek,* May 14, pp. 72–91.

LaRocco, J. W., and Jones, A. P. (1978). Co-worker and leader support as moderators of stress-strain relationships in work situations. *Journal of Applied Psychology, 63,* 629–634.

Lasch, C. (1978). *The culture of narcissism: American life in an age of diminishing expectations.* New York: Norton.

Laslett, P. (1964). The world we have lost. In E. Josephson and M. Josephson (eds.), *Man alone: Alienation in modern society,* 86–93. New York: Dell.

Lawrence, A., and Chown, P. (1985). *Plant closings and technological change: A guide for union negotiations.* Institute of Industrial Relations, Berkeley: University of California Press.

Lazarus, R. S. (1966). *Psychological stress and the coping process.* New York: McGraw-Hill.

Lazarus, R. S. (1974). Cognitive and coping processes in emotion. In B. Weiner (ed.), *Cognitive views of human motivation,* 21–32. New York: Academic Press.

Lazarus, R. S. (1975a). A cognitively oriented psychologist looks at biofeedback. *American Psychologist, 30,* 553–561.

Lazarus, R. S. (1975b). The self-regulation of emotion. In L. Levi (ed.), *Emotions— Their parameters and measurement,* 47–68. New York: Ravel Publishing.

Lazarus, R. S. (1981). The stress and coping paradigm. In C. Eisdorfer, D. Cohen, A. Kleinman, and P. Maxim (eds.), *Models for Clinical Psychpathology,* 177–214. New York: Spectrum.

Lazarus, R. S., Opton, E. M., Nomikos, M. S., and Rankin, N. O. (1965). The principle of short-circuiting of threat: Further evidence. *Journal of Personality, 33,* 622–635.

Lears, J. (1981). *No place of grace.* New York: Pantheon.

Lebeaux, E. (1971). Life on AFDC budgets of despair. In R. Perrucci and M. Pilisuk (eds.), *The triple revolution emerging: Social problems in depth,* 508–516. Boston: Little, Brown.

Lee, G. R. (1980). Kinship in the 70s: A decade review of research and theory. *Journal of Marriage and the Family, 42,* 923–934.

Leinhardt, S. (1977). *Social networks: A developing paradigm.* New York: Academic Press.

Lerner, R. M., and Ryff, R. (1978). Implementation of the life span view of human development: The sample case of attachment. In P. B. Baltes (ed.), *Life span development and behavior*, Vol. 1, 2–45. New York: Academic Press.

Lever, J. (1976). Sex differences in the games children play. *Social Problems, 23*, 478–487.

Levinson, D. J. (1978). *The seasons of a man's life*. New York: Alfred Knopf.

Levy, L. H. (1976). Self-help groups: Types and psychological processes. *Journal of Applied Behavioral Sciences, 12*(3), 310–322.

Lewin, K. (1946). Behavior and development as a function of the total situation. In L. Carmichael (ed.), *Manual of child psychology*, 791–844. New York: John Wiley and Sons.

Lewis, O. (1966a). The culture of poverty. *Scientific American, 215*(4), 19–25.

Lewis, O. (1966b). *La vida*. New York: Random House.

Liddell, H. (1950). Some specific factors that modify tolerance for environmental stress. *Proceedings of Academic Research in Nervous and Mental Disorders, 29*, 155–159.

Liem, R., and Liem, J. (1978). Social class and mental illness reconsidered: The role of economic stress and social support. *Journal of Health and Social Behavior, 19*, 139–156.

Lifton, R. J. (1982). Beyond psychic numbing: A call to awareness. *American Journal of Orthopsychiatry, 52*(4), 619–729.

Lin, N., Ensel, W., Simeone, R., and Kuo, W. (1979). Social support, stressful life events and illness. A model and an empirical test. *Journal of Health and Social Behavior, 20*, 108–119.

Linton, R. (1936). *The study of man*. New York: Prentice-Hall.

Lipowski, Z. (1977). Psychosomatic medicine in the seventies: An overview. *American Journal of Psychiatry, 134*, 233–244.

Litwak, E. (1960a). Geographic mobility and extended family cohesion. *American Sociological Review, 25*, 385–394.

Litwak, E. (1960b). Occupational mobility and extended family cohesion. *American Sociological Review, 25*, 9–21.

Litwak, E., and Szelenyi, I. (1969). Primary group structures and their functions: Kin, neighbors, and friends. *American Sociological Review, 34*, 465–474.

Lofland, L. (1982). Loss and human connection: An exploration into the nature of the social bond. In W. Eckes, and F. S. Knowles (eds.), *Personality roles and social behavior*, 219–242. New York: Springer-Verlag.

London, P. (1978). The intimacy gap. *Psychology Today*, (May), 40–42.

Long, K., Rosenfeld, S., Krauss, G., and Holman, H. (1980). Outcomes of arthritis community education: A randomized controlled study. Paper presented at the 108th annual meeting of the American Public Health Association, 23 October, Detroit.

Longfellow, C. M. (1979). The role of support in moderating the effects of stress and depression. Paper presented at the Society for Research in Child Development, August, San Francisco.

Lopata, H. Z. (1973). *Widowhood in an American city*. Cambridge, MA: Schenkman Publishing Co.

Lowenthal, M. F., and Haven, C. (1968). Interaction and adaptation: Intimacy as a critical variable. In B. Neugarten (ed.), *Middle age and aging,* 390–400. Chicago: University Press.

Lowenthal, M. F., Thurnher, M., and Chiriboga, D. (1975). *Four stages of life.* San Francisco: Jossey-Bass.

Lyman, S. (1970). *The Asian in the West.* Reno: University of Nevada.

Macarov, D. (1980). *Work and welfare: The wholly alliance.* Beverly Hills, Calif.: Sage.

Maccoby, E., and Jacklin, C. (1974). *The psychology of sex differences.* Stanford: Stanford University Press.

Mack, J. E. (1982). The perception of US-Soviet intentions and other psychological dimensions of the nuclear arms race. *American Journal of Orthopsychiatry, 52*(4), 590–599.

Macy, J. R. (1981). Despair work. *Evolutionary Blues.* Arcata, Calif.

Macy, J. R. (1982). *Despair and personal power in the nuclear age.* Philadelphia: New Society Publications.

Marcuse, H. (1968). *One dimensional man.* Boston: Beacon Press.

Maris, P. (1974). *Loss and change.* New York: Pantheon.

Marmot, M., and Syme, S. (1976). Acculturation and coronary heart disease. *American Journal of Epidemiology, 104*(3), 225–247.

Marty, M. E., and Vaux, K. L., eds. (1982). *Health medicine and the faith traditions.* Philadelphia: Fordress Press.

Maslach, C., and Jackson, S. E. (1984). Burnout in organizational settings. In S. Oskamp (ed.), *Applied social psychology manual,* Vol. VI, 133–153. Beverly Hills, Calif.: Sage.

Maslow, A. (1943). Dynamics of personality organization. *Psychological Review, 50,* 514–558.

Mauss, M. (1954). *The gift: Forms and functions of exchange in archaic societies.* London: Cohen and West.

Mayeroff, M. (1971). *On caring.* New York: Harper and Row.

McAdoo, J. L. (1979). Well-being and fear of crime among black elderly. In D. E. Gelfand and A. J. Kutzick (eds.), *Ethnicity and aging: Theory, research and policy,* 28–44. New York: Springer Publishing Co.

McClelland, D. (1961). *The achieving society.* Princeton, N.J.: Van Nostrand.

McClelland, D. (1975). *Power: The inner experience.* New York: Irvington.

McClelland, D., and Burnham, D. (1976). Power: The great motivator. *Harvard Business Review, 54*(2), 100–110.

McIntosh, M. (1979). The welfare state and the needs of the dependent family. In S. Burman (ed.), *Fit work for women,* 153–172. Sydney: Australian National University Press.

Mead, G. H. (1934). *Mind, self and society from the standpoint of a social behaviorist.* Chicago: University of Chicago Press.

Mead, M. (1932). *The changing culture of an Indian tribe.* New York: Columbia University Press.

Mead, M. (1953). *Cultural patterns and technological change: A manual.* Paris: UNESCO.

Mead, M. (1961). *Cooperation and competition among primitive peoples.* Boston: Beacon Press.

Mead, M. (1972) *Blackberry winter: My early years.* New York: Morrow.

Mead, M. (1978). *Culture and commitment: The new relationship between the generations in the 1970s.* New York: Columbia University Press.

Mead, M., and Wolfenstein, M. (1955). *Childhood in contemporary cultures.* Chicago: University of Chicago Press.

Mechanic, D. (1976). Stress, illness, and illness behavior. *Journal of Human Stress, 2*(2), 2–6.

Mechanic, D. (1977). Illness behavior, social adaptation, and the management of illness: A comparison of educational and medical models. *Journal of Nervous Mental Disease, 165,* 79–87.

Meyers, J., Lindenthal, J., and Pepper, M. (1975). Life events, social integration psychiatric symptomatology. *Journal of Health and Social Behavior, 16,* 421–429.

Miley, W. M. (1980). Self awareness and altruism. *Psychological Research, 30,* 3–8.

Miller, A. R. (1977). Interstate migrants in the United States: Some social-economic differences by type of move. *Demography, 4,* 1–17.

Miller, C. (1976). Societal change and public health: A rediscovery. *American Journal of Public Health, 66,* 54–60.

Miller, J. B. (1976). *Toward a new psychology of women.* Boston: Beacon Press.

Miller, R. S., and Lefcourt, H. M. (1982). The assessment of social intimacy. *Journal of Personality Assessment, 46*(5), 514–518.

Miller, R. S., and Lefcourt, H. M. (1983). Social intimacy: An important moderator of stressful life events. *American Journal of Community Psychology, 11,* 127–139.

Minkler, M. (1981). Application of social support theory to education: Implications for work with the elderly. *Health Education Quarterly, 8*(2), 147–165.

Minkler, M. (1982). Social support and health: Programmatic implications. *Patient Education Newsletter,* (June), 32–33.

Minkler, M. (1983). Blaming the aged victim: The politics of scapegoating in times of fiscal conservatism. *International Journal of Health Services, 13*(1), 155–168.

Minkler, M., and Estes, C. L. (1984). *Readings in the political economy of aging.* Farmingdale, NY: Policy, Politics, Health and Medicine Series, Baywood.

Minuchin, S., and Montalvo, B. (1967). *Families of the slums: An exploration of their structure and treatment.* New York: Basic Books.

Minuchin, S., Rosmon, B., and Baker, L. (1978). *Psychosomatic families: Anorexia nervosa in context.* Cambridge, Mass.: Harvard University Press.

Mishler, E., and Scotch, N. (1963). Sociocultural factors in the epidemiology of schizophrenia: A review. *Psychiatry, 26,* 315–351.

Mitchell, J. (1972). *Women's estate.* New York: Pantheon.

Mitchell, R. E., and Trickett, E. J. (1980). Social networks as mediators of social support: An analysis of the effects and determinants of social networks. *Community Mental Health Journal, 16,* 27–44.

Moos, R. (1979). Social-ecological perspectives on health. In C. G. C. Stone, F. Cohen, and N. E. Adler (eds.), *Health psychology: A Handbook,* 523–548. San Francisco: Jossey-Bass.

Moos, R., and Billings, A. (1982). Conceptualizing and measuring coping resources and processes. In L. Goldberger and S. Breznitz (eds.), *Handbook of stress: Theoretical and clinical aspects,* 212–230. New York: MacMillan.

Mori, S. O. (1982). Kimochi: Good feelings for Japanese-American elders. *Generations, 3,* (Spring), 46–52.

Morris, M. G. (1968). Psychological miscarriage: An end to mother love. In R. Perrucci and M. Pilisuk (eds.), *The triple revolution: Social problems in depth*, 241–251. Boston: Little and Brown.

Moustakas, C. E. (1972). *Loneliness and love*. Englewood Cliffs, N.J.: Prentice-Hall.

Moustakas, C. E. (1975). *Portraits of loneliness and love*. Englewood Cliffs, N.J.: Prentice-Hall.

Mueller, D. P. (1980). Social networks: A promising direction for research on the relationships of the social environment to psychiatric disorder. *Social Science and Medicine, 14a*, 147–161.

Mueller, D. P., Edwards, D. W., and Yarvis, R. M. (1977). Stressful life events and psychiatric symptomalogy: Change or undesirability? *Journal of Health and Social Behavior, 18*, 307–317.

Mumford, E., Schlesinger, H., and Glass, G. (1982). The effects of psychological intervention on recovery from surgery and heart attacks: An analysis of the literature. *American Journal of Public Health, 72*(2), 141–151.

Mumford, L. (1967) *The myth of the machine*. London: Sacker and Warburg.

Murdock, G. P. (1949). *Social structure*. New York: Macmillan.

Murray, H. A. (1939). *Explorations in personality*. New York: Oxford University Press.

Murray, H. A. (1981). *Endeavors in psychology: Selections from the personology of Henry A. Murray*. New York: Harper and Row.

Mussen, P. H., Conger, J. J., and Kagan, J. (1969). *Child development and personality*. New York: Harper and Row.

Myasaka, T., and Kavata, C. (1979). The neighborhood organization: An important factor in organizing a community for health education. *International Journal of Health Education, 22*(2), 78–91.

National Indian Council on Aging. (1981a). American Indian elderly: A national profile. Research Report. Albuquerque, N. Mex.: National Indian Council on Aging.

National Indian Council on Aging. (1981b). Indian elderly and entitlement programs: An accessing demonstration project. Research Report. Albuquerque, N. Mex.: National Indian Council on Aging.

Navarro, V. (1982). The crisis of the international capitalist order and its implications for the welfare state. *International Journal of Health Services, 12*(2), 169–180.

Nesser, W. B., Tyroler, H. A., and Cassel, J. C. (1971). Social disorganization and stroke mortality in the black population of North Carolina. *American Journal of Epidemiology, 93*, 166–175.

Newcomb, T. (1961). *The acquaintance process*. New York: Holt, Rinehart and Winston.

Newcomber, D. (1972). The family of the future? A kinship model. *Social Action, 39*(4), 24–30.

Nisbet, R. A. (1977). *The social bond: An introduction to the study of society*, 2d ed. New York: Knopf.

Norbeck, J. S. (1981). Social support: A model for clinical research and application. *Advances in Nursing Science, 3*(4), 43–59.

Nordstrom, M. (In press). Sex differences and the experiences of the physical environments. In M. P. Safir, M. T. Mednick, D. Izraeli, and J. Bernard (eds.), *Women's worlds: From the new scholarship*. New York: Praeger.

Nowr, A. K., and Czaczkes, J. W. (1972). Personality factors in chronic hemodialysis patients causing noncompliance with medical regimen. *Psychosomatic Medicine, 34*(4), 333–344.

Nuckolls, K., Cassell, J., and Kaplan, B. (1972). Psychosocial assets, life crisis and the prognosis of pregnancy. *American Journal of Epidemiology, 95,* 431–441.

Oakley, A. (1974). *The sociology of housework*. London: M. Robertson.

Orford, J. (1975). Alcoholism and marriage: The argument against specialism. *Journal of Studies in Alcohol, 36*(11), 872–891.

Orme-Johnson, D. (1973). Autonomic stability and transcendental meditation. *Psychosomatic Medicine, 35,* 31–349.

Osgood, C. E., and Tannenbaum, P. H. (1955). The principle of congruity in the prediction of attitude change. *Psychological Review, 62,* 42–55.

Ovington, M. W. (1969). *Half a man: The status of the negro in New York*. New York: Schocken Books. (Original published in 1911).

Packard, V. (1972). *A nation of strangers*. New York: McKay Publishers.

Parke, R. D., and Collmer, C. W. (1975). Child abuse: An interdisciplinary analysis. In E. M. Hetherington (ed.), *Review of Child Development Research*, Vol. 5, 518–590. Chicago: University of Chicago Press.

Parkes, C. M. (1972). *Bereavement: Studies of grief in adult life*. New York: International Universities Press.

Parkes, C. M., Benjamin, B., and Fitzgerald, R. G. (1969). Broken heart: A study of increased mortality among widowers. *British Medical Journal, 1,* 740–743.

Parlee, M. B. (1979). The friendship bond. *Psychology Today, 11*(3), 43–54.

Pattison, E. M. (1977). A theoretical empirical base for social systems therapy. In E. Foulks, R. Wintrob, J. Westermeyer, and A. Favazza (eds.), *Current perspectives in cultural psychiatry,* 217–254. New York: Spectrum.

Pattison, E. M., DeFrancisco, D., Wood, P., Frazier, H., and Crowder, J. A. (1975). Psychosocial kinship model for family therapy. *American Journal of Psychiatry, 132,* 1246–1251.

Pearlin, L., and Schooler, C. (1978). The structure of coping. *Journal of Health and Social Behavior, 19,* 2–21.

Pelletier, K. (1977). *Mind as healer, mind as slayer: A holistic approach to preventing stress disorders*. New York: Delta.

Peplau, L. A., and Perlman, D., eds. (1982). *Loneliness: A sourcebook of current theory, research and therapy*. New York: John Wiley and Sons.

Pepper, B., and Ryglewicz, H. (1982). Testimony for the neglected: The mentally ill in the post deinstitutionalized age. *American Journal of Orthopsychiatry, 52*(3), 388–392.

Perlman, D., and Peplau, L. A. (1983). Loneliness research: Implications for interventions. Paper presented for a workshop on Preventive Interventions to Reduce the Harmful Consequences of Loneliness, sponsored by the Office of Prevention, National Institute of Mental Health, 21 August, Santa Barbara, Calif.

Perrucci, R., and Pilisuk, M. (1970). Leaders and ruling elites: The interorganizational bases of community power. *American Sociological Review, 35,* 1040–1057.

Phillips, R. (1975). Role of lifestyle and dietary habits in risk of cancer among Seventh-day Adventists. *Cancer Research, 34,* 3513–3522.

Pilisuk, M. (1962). Cognitive balance and self relevant attitudes. *Journal of Abnormal and Social Psychology, 65,* 95–103.

Pilisuk, M. (1968a). Cognitive balance, primary groups and the patient-therapist relationship. *Behavioral Sciences, 8,* 137–145.

Pilisuk, M. (1968b). Depth, centrality and tolerance in cognitive consistency. In R. Abelson, E. Aronson, W. McGuire, T., Newcomb, M. Rosenberg, and P. Tannenbaum (eds.), *Theories of cognitive consistency: A sourcebook,* 693–700. Chicago: Rand McNally, and Co.

Pilisuk, M. (1980). The future of human services without funding. *American Journal of Orthopsychiatry, 50*(2), 200–204.

Pilisuk, M. (1982). Delivery of social support: The social innoculation. *American Journal of Orthopsychiatry, 52*(1), 20–31.

Pilisuk, M., Chandler, S., and D'Onofrio, C. (1982–1983). Reweaving the social fabric: Antecedents of social support facilitation. *International Quarterly of Community Health Education, 3*(1), 45–66.

Pilisuk, M., and Froland, C. (1978). Kinship, social networks, social support and health. *Social Science and Medicine, 12B,* 273–280.

Pilisuk, M., and Minkler, M. (1980). Supportive networks: Life ties for the elderly. *Journal of Social Issues, 16*(2), 93–116.

Pilisuk, M., and Minkler, M. (1985). Supportive ties: Economic and political considerations. *Social Policy, 15*(3), 6–11.

Pilisuk, M., Montgomery, M. B., and Parks, S. H. (1985). Health status and supportive relationships among older adults. Unpublished manuscript. University of California, Davis.

Pilisuk, M., and Ober, L. (1976). Torture and genocide as a public health problem. *American Journal of Orthopsychiatry, 46*(3), 388–392.

Pilisuk, M., and Parks, S. H. (1980). Structural dimensions of social support groups. *The Journal of Psychology, 106,* 157–177.

Pilisuk, M., and Parks, S. H. (1981). The place of network analysis in the study of supportive social associations. *Basic and Applied Social Psychology, 2*(2), 121–135.

Pilisuk, M., and Parks, S. H. (1982). Friendship can be good for your health: Part II. *Human Relations, 7*(9), 1–3.

Pilisuk, M., and Parks, S. H. (1983). Social support and family stress. In H. McCubbin, M. B. Sussman, and J. M. Patterson (eds.), *Social stress and the family,* 137–157. New York: Hayworth Press.

Pilisuk, M., Parks, S. H., Kelly, J., and Turner, E. (1982). The helping network approach: Community promotion of mental health. *Journal of Primary Prevention, 3*(2), 116–132.

Pilisuk, M., and Pilisuk, P. E. (1973). *How we lost the war on poverty.* New York: Dutton.

Pines, A. (1983). On burnout and the buffering effects of social support. In B. A. Farber (ed.), *Stress and burnout in the human service professions*, 155–174. Elmsford: Pergamon.

Pittman, D., and Snyder, C. (1962). *Society, culture and drinking patterns*. New York: John Wiley and Sons.

Piven, F. T, and Cloward, R. A. (1971). *Regulating the poor: The functions of public welfare*. New York: Pantheon.

Piven, F. T., and Cloward, R. A. (1977). *Poor people's movements: Why they succeed and how they fail*. New York: Pantheon.

Porritt, D. (1979). Social support in crisis: Quantity or quality? *Social Science and Medicine, 13*, 715–721.

Poster, M. (1978). *Critical theory of the family*. London: Pluto Press.

Poulshock, S. W., Deimling, G. T., and Silverston, B. (1982). A survey of families caring for elderly: Focus upon stress effects. Paper presented to at the American Orthopsychiatric Association, April, San Francisco.

Pratt, L. (1976). *Family structure and effective health behavior*. Boston: Houghton-Mifflin.

Pringle, B. (1974). Family clusters as a means of reducing isolation among urbanites. *The Family Coordinator, 23*(2), 175–180.

Rahe, R. H., Mahan, J. L., and Arthur, R. J. (1970). Prediction of near-future health change from subjects' preceding life changes. *Journal of Psychosomatic Research, 14*, 401–406.

Rank, O. (1932). *Art and artist*. New York: Alfred Knopf.

Raphael, B. (1977). Preventive intervention with the recently bereaved. *Archives of General Psychiatry, 34*, 1450–1457.

Redfield, J. R., and Stone, A. (1979). Individual viewpoints of stressful life events. *Journal of Consultation and Clinical Psychology, 47*, 147–154.

Regan, M., and Roland, H. (In press). Rearranging family and career priorities: Professional women and men of the 80's. *Journal of Marriage and the Family*.

Reina, R. E. (1962). Two patterns of friendship in a Guatemalan community. In B. H. Stoodley (ed.), *Society and self*, 215–222. New York: The Free Press.

Reinharz, S. (1983). Consulting to the alternative work setting: A suggested strategy for community psychology. *Journal of Community Psychology, 11*, 199–212.

Reisman, J. M. (1979). *Anatomy of friendship*. New York: Irvington Publishers.

Reiss, I. L. (1971). *The family system in America*. New York: Holt, Rinehart and Winston.

Reuveni, U. (1975). Network intervention with a family in crisis. *Family Process, 14*(2), 193–203.

Revenson, T. A., Wollman, C. A., and Felton, B. J. (1983). Social supports as stress buffers for adult cancer patients. *Psychosomatic Medicine, 40*(4), 321–332.

Riesman, D., Glazer, N., and Denney, R. (1969). *The lonely crowd: A study of changing American character*. New Haven: Yale University Press.

Riessman, F. (1984). Self-helpers. *The Nation*, (1 June) p. 561.

Riley, D. (1981). Left critiques of the family. In B. Antonis, V. Binney, P. Brown, J.

Caplan, K. Granwood, and L. Jordanova (eds.), *Women in society: Interdisciplinary essays*, 75–92. London: Virago Press.

Roberto, K. A., and Scott, J. P. (1984–1985). Friendship among older women. *International Journal of Aging and Human Development, 19*(1), 1–10.

Robertson, J. (1952). *A two-year-old goes to the hospital.* New York: New York University Film Library. Film.

Rodin, J. (1978). Somatopsychics and attribution. *Personality and Social Psychology Bulletin, 4,* 531–540.

Rodin, J. (1980). Personal control through the life course. Paper presented at the American Psychology Association Meeting on Implications of the Life-span Perspective for Social Psychology, Montreal, P.Q., Canada.

Rook, K. S. (1983). Interventions for loneliness: A review and analysis. Paper presented for a workshop on Preventive Interventions to Reduce the Harmful Consequences of Loneliness, sponsored by the Department of Psychology, UCLA, in cooperation with the Office of Prevention, National Institute of Mental Health, Santa Barbara.

Rosenberg, S. G. (1971). Patient education leads to better care for heart patients. *HSMHA Health Reports, 86*(9), 793–802.

Rosenmayr, L., and Köckeis, E. (1970). Family relations of the elderly. In C. C. Harris (ed.), *Readings in kinship in urban society,* 367–386. New York: Pergamon Press.

Rosenmayr, L. (1977). The family—A source of hope for the elderly? In E. Shanas and M. B. Sussman (eds.), *Family, bureaucracy and the elderly,* 132–157. Durham, N.C.: Duke University Press.

Rosenmayr, L. (1980). Achievements, doubts and prospects of the sociology of aging. *Human Development, 23,* 60.

Rosow, I. (1974). *Socialization to old age.* Berkeley: University of California Press.

Ross, C. E., Mirowsky, J., and Ulbrich, P. (1983). Distress and the traditional female role: A comparison of Mexicans and Anglos. *American Journal of Sociology, 89*(3), 670–683.

Ross, C. K. (1981). Factors influencing successful preventive health education. *Health Education Quarterly, 8*(3), 187–208.

Ross, R. J. S. (1982). Citizens, experts and the limits of local control. Paper presented at the Society for the Study of Social Problems Annual Meeting, September, San Francisco.

Rossi, P. H., and Shlay, A. B. (1982). Residential mobility and public policy issues: "Why Families Move" revisited. *Journal of Social Issues, 38*(3), 21–34.

Roszak, T. (1969). *The making of a counter culture: Reflections on technocratic society and its youthful opposition.* Garden City, N.J.: Doubleday.

Roszak, T. (1972). *Where the wasteland ends: Politics and transcendence in postindustrial society.* Garden City, N.Y.: Doubleday.

Rothman, J. (1970). Three models of community organization practice. In F. M. Cox, J. L. Erlich, J. Rothman, and J. E. Tropman (eds.), *Strategies of community organization,* 20–37. Itasca, Ill.: Peacock Publishing.

Rubenstein, C. M., Shaver, P., and Peplau, L. A. (1979). Loneliness. *Human Nature, 2,* 59–65.

Rubin, Z. (1980). *Children's friendships.* Cambridge, Mass.: Harvard University Press.

Rudin, S. (1965). The personal price of national glory. *TransAction, 2*(6), 4–9.

Russell, D., Peplau, L. A., and Ferguson, M. (1978). Developing a measure of loneliness. *Journal of Personality Assessment, 42*(3), 290–294.

Ryan, W. (1976). *Blaming the victim.* New York: Random House.

Sachar, E. J. (1975). Neuroendocrine abnormalities in depressive illness. In E. K. Sachar (ed.), *Topics in psychoendocrinology,* 135–156. New York: Grune and Stratton.

Sadler, W. J., and Johnson, T. (1980). From loneliness to anomie. In J. Hartog, J. R. Audy, and Y. A. Cohen (eds.), *The anatomy of loneliness,* 34–64. New York: International Universities Press.

Sagan, C. (1983). Planet earth: A universal anomaly. *Gray Panther Network,* (January-February), 4–7.

Sahlins, M. D. (1967). *Social stratification in Polynesia.* Seattle: University of Washington Press.

Sahlins, M.D. (1972). *Stone age economics.* Chicago: Aldine.

Salzinger, L. L. (1982). The ties that bind: The effect of clustering on dyadic relationships. *Social Networks, 4,* 117–145.

Sandler, I. N, and Lakey, B. (1982). Locus of control as a stress moderator: The role of control perceptions and social support. *American Journal of Community Psychology, 10,* 65–80.

Sandner, D. (1979). *Navajo symbols of healing,* New York: Harcourt, Brace Jovanovich.

Sarason, I. G., Johnson, J. H., and Siegel, J. M. (1978). Assessing the impact of life changes: Development of the life experience survey. *Journal of Consultation and Clinical Psychology, 46,* 932–946.

Sarason, S. B. (1974). *The psychological sense of community.* San Francisco: Jossey-Bass.

Sarason, S. B. (1976). Community psychology: Networks and Mr. Everyman. *American Psychologist,* (May), 317–328.

Satir, V. (1967). *Conjoint family therapy.* Palo Alto: Science and Behavior Books.

Schachter, S. (1951). Deviation, rejection, and communication. *Journal of Abnormal and Social Psychology, 46,* 190–207.

Schell, J. (1982). *The fate of the earth.* New York: Knopf.

Schiller, H. I. (1969). *Mass communications of the American empire.* Boston: Beacon Press.

Schoen, D. A. (1977). Network-related intervention. Paper prepared for the Network Development Staff, National Institute of Education, March, Washington, D.C.

Schoenberg, B. M. (1980). *Bereavement counseling.* Westport, Conn.: Greenwood Press.

Schultz, R., and Hanusa, B. (1978). Long-term effects of control and predictability enhancing interventions: Findings and ethical issues. *Journal of Personality and Social Psychology, 38*(11), 1194–1201.

Schwartz, M. D. (1977). An information and discussion program for women after a mastectomy. *Archives Surgery, 112,* 276–281.

Schwebel, M. (1982). Effects of the nuclear war threat on children and teenagers:

Implications for professionals. *American Journal of Orthopsychiatry, 52*(4), 608–618.

Seligman, M. E. (1975). *Helplessness: On depression, development and death.* San Francisco: W. H. Freeman.

Sena-Rivera, J. (1980). *La Familia Hispana* as a natural support system: Strategies for prevention in mental health. In R. Valle and W. Vega (eds.), *Hispanic natural support systems: Mental health promotion perspectives,* 75–82. Sacramento: State of California, Department of Mental Health.

Sennett, R. (1970a). The brutality of modern families. *Transaction, 7*(11), 29–37.

Sennett, R. (1970b). *The uses of disorder: Personal identity and city life.* New York: Vintage.

Sennett, R. (1976). Destructive Gemeinschaft. *Partisan Review, 43*(3), 341–361.

Severy, J. (1974). Reply to Wispe and rejoinder. *Journal of Social Issues, 30*(2), 189–201.

Shanas, E. (1979). The family as a social support system in old age. *The Gerontologist, 19,* 169–174.

Sharf, L. S. (1980). *To work and to wed: Female unemployment and feminism and the Great Depression.* Westport, Conn.: Greenwood Press.

Shorter, E. (1975). *The making of the modern family.* New York: Basic Books.

Shulman, N. (1975). Life-cycle variation in patterns of close relationships. *Journal of Marriage and the Family,* (November), 813–827.

Shumaker, S. A., and Stokols, D. (1982). Residential mobility as a social issue and research topic. *Journal of Social Issues, 38*(3), 1–20.

Signell, K. A., and Scott, P. A. (1971). Mental health consultation: An interaction model. *Community Mental Health Journal, 7*(4), 27–32.

Silver, G. (1974). *Family medical care: A design for health maintenance.* Cambridge, Mass.: Ballinger Publishing Co.

Silverman, P. R. (1984). *Natural help groups: A guide for mental health workers.* Washington, D.C.: National Institute of Mental Health.

Simmel, G. (1950). *The sociology of Georg Simmel.* (K. H. Wolf, trans.) New York: Free Press.

Skinner, B. F. (1953). *Science and human behavior.* New York: Macmillan.

Skjei, F. W. (1981). *The male ordeal: Role crisis in a changing world.* New York: Pulman.

Skolnick, A. (1972). *The intimate environment: Exploring marriage and the family.* Boston: Little, Brown.

Skolnick, A. (1973). *Exploring marriage and the family.* Boston: Little, Brown.

Skolnick, A., and Skolnick, J. H. (1971). *Family in transition.* New York: Holt, Rinehart and Winston.

Slater, P. (1976). *Pursuit of loneliness: American culture at the breaking point.* Boston: Beacon Press.

Smith, M. S., and Bissell, J. S. (1970). Report analysis: The impact of Head Start. *Harvard Educational Review, 40,* 51–105.

Sokolovsky, J., Cohen, C., Berger, D., and Geiger, J. (1978). Personal networks of ex-mental patients in a Manhattan SRO hotel. *Human Organization, 37,* 5–15.

Solomon, G. F., and Amkraut, A. A. (1983). Emotions, immunity, and disease. In L. Temoshok, C. Van Dyke, and L. Zegans (eds.), *Emotions in health and illness:*

Theoretical and research foundations, 167–186. New York: Academic Press.

Speck, F. (1933). Ethical attributes of the Labrador Indians. *American Anthropologist, 35,* 559–94.

Speck, R., and Attneave, C. (1973). *Family networks.* New York: Pantheon.

Spencer, E. C., and Croley, H. T. (1977). Administrative consultation. In A. Kadushin (ed.), *Consultation in social work practice,* 51–68. New York: Columbia University Press.

Spiegel, J. (1982). An ecological model of ethnic families. In J. McGoldrick, J. Pearce, and J. Giordano (eds.), *Ethnicity and family therapy,* 31–51. New York: Guilford Press.

Spitz, R. (1974). *Grief: A peril in infancy.* New York: New York University Film Library. Film.

Stack, C. (1974). *All our kin.* New York: Harper and Row.

Stallard, K., Ehrenreich, B., and Sklar, H. (1983). *Poverty in the American dream: Women and children first.* Institute for New Communications. New York: South End Press.

Stearns, P. N. (1977). *Old age in European society.* New York: Holmes and Meier.

Stearns, P. N. (1983). *Old age in pre-industrial society.* New York: Holmes and Meier.

Steele, R. (1970). Parental abuse of infants and small children. In T. Benedek, and E. J. Anthony (eds.), *Parenthood: It's psychology and psychopathology,* 449–478. Boston: Little Brown.

Stein, M., Schiavi, R. C., and Camerino, M. (1976). Influence of brain and behavior on the immune system. *Science, 191,* 435–440.

Stevens-Long, J. (1979). *Adult life developmental processes.* Palo Alto: Mayfield Publishing.

Stokes, J. P. (1983). Predicting satisfaction with social support from social network structure. *American Journal of Community Psychology, 11,* 141–152.

Stokols, D., and Shumaker, S. A. (1982). The psychological context of residential mobility and well-being. *Journal of Social Issues, 38*(3), 149–172.

Stoller, R. J. (1964). A contribution to the study of gender identity. *International Journal of Psychoanalysis, 15,* 220–226.

Storm, H. (1972). *Seven arrows.* New York: Ballantine.

Stout, C., Morrow, J., Brand, N., and Wolf, S. (1964). Unusually low incidence of death from myocardial infraction. *Journal of American Medical Association, 188,* 845–855.

Stueve, A., and Fischer, C. S. (1978). *Social networks and older women.* Working paper 292, Institute of Urban and Regional Development, University of California, Berkeley.

Sullivan, H. S. (1953). *The interpersonal theory of psychiatry.* New York: Norton.

Sussman, M. B. (1965). Relationships of adult children with their parents in the United States. In E. Shanas and F. Streib (eds.), *Social structure and the family: Generational relations,* 62–92. Englewood Cliffs, N.J.: Prentice-Hall.

Sussman, M. B., and Burchinal, L. (1962). Kin family network: Unheralded structure in current conceptualizations of family functioning. *Marriage and Family Living, 24,* 320–332.

Swan, G. E. (1982). Lifestyle revolution. *San Francisco Chronicle,* 15 November.

Swift, C. (1979). The prevention equation and self-help groups. *Self-Help Reporter,* *3*(4), 1–2.

Syme, S., and Berkman, L. (1976). Social class, susceptibility and sickness. *American Journal of Epidemiology, 104*(1), 1–8.

Syme, S. L., Hyman, M. M., and Enterline, P. E. (1965). Cultural mobility and the occurrence of coronary heart disease. *Journal of Health and Human Behavior, 6,* 178–189.

Talwar, G. P., Harnjan, S. V. S., Saxena, R. K., Pandian, M. R., Gupta, P. D., and Bhattarai, G. B. (1975). *Regulation of growth of differentiated function in eukaroyte cells.* New York: Raven Press.

Tharp, R. (1963). Dimensions of marriage roles. *Marriage and Family Living, 25,* 389–404.

Thibaut, J., and Kelley, H. (1959). *The social psychology of groups.* New York: John Wiley and Sons.

Thomas, L. (1974). *The lives of a cell: Notes of a biology watcher.* New York: Viking Press.

Tillich, P. (1954). *Love, power and justice.* New York: Oxford.

Tillman, W., and Hobbes, G. (1949). The accident prone automobile driver: A study of the psychiatric and social background. *American Journal of Psychiatry, 106,* 321.

Tilly, L., and Scott, J. (1978). *Women's work and family.* New York: Holt, Rinehart and Winston.

Toledo, J. R., Hughes, H., and Sims, J. (1979). Management of noncompliance to medical regimen: A suggested methodological approach. *International Journal of Health Education, 22*(4), 407–418.

Tolsdorf, C. (1976). Social networks, support and coping: An exploratory study. *Family Relations, 5*(4), 407–418.

Tracy, G. S., and Gussow, Z. (1976). Self-help health groups: A grass-roots response to a need for services. *Journal of Applied Behavioral Sciences, 12*(3), 381–396.

Treas, J. (1977). Family support systems for the aged: Some social and demographic considerations. *The Gerontologist, 17*(6), 486–491.

Troll, L. E. (1971). The family of later life: A recent review. *Journal of Marriage and the Family, 33,* 263–290.

Troll, L. E., Miller, S., and Atchley, R. (1979). *Families in later life.* Belmont, Calif.: Wadsworth Publishing Co.

Troll, L. E., and Smith, J. (1976). Attachment through the life-span: Some questions about dyadic bonds among adults. *Human Development, 19,* 1156–1170.

Turk, H. (1970). Interorganizational networks in urban society: Initial perspectives and comparative research. *American Sociological Review, 35,* 1–20.

Turner, R. J. (1982). Social support as a contingency in psychological well-being. *Journal of Health and Social Behavior, 22,* 357–367.

Turner, V. (1967). *The forest of symbols.* Ithaca: Cornell University Press.

Unger, O. G. (1980). Supporting families under stress: The role of social networks. *Family Relations, 28,* 566–574.

United States Department of Commerce, Bureau of the Census. (1982). *Money, in-*

come and poverty, status of families and persons in the U.S., 1982 current population report. Washington, D.C.: Government Printing Office.

United States Department of Commerce, Bureau of the Census. (1985). *Statistical abstract of the United States.* Washington, D.C.: Government Printing Office.

Vaillant, G. E. (1977). *Adaptation to life.* Boston: Little, Brown.

Valentine, C. (1970). *Culture and poverty.* Chicago: University of Chicago Press.

Van Dyke, C., and Kaufman, I. C. (1983). Psychobiology of bereavement. In L. Temoshok, C. Van Dyke, and R. Zegans (eds.), *Emotions in health and illness,* 37–50. New York: Grune and Stratton.

Van Wagner, K., and Swanson C. (1979). From Machiavelli to Ms.: Differences in male-female power styles. *Public Administration Review,* (January–February), 65–72.

Veninga, R., and Fredlund, D. (1974). Teaching the group approach. *Nursing Outlook, 22*(6), 25–30.

Verbrugge, L. M. (1977). The structure of adult friendship choices. *Social Forces, 56,* 576–597.

Verdon, M. (1981). Kinship, marriage and the family: An operational approach. *American Journal of Sociology, 86,* 796–818.

Verzaro, M., and Hennon, C. B. (1980). Single-parent families: Myth and reality. *Journal of Home Economics, 72*(3), 32–36.

Vinokur, A., and Selzer, M. L. (1975). Desirable versus undesirable life events: Their relationship to stress and mental distress. *Journal of Personality and Social Psychology, 32,* 329–337.

Visher, E. B., and Visher, J. S. (1979). *Stepfamilies: A guide to working with stepparents and stepchildren.* New York: Brunner/Mazel.

Vithoulkas, G. (1979). *Homoeopathy in medicine of the new nation.* New York: Arco Publishing Co.

Viviano, F. (1982). Is the sunbelt boom hurting family life. Pacific News Release, *The California Aggie,* (January 11), Davis, Calif.

Vogel, E. (1963). *Japan's new middle class.* Berkeley: University of California Press.

Vogel, E. (1968) The salary man. In J. A. Kahl (ed.), *Comparative perspectives on stratification,* 18–36. Boston: Little, Brown.

Walker, K. W., MacBride, A., and Vachon, M. L. S. (1977). Social support and the crisis of bereavement. *Social Science and Medicine, 11,* 35–41.

Walster, E., Berscheid, E., and Walster, G. (1973). New directions in equity research. *Journal of Personality and Social Psychology, 2,* 151–175.

Walster, E., Walster, C., and Berscheid, E. (1978). *Equity theory and research.* Boston: Allyn and Bacon.

Washington Post. (1982). Traditional family still predominates, 18 November.

Weeks, D. G., Michela, J. L., Peplau, L. A., and Eragg, M. E. (1980). The relationship between loneliness and depression: A structural equation analysis. *Journal of Personality and Social Psychology, 39,* 1238–1244.

Weiss, J. (1972). Influence of psychological variables on stress induced pathology. In R. Porter and J. Knight (eds.), *Physiology, emotion and psychosomatic illness,* 253–279. Ciba Foundation Symposium, No. 8. New York: Elsevier.

Weiss, R. S. (1969). The fund of sociability. *Transaction,* (July–August), 36–43.

Weiss, R. S. (1973). *Loneliness: The experience of emotional and social isolation.* Cambridge, Mass.: MIT University Press.

Wellman, B. (1979). The community question: The intimate networks of East Yorkers. *American Journal of Sociology, 84*(5), 1201–1231.

Wellman, B. (1980). A guide to network analysis. Working paper series #1, Structural Analysis Programs, Department of Sociology, University of Toronto.

Werner, E. (1984). *Kith, kin and hired hands.* Baltimore: University Park Press.

Westermeyer, J. (1980). Mental illness in a peasant society: Social outcomes. *American Journal of Psychiatry, 137,* 1390–1394.

Westermeyer, J., and Pattison, E. M. (1981). Social networks and mental illness in a peasant society. *Schizophrenia Bulletin, 7*(1), 125–134.

Whitaker, C. (1965). Acting out in family psychotherapy. In L. E. Abt (ed.), *Acting out: Theoretical and clinical aspects,* 189–197. New York: Grune and Stratton.

Whyte, W. H. (1956). *The organization man.* New York: Simon and Schuster.

Wilcox, B. L. (1981a). Social support in adjusting to marital disruption: A network analysis. In B. H. Gottlieb (ed.), *Social networks and social support,* 97–116. Beverly Hills, Calif.: Sage Publications.

Wilcox, B. L. (1981b). Social support, life stress and psychological adjustment: A test of the buffering hypothesis. *American Journal Community Psychology, 9*(4), 371–386.

Wilensky, H. (1975). *The welfare state and equality.* Berkeley: University of California Press.

Winder, A., and Kanno, N. B. (1980–1981). Collaboration: An alternative value and its implications for health education. *International Quarterly of Community Health Education, 1*(2), 183–194.

Wispe, L. G. (1972). Positive forms of social behavior: An overview. *Journal of Social Issues, 28*(3), 1–19.

Wolff, C. T., Friedman, S. B., Hofer, M. A., and Mason, J. (1964). Relationship between psychological defenses and mean urinary 17-hydroxycordicosteroid excretion rates: A predictive study of parents of fatally ill children. *Psychosomatic Medicine, 26,* 576–591.

Wolff, H. G., Wolf, S. W., and Goudell, H. (1968). *Stress and disease.* Springfield, Ill.: Thomas Publications.

Woods, J., and Robertson, J. F. (1978). Friendship and kinship interaction: Differential effect on the morale of the elderly. *Journal of Marriage and the Family,* (May), 237–242.

Wyman, L. (1965). The religion of the Navajo Indians. In V. Ferm (ed.) *Ancient religions,* 341–362. New York: Citadel Press.

Yankelovich, D. (1981). *New rules: Searching for self-fulfillment in a world turned upside down.* New York: Random House.

Young, J. B. (1981). Cognitive therapy and loneliness. In G. Emery, S. D. Hollon, and R. C. Bedrosian (eds.), *New directions in cognitive therapy,* 139–159. New York: Guilford Press.

Young, W. C. (1972). Project unique: Integrated quality urban, suburban education.

In A. H. Passow (ed.), *Opening opportunities for disadvantaged learners*, 260–285. New York: Teachers College Columbia University.

Youniss, J. (1980). *Parents and peers in social development*. Chicago: University of Chicago Press.

Youniss, J. (1984). Morality, communicative relations, and the development of reciprocity. In W. Edelstein and J. Habermas (eds.), *Structuralism and development*, 34–60. Frankfurt: Suhrkamp.

Zandler, A. F. (1982). *Making groups effective*. San Francisco: Jossey-Bass.

Zborowski, M., and Herzog, E. (1972). *Life is with people: The culture of the shtetl*. New York: Schocken.

INDEX